Directory of Real Estate Development and Related Education Programs

ELEVENTH EDITION

Urban Land Institute

About ULI

The mission of the Urban Land Institute is to provide leadership in the responsible use of land and in creating and sustaining thriving communities worldwide.

Established in 1936, the Institute today has more than 40,000 members worldwide, representing the entire spectrum of the land use and development disciplines. ULI relies heavily on the experience of its members. It is through member involvement and information resources that ULI has been able to set standards of excellence in development practice. The Institute has long been recognized as one of the world's most respected and widely quoted sources of objective information on urban planning, growth, and development.

Richard M. Rosan
President, ULI Worldwide

ULI Staff

Rachelle Levitt	Executive Vice President Global Information Group/Publisher
Dean Schwanke	Senior Vice President Publications and Awards
David Takesuye	Director, Awards and Competitions Project Director
Michelle Lopez	Senior Associate, Education
Nancy H. Stewart	Director, Book Program
James A. Mulligan	Managing Editor
Sandy Chizinsky	Copy Editor
Betsy VanBuskirk	Creative Director
Susan S. Teachey/ON-Q Design, Inc.	Layout Artist
Craig Chapman	Director, Publishing Operations
Karrie Underwood	Administrative Manager/ Desktop Publishing Assistant

Recommended bibliographic listing:
ULI–the Urban Land Institute. *The Directory of Real Estate Development and Related Education Programs.* Eleventh Edition. Washington, D.C.: ULI–the Urban Land Institute, 2008.
ULI Catalog Number D112
ISBN 978-0-87420-097-3
Printed in the United States of America.

Foreword: About Real Estate Development Education

Three decades ago, ULI began looking at the relationship between real estate development and university education, and established a committee to develop programs that would support graduate-level education in real estate development. ULI members believed that students studying urban and regional planning and allied subjects could enhance their effectiveness by learning about real estate development from the perspective of the private sector, particularly as regulations were becoming more complex and public and private sector interaction was increasing. Thus, when ULI began its efforts in the university education arena, its first step was to provide curriculum grants to graduate-level planning programs that were interested in introducing the developers' perspective into a curriculum that was largely oriented to the public sector.

Developers also saw a need for graduates with sophisticated and specialized skills who could deal with the increasing complexities of the development industry. They realized even then that the changes taking place in the industry would be far-reaching, and that the development professionals of the future would need more than an entrepreneurial spirit to succeed. Formal education could provide an understanding of the interdisciplinary elements that are a normal part of every development project.

Meanwhile, as the result of heightened interest on the part of both students and academic institutions in real estate development education, several universities began new programs in their professional schools. Many existing real estate programs also began to realize that to achieve a high level of professional knowledge, their students required an integrated curriculum that would bring together business, design, finance, law, planning, and related courses. ULI supported the development of interdisciplinary programs, whether these were free-standing real estate development programs or new, cross-disciplinary curricula within existing programs. (Despite ULI's support, however, only a handful of current programs are truly interdisciplinary.)

Over the years, graduate-level education in real estate development has had its ups and downs—often because of the vagaries of the industry—but many programs that were begun in the mid-1980s and early 1990s are thriving. It now appears, however, that the market and students' needs have brought about a small change in real estate education, this time through the design schools. The past few years have revealed a glimmer of interest in bringing real estate into the design professions, often at the request of students. ULI was fortunate to receive an endowment from developer Gerald D. Hines to fund an annual interdisciplinary student urban design competition. This competition has fostered interdisciplinary activity at universities across the country, including the formation of several interdisciplinary real estate clubs and other student groups that bring together design and real estate/business students.

Overall, the ULI university education program functions as a resource for real estate development faculty—who, because they are housed in many different departments and programs, do not have a centralized professional body. Similarly, this directory is intended as a centralized resource for students who wish to study real estate development and related areas.

In addition to publishing this directory, ULI currently supports university education through the following activities:

• **Textbooks (www.uli.org/bookstore).** In 2007, ULI published an extensively revised and updated fourth edition of its comprehensive real estate development textbook, *Real Estate Development: Principles and Process.* Covering each stage of the process step by step, the textbook explains the basics of idea conception, feasibility, planning, financing, market analysis, contract negotiation, construction, marketing, and asset management. ULI has also published many other books that are used as textbooks, including *Business Park and Industrial Development Handbook*, 2nd ed. (2001); *Developing Sustainable Planned Communities* (2007); *Dynamics of Real Estate Capital Markets* (2006); *Growing Cooler* (2008); *Inside Track to Careers in Real Estate* (2006); *Mixed-Use Development Handbook*, 2nd ed. (2003); *Multifamily Housing Development Handbook* (2000); *Office Development Handbook*, 2nd ed. (1998); *Professional Real Estate Development: The ULI Guide to the Business*, 2nd ed. (2003); *Real Estate Market Analysis* (2001); *Residential Development*, 3rd ed. (2003); *Resort Development*, 2nd ed. (2008); and *Retail Development*, 4th ed. (2008).

• **Development Case Studies (www.uli.org/casestudies).** The ULI Development Case Studies—formerly known as Project Reference Files—feature detailed descriptions of proven, innovative, and financially successful real estate development projects throughout the world. Subscribers have access to nearly 500 existing case studies and 24 new case studies each year, issued quarterly. Often used by educators in the classroom, ULI Development Case Studies provide in-depth information, including key features and strategies; project data on costs, rents, and more; fully downloadable photos; and site and floor plans. To allow simultaneous access for multiple users, university libraries are permitted to obtain site licenses.

• **ULI Gerald D. Hines Student Urban Design Competition (www.udcompetition.uli.org).** Once a year, ULI offers graduate students in the United States and Canada the opportunity to participate in a two-week design and development charrette. Interdisciplinary teams are charged with solving a large-scale development problem on a real site. The winning team receives $50,000 in prize money.

• **Careers in Real Estate program.** In conjunction with the ULI annual spring and fall meetings, ULI sponsors a Careers in Real Estate program, which features a panel of executive recruiters and ULI members who explore employment strategies; the emphasis is on geographic opportunities, career building blocks, and options available at the entry and beginning management levels.

• **ULI Fellows program.** ULI provides assistance to 24 university faculty members who are noted for their research in areas of interest to the development profession. This program strengthens ULI's connection to outstanding individual instructors and university programs, and includes several faculty from outside the United States.

• **Graduate Student Fellows program.** ULI Foundation members may sponsor graduate students at universities of their choice to receive free ULI memberships for two years; students also have the opportunity to attend two ULI meetings and one conference/workshop annually, with all expenses paid. Student fellows also have the privilege of participating in many ULI events not normally open to students, including product councils.

• **Special membership rates and categories.** Student membership rates are available with proof of current enrollment. In addition, ULI offers a special membership category (Young Leader) for people under 35, to encourage new professionals, including recent graduates, to become part of the Institute early in their careers.

About the Directory

This is the 11th edition of the ULI directory published since 1988. Since the first edition, many new programs have been started, others have ended, and much more interest has been generated by programs outside the United States.

The study of real estate and real estate development takes many forms—from one- or two-year degree programs to real estate concentrations in planning, business, or architecture schools. The evolution of real estate development programs has taken several paths, giving rise to various educational models. This directory lists all types, from the master's in business administration with a specialization in real estate development or real estate finance to the one- or two-year specialized master of real estate development. While the directory's primary focus is on graduate programs, if a university has graduate and undergraduate programs, both programs are listed.

Generally, the directory provides information about two degree formats: the traditional degree, which allows the student to specialize in one area of real estate development (planning, business, architecture, or finance); and the interdisciplinary degree, which is focused wholly on real estate studies. Traditional degrees are usually offered in business or planning. Business degrees with real estate concentrations typically provide students with the opportunity to pursue a general management degree, but to specialize in real estate development or some segment of the real estate industry through a sequence or group of electives. Students in such programs typically graduate with a master's in business administration or a master of science in business. Business school programs usually emphasize the business side of real estate development— financing, marketing, or development company management.

Students seeking planning degrees usually graduate with a master's in community planning, a master's in regional planning, or a master's in urban planning with a real estate emphasis. Planning programs tend to emphasize land use planning, transportation or infrastructure development, land use law and policy, and other planning topics; students who take a concentration in real estate development will learn how it relates to planning .

Interdisciplinary programs—whether one- or two-year programs that award a degree in real estate development, or jointly sponsored programs—offer students courses in all disciplines that are relevant to development. Students in such programs graduate with a real estate development degree, such as a master's in real estate development or a master's in real estate, or with a joint degree— for example, a master's in business administration/master's in community planning. Real estate development degrees are offered at only a handful of universities.

Programs in related fields, which are designed to broaden students' education by exposing them to real estate development, rather than to prepare them for careers in the field, are also available. Examples include architecture programs, some planning programs, and, in some cases, law programs. Such courses of study are often required for professional licensure.

This directory includes degree programs from around the world. It is important to note that while the directory is relatively comprehensive, it is not exhaustive. Participation in the directory is strictly voluntary. (Other universities that offer real estate programs are listed at the end of the directory.)

All students considering a career in real estate development are advised to talk with developers, real estate lawyers, architects, financiers, asset managers, corporate real estate directors, and planners to gain a full picture of the career options open to them and of the educational requirements for those careers. Students should then discuss career goals with program faculty to ensure that the curriculum offered will provide the skills and knowledge needed to succeed in their chosen field.

Dean Schwanke
Senior Vice President
Global Information Group

Hyperlinks

Internet links to the education programs listed in this book may be accessed via the ULI Web site at www.uli.org; go to Meetings/ Education to find the link.

Contents

Guide to Degree Programs

BA: Bachelor of Arts
Universidad de Alicante

University of Northern Iowa

University of Western Ontario

BBA: Bachelor of Business Administration
Baruch College, The City University of New York

Baylor University

University of Georgia

University of Michigan

University of San Diego

Temple University

University of Texas at Austin

University of Texas at San Antonio

Wichita State University

University of Wisconsin at Madison

BPSD: Bachelor of Property and Sustainable Development
Bond University

BS: Bachelor of Science
Arizona State University

Florida State University

Indiana University

Old Dominion University

Penn State University

University of Pennsylvania

BSCM: Bachelor of Science in Construction Management
Southern Polytechnic State University

BSBA: Bachelor of Science in Business Administration
University of Colorado

University of Denver

Marquette University

University of Nebraska at Omaha

University of Nevada, Las Vegas

Old Dominion University

BSc: Bachelor of Science
Dublin Institute of Technology

National University of Singapore

University of Reading

BUDP: Bachelor of Urban Design and Planning
Bond University

DDes: Doctor of Design
Harvard University

JD/MBA: Joint Law and MBA
University of Colorado

LLM (Master of Laws) in real estate law
The John Marshall Law School

MAcc: Master of Accounting
University of Michigan

MArch: Master of Architecture
University of Washington

MBA: Master of Business Administration
Baruch College, The City University of New York

Baylor University

Columbia University

Florida State University

University of Florida

University of Georgia

Indiana University

University of Michigan

University of North Carolina at Chapel Hill

University of North Carolina at Charlotte

Penn State University

University of Pennsylvania

Roosevelt University

University of San Diego

University of Texas at Austin

University of Texas at San Antonio

Virginia Commonwealth University

University of Washington

Wichita State University

University of Wisconsin–Madison

York University

MCRP: Master of City and Regional Planning
University of North Carolina at Chapel Hill (Department of City and Regional Planning)

MDesS: Master in Design Studies
Harvard University

MPA: Master of Public Administration
University of Washington

MPhil: Master of Philosophy in Real Estate Finance
University of Cambridge

MPS: Master of Professional Studies
Cornell University

MPV: Master of Property Valuation
Bond University

MRE: Master of Real Estate
University of Amsterdam

Texas A&M University

MRED: Master of Real Estate Development
Clemson University

University of Maryland

University of Southern California

MS: Master of Science
Baruch College, The City University of New York

Georgia Institute of Technology

The Johns Hopkins University

New York University

University of Texas at San Antonio

Virginia Commonwealth University

MSAE: Master of Science in Applied Economics
Marquette University

MSB: Master of Science in Business
Virginia Commonwealth University

MSc: Master of Science
Dublin Institute of Technology

National University of Singapore

University of Reading

Royal Institute of Technology

MSCM: Master of Science in Construction Management
New York University

MSLD: Master of Science in Land Development
Texas A&M University

MSRE: Master of Science in Real Estate
University of Amsterdam

University of Florida

New York University

Roosevelt University

University of San Diego

Florida A&M University

University of Washington

MSRECM: Master of Real Estate and Construction Management

University of Denver

MSRED: Master of Science in Real Estate Development

Massachusetts Institute of Technology

MUP: Master of Urban Planning

Bond University

University of Washington

MUPDD: Master of Urban Planning Design and Development

Cleveland State University

PhD: Doctor of Philosophy

Baruch College, The City University of New York

University of Florida

University of Georgia

National University of Singapore

University of North Carolina at Chapel Hill

Penn State University

University of Texas at Austin

University of Wisconsin–Madison

Certificates

BSBA with a Certificate in Real Estate

University of Colorado

Certificate in Land Development

Southern Polytechnic State University

Certificate in Real Estate

University of Michigan

CREDD: Certificate in Real Estate Design and Development

University of Pennsylvania

Graduate Certificate in Real Estate

Virginia Commonwealth University

Graduate Certificate in Urban Real Estate Finance and Development

Cleveland State University

Graduate Certificate of Real Estate Development

University of Maryland

Guide to Programs by State and Country

Arizona
Arizona State University

California
University of San Diego
University of Southern California

Colorado
University of Colorado
University of Denver

Florida
Florida State University
University of Florida

Georgia
Georgia Institute of Technology
University of Georgia
Southern Polytechnic State University

Illinois
The John Marshall Law School
Roosevelt University

Indiana
Indiana University

Iowa
University of Northern Iowa

Kansas
Wichita State University

Maryland
The Johns Hopkins University
University of Maryland

Massachusetts
Harvard University
Massachusetts Institute of Technology

Michigan
University of Michigan

Nebraska
University of Nebraska at Omaha

Nevada
University of Nevada, Las Vegas

New York
Baruch College, The City University
 of New York
Columbia University
Cornell University
New York University

North Carolina
University of North Carolina at Chapel Hill
University of North Carolina at Charlotte

Ohio
Cleveland State University

Pennsylvania
Penn State University
University of Pennsylvania
Temple University

South Carolina
Clemson University

Texas
Baylor University
Texas A&M University
University of Texas at Austin
University of Texas at San Antonio

Virginia
Old Dominion University
Virginia Commonwealth University

Washington
University of Washington

Wisconsin
Marquette University
University of Wisconsin–Madison

Australia
Bond University

Canada
University of Western Ontario
York University

Ireland
Dublin Institute of Technology

The Netherlands
University of Amsterdam

Singapore
National University of Singapore

Spain
Universidad de Alicante

Sweden
Royal Institute of Technology

United Kingdom
University of Cambridge
University of Reading

Universidad de Alicante

Paloma Taltavull de La Paz, Program Head
Applied Economic Analysis
Instituto de Economía Internacional
Campus de San Vicente del Raspeig s/n
03080 Alicante, Spain
34 96 590 9693; fax 34 96 590 9322
paloma@ua.es
www.iei.ua.es/dei

Degree	Year Program Began	Credit Hours	Years to Complete	Full-Time Students (2006–2007)	Part-Time Students (2006–2007)	Degrees Conferred (2006)
Titulo Propio en Estudio Inmobiliarios (Real estate undergraduate)	1997	230	3	60	22	18

Degree	Application Deadline	Minimum Undergraduate GPA	Departmental Requirements
Titulo Propio en Estudio Inmobiliarios	9/30/2008	University Exam approved	Curriculum vitae

Number of Faculty/FTE	Specialized Degree Accreditation	In-State Undergraduate Tuition
45/56	BA in real estate studies	€3,500

Degree Specialization

Titulo Propio en Estudio Inmobiliarios' is designed to give real estate professionals an up-to-date education that reflects the current requirements of the Spanish real estate market.

Program Description

The Titulo Propio en Estudio Inmobiliarios' (DEI) was designed to address a gap in real estate education in the Spanish university system. The goal is to assist real estate professionals (notaries, real estate managers, real estate brokers, real estate advisers, and assessors) in all aspects of their work. To meet the wide-ranging needs of real estate professionals, the specially designed program combines four main disciplines: economy and finance, law, building construction, and new technologies.

Core Curriculum

The core curriculum is based on economics and finance (including the nature of the mortgage market), law, building construction, and technological tools.

Financial Aid

Tuition fees are the only source of funds. Resources for teaching and research—including lecture rooms, information technology laboratories, and designing/drawing rooms—are provided by the Instituto de Economia Internacional.

Lecture Series

Regular lectures are offered on the 44 different subjects covered in the program. The program also includes professional conferences that cover important topics, such as the role of professionals in the Spanish real estate market; changes in the Spanish real estate finance market; new regulations; and new markets, such as golf courses and rental housing.

International Programs

Through agreements with various universities in Europe (in the United Kingdom, Ireland, the Netherlands, Austria, and Poland, among other countries), ten students are permitted to study abroad each year. The program also offers seminars on international real estate topics; in 2007–2008, for example, the seminar focused on international standards in valuation.

Program Advisory Group

The program will be redesigned to fully conform to the Bolognia requirements. The advisory group for the redesign is made up of the coordinators for various program areas: two professors in real estate law, two in architecture, one in new technologies, two in economics and finance, one in business administration, and one in language.

Internship Placement Assistance

Placement assistance is provided if it is required. Contact dei@ua.es.

Job Placement Assistance

After completing their degree, students have the opportunity to spend three to six months in a real estate company. Contact dei@ua.es.

Clubs/Alumni Associations

The alumni association is Asociación de antiguos alumnus. Further information is available through the DEI secretary.

University of Amsterdam

P. van Gool
Faculty of Economics
Amsterdam School of Real Estate
Jollemanhof 5
Amsterdam, 1019 GW
The Netherlands
31 (0) 20 6681129; fax 31 (0) 20 6680361
Contact: Mrs. S.N.L. de Maat
s.demaat@asre.uva.nl
www.asre.nl

Degree	Year Program Began	Credit Hours	Years to Complete	Thesis or Final Product	Part-Time Students (2006–2007)	Degrees Conferred (2006)
MRE	1989	67.5	2	Masterproof	118	55
MSRE	2000	65	2	Master's thesis	198	34

Degree	Application Deadline	Departmental Requirements
MRE	April 1	Resume, diplomas, 1 letter of reference, personal statement, intake conversation
MSRE	June 1	Resume, diplomas, 1 letter of reference, personal statement

Degree	Specialized Degree Accreditation	In-State Graduate Tuition	Out-of-State Graduate Tuition
MRE	RICS, NVAO	€37,400	€37,400
MSRE	NVAO	€23,900	€23,900

Degree Specializations

MRE; MSRE in investment; MSRE in management; MSRE in project development; MSRE in area development.

Program Description

The MRE is intended for real estate specialists who want to move on from specific jobs to more general, strategically oriented management positions. This intensive program has broad aims and focuses on strategic questions. The teaching approach is based on extensive interaction between students and professors and among the students themselves. The professional network that the students create during the program is an essential aspect of the educational experience.

MSRE students choose a profile (an area of concentration) at the start of the program. A profile has two compulsory subjects and one optional subject, chosen from among seven modules. The MSRE program concludes with an extensive research thesis. Students choose from among the following courses: investment analysis, asset management, project development, area development, valuation, market analysis, and feasibility analysis.

Lecture Series

The Amsterdam School of Real Estate organizes one lecture a week, which is delivered by a professor or by a lecturer from a real estate company.

International Programs

MRE: A one-week summer course in New York and a three-day field trip to a European city.

MSRE: Four-day field trips to Europe.

Program Advisory Group

Starts in 2008.

Clubs/Alumni Associations

MRE: The Amsterdam School of Real Estate Alumni Association has almost 500 members and organizes several activities every year.

MSRE: The MSRE Alumni association was founded in 2006 and now has almost 100 members.

Faculty

Johan Conijn, housing market.

Peter van Gool, real estate economics.

Ed F. Nozeman, real estate development.

Affiliated Faculty

Andrew Baum, real estate investment analysis.

Roel A.M. van de Bilt, financial risk management.

Hamith M.I.Th. Breedveld, contracts.

René J.V.M. Buck, economic geography.

Rob E.F.A. Crassee, corporate real estate management.

Jan van Duijvendijk, development law.

Albert D. Flesseman, rental law.

Boris van der Gijp, office market.

Peter de Haas, international investment markets.

Tineke ten Have, institutional valuation.

Frans G. van Hoeken, valuation.

Adriaan Hoogvliet, housing market strategy.

Joop Kluft, financial law.

Mildred E.D.M. Knegt, administrative law.

Hans Op 't Veld, performance measurement.

Lars Rompelberg, regional development financing.

Patrick H.J. Ruwiel, asset management.

Wim J.M. Scheffers, concept development.

Jan-Willem Speetjens, retail market.

Guido J. Wallagh, regional development.

Other

MRE and MRSE: The language of the programs is Dutch.

The MSRE modules may be regarded as stand-alone programs.

Arizona State University

Jay Q. Butler, Professor
Morrison School of Management and Agribusiness
7001 East Williams Field Road
Mesa, AZ 85212
480-727-1585; fax 480-727-1961
jay.butler@asu.edu
morrisonschool@asu.edu
http://poly.asu.edu/msma

Degree	Year Program Began	Credit Hours	Years to Complete	Full-Time Students (2006–2007)	Part-Time Students (2006–2007)	Degrees Conferred (2006)
BS in real estate	1950	120	4	50	23	14

Degree	Minimum High School GPA	Departmental Requirements
BS	2.0	Resume, personal statement, 3 letters of reference

In-State Undergraduate Tuition	Out-of-State Undergraduate Tuition
$2,830	$8,974

Degree Name and Specialization

BS in real estate.

Program Description

The real estate program is in the Morrison School of Management and Agribusiness at Arizona State University's Polytechnic campus. The program's mission is to creatively and effectively provide timely information to enable members of the real estate industry to make informed decisions. Its educational mission is to integrate creative classroom instruction and business-world applications, so that students are prepared for leadership roles in the rapidly changing real estate industry. The program represents a unique academic and business partnership that serves students and the real estate industry by providing educational and informational opportunities. The real estate industry has provided support through scholarships, internships, career opportunities, and research issues.

Core Curriculum

Thirty semester hours in prebusiness skills; 41–44 semester hours in general studies; 9 semester hours in program requirements; 18 semester hours in major requirements; 22 semester hours in business core; and 3 semester hours for capstone. Minimum of 120 hours.

Financial Aid

Our school offers several scholarships, three of which are specifically for real estate students: the Dick Baxter Real Estate Scholarship, the Ed Thirkhill Memorial Scholarship, and the Catteneo Family Scholarship. Contact financialaid.poly@asu.edu.

Lecture Series

Because we use a lot of professionals in our classrooms, we do not have a formal lecture series. We have had and will continue to have ongoing lunch meetings with professionals.

Internship Placement Assistance

Our program does offer internship assistance, but it is not required for coursework. Contact Otis J. White at 480-727-1513, or otis.white@asu.edu.

Job Placement Assistance

ASU offers job placement assistance through Career Services. We also post part-time and full-time employment opportunities on the student electronic bulletin board. Contact Justin Finnerty at 480-727-4411, or CareerPreparation@asu.edu.

Clubs/Alumni Associations

Sun Devil Real Estate Alumni Club.

Other

Every semester, we offer a special-topics course taught by real estate professionals. For example, we have had property management taught by members of the local IREM chapter, and real estate marketing taught by people from Westcor.

Faculty

Walter Smith, associate professor of business. PhD, economics, University of California at Berkeley; MBA, Boston University; BA, University of Wisconsin. Real estate finance and valuation.

Affiliated Faculty

David L. Forsyth, lecturer. JD, Arizona State University; BS, accountancy, Northern Arizona University. Real estate law.

Gerard Vick. MS, business, University of Wisconsin; JD, Concord Law School; BS, forestry and resource management, University of California at Berkeley. MAI. Appraisal.

Baruch College, The City University of New York

Ko Wang, Program Head
Department of Real Estate
Zicklin School of Business
137 East 22nd Street
Box C-406
New York, NY 10010
646-660-6937; fax 646-660-6931
Contact: Margo Weaker
margo_weaker@baruch.cuny.edu; Zicklin_realestate@baruch.cuny.edu
http://zicklin.baruch.cuny.edu/faculty/realestate/

Degree	Year Program Began	Credit Hours	Years to Complete	Thesis or Final Product	Full-Time or Part-Time Students (2006–2007)
BBA, real estate major	2006	124	4	No	266
BBA, real estate minor	2004	9	N/A	No	
MBA in real estate	2007	57	2	No	
MS in real estate	2008	30	1	Yes	
PhD	2007	60	4	Yes	

Degree	Application Deadline	Average Undergraduate GPA	Average GRE or GMAT Score	Departmental Requirements
BBA, major in real estate	Fall: February 1 Spring: October 1	N/A	N/A	Students who wish to major in the Zicklin School of Business must complete the following courses with an overall GPA of at least 2.25: ACC 2101, CIS 2200, ECO 1001, ECO 1002, ENG 2100, LAW 1101, MTH 2205 (or equivalent), and STA 2000 (or equivalent). In addition, they must have completed a minimum of 45 credits overall (including the above eight courses) with an overall GPA of at least 2.25. Included in the 45 credits must be either ENG 2150 or COM 1010.

Number of Faculty	Specialized Degree Accreditation	In-State Graduate Tuition	Out-of-State Graduate Tuition	In-State Undergraduate Tuition	Out-of-State Undergraduate Tuition
8 full time; 5 adjunct	All AACSB	Full-time MBA: $4,400/term Part-time MBA: $400/credit Full-time MS: $3,200/term Part-time MS: $270/credit	MBA: $600/credit; MS: $500/credit	Full-time: $2,000/term Part-time: $170/credit	$360/credit

Degree Specializations

BBA, major in real estate; BBA, minor in real estate; MBA in real estate; MS in real estate; PhD in business with a real estate track.

Program Description

The Department of Real Estate seeks talented and motivated students who are interested in understanding the economic and behavioral aspects of real estate markets. Our mission is to produce future leaders in real estate and related fields. To achieve this goal, the department recruits faculty members with an established record of (or with great potential to produce) top-notch research, and the ability to interact effectively with industry leaders.

Our real estate program not only prepares students to enter one of the most exciting and fastest-growing career fields in New York, but also ensures that students acquire the skills to succeed in related industries in the business world. Given the pervasive impact of real estate on both the public and the business sectors, the study of real estate helps students understand the important concepts and issues that must be addressed in crucial business and public policy decisions.

Core Curriculum

BBA, major in real estate: 30 credits in required business courses; BBA, major in real estate, investment track: 24 credits (12 credits of required courses and 12 credits of elective courses); BBA, major in real estate, development track: 24 credits (18 credits of required courses and 6 credits of elective courses); BBA, minor in real estate: 9 credits; MBA in real estate: 33 credits in core and breadth courses; MS in real estate: 18 credits in required courses; 4 credits in electives.

Financial Aid

Baruch College participates in all federal and state financial aid programs. It also offers the Joseph Moinian Real Estate Award, and three scholarships: the Mortgage Bankers Association of New York Scholarship; the Association of Real Estate Women Charitable Fund Scholarship; and the WX (Women Executives in Real Estate) Scholarships. For more information, see www.baruch.cuny.edu/financialaid/ or call Nancy West at 646-312-1360.

Lecture Series

The Department of Real Estate works with both the undergraduate and graduate real estate clubs to schedule outside speakers from the real estate industry to speak at events throughout the year. The department also works with Executives on Campus and the Graduate Career Management Center to recruit speakers for its real estate panels. Executives on Campus presents a real estate panel each semester, and the Graduate Career Management Center presents a real estate panel every fall during Career Week.

Program Advisory Group

Visiting Scholars are friends of our students, faculty members, and of the Department of Real Estate. They are well established and respected in the real estate industry. All of them have PhD degrees, and many are well published in both academic and practitioner-oriented journals. The scholars speak to students and serve as guest lecturers in real estate classes. In the future, they may also co-teach classes with faculty members. Most importantly, they provide our faculty members with the most up-to-date information about issues and practices in the real world, helping to ensure that our courses are not only rigorous but relevant. The department is also in the process of establishing an advisory committee.

Internship and Job Placement Assistance

The Department of Real Estate works closely with both the undergraduate and graduate career centers to promote internships and jobs. Both the graduate and undergraduate career centers provide students with numerous tools and resources to assist in their search for internships and full-time jobs. Programs and resources include career workshops, self-assessment, individual consultations, online career libraries and databases, corporate panels and presentations, on- and off-campus recruiting, and mentoring programs. Both centers also post real estate internships and job opportunities on their Web sites. For undergraduates: Starr Career Center, 646-312-4670 or careerdc@baruch.cuny.edu. For graduate students: Graduate Career Management Center, 646-312-1330, or graduate-career_services@baruch.cuny.edu.

Clubs/Alumni Associations

For information on the Graduate Real Estate Club, contact Ben Polen, president (BenPolen@gmail.com). For information on the Undergraduate Real Estate Club, contact Igor Zaytsev, president (iz032156@baruch.cuny.edu).

Other

The real estate program at Baruch will be one of the most comprehensive programs in the most intense real estate location (New York City) in the country. The department's offerings cover all aspects of real estate and provide a range of degree options. The department recruits outstanding faculty members to ensure that it becomes a center of excellence in pro-

ducing and disseminating cutting-edge real estate knowledge. The department also has two important allies in the career world: Margo Weaker, Director of Real Estate Student Services, and Dr. David Shulman, Visiting Scholar. Both are actively involved in outreach to real estate firms to promote student internships and jobs for Baruch students.

Faculty

Jeffrey Beal, adjunct lecturer. BBA, University of Michigan; BPS, New York Institute of Technology. Certified General Appraiser, Real Estate Solutions. Appraising, eminent domain, taxation, litigation support, partial interests, zoning.

Donna Burton, adjunct lecturer. BA, Boston College; MBA, Clark Atlanta University. Portfolio Manager, New Plan Excel Realty Trust, Inc. Portfolio management in real estate finance.

David Frame, assistant professor of real estate. BSc, University of Minnesota; PhD, Carnegie Mellon University. Housing economics, migration, urban development, public policy.

John Goering, professor of public affairs and real estate. BA, Fordham University; MA, Brown University; PhD, Brown University. Real estate market analysis; development; housing and land use; undergraduate and graduate real estate and public affairs education.

Robert Maniscalco, adjunct assistant professor. BS, University of Connecticut; JD, Cornell Law School. Attorney, Reid and Maniscalco. Business law in real estate.

Michael Schwartz, adjunct assistant professor. AAS, New York City College of Technology; BA, Brooklyn College; JD, University of Illinois College of Law; LLM, New York University School of Law. Business law and real estate transactions.

David Scribner, Jr., substitute adjunct professor of real estate. BA, Columbia University; MBA, University of Connecticut; PhD, University of Florida. Real estate counseling, market analysis, valuation, behavioral and urban economics, undergraduate and graduate real estate education.

Ko Wang, Newman Chair in Real Estate Finance. LLB, Chinese Culture University; MS, MBA, PhD, University of Texas at Austin. Real estate investment, corporate finance, real estate markets, real estate investment trusts.

Jay Weiser, associate professor of law and real estate education. BA, Columbia University; JD, Columbia Law School; MA, Stanford University. Bankruptcy; contracts; empirical studies; environmental issues; privacy law; law and economics.

Gerd Welke, assistant professor of real estate. BSc, MSc, University of the Witwatersrand; PhD, physics, State University at Stony Brook; PhD, real estate, Haas School of Business, University of California. Real estate finance, real estate portfolio management.

Rui Yao, associate professor of real estate. BS, Peking (Beijing) University; PhD, Kenan-Flagler Business School, University of North Carolina at Chapel Hill. Asset allocation, real estate finance, housing economics.

Affiliated Faculty

David Bellman, adjunct professor. BS, George Washington University. Senior vice president, construction, AvalonBay Communities, Inc. Mid- and high-rise construction.

Hilary Botein, assistant professor. PhD, Columbia University; JD, Northeastern University School of Law. Development of low-income housing; U.S. community development policies and programs.

Baylor University

Dr. J. Allen Seward, Department Chair
Department of Finance, Insurance, and Real Estate
Hankamer School of Business
One Bear Place #98004
Waco, TX 76798
254-710-4542; fax 254-710-1092
Contact: Dr. Charles J. Delaney
Charles_Delaney@Baylor.edu
http://business.baylor.edu/fin

Degree	Year Program Began	Credit Hours	Years to Complete	Full-Time Students (2006–2007)	Degrees Conferred (2006)
BBA in real estate	1954–1955	79	4	112	63

Degree	Application Deadline
BBA in real estate	See http://businessbaylor.edu/undergrad

Number of Faculty/FTE	Specialized Degree Accreditation	In-State Graduate Tuition	Out-of-State Graduate Tuition	In-State Undergraduate Tuition	Out-of-State Undergraduate Tuition
BBA: 2 MBA: 1	AACSB	$925/semester	$925/semester	$22,200/year flat rate 12+ hours	$22,200/year flat rate 12+ hours

Degree Specializations

BBA in real estate.
MBA with one real estate elective.

Program Description

The real estate major within the BBA degree is designed to prepare students for the many careers in real estate and to provide them with the necessary foundation for graduate study in the field. Requirements for the major are four real estate courses, including three required courses—principles of real estate, real estate appraisal, and real estate investments—and one elective course from the following list: real estate law of agency and contracts, real estate finance, and real estate management. As part of the curriculum, students are introduced to ARGUS, the real estate industry's leading property analysis software. Satisfactory completion of three courses—principles of real estate, real estate law of agency and contracts, and one other real estate course—will qualify a student to take the Texas real estate sales license examination administered by the Texas Real Estate Commission. (See the Real Estate Major Advising Sheet at http://baylor.edu/business/finance.)

Core Curriculum

The BBA in real estate requires 36 hours of core business courses in accounting, finance, business law, information systems, marketing, management, business writing, and business strategy, plus 13 to 14 hours of real estate courses and 15 hours of electives (which may be additional real estate or other business courses). See http://business.baylor.edu/undergrad.

Financial Aid

Scholarships, grants, loans, and on-campus employment are available through the university Student Financial Aid Office. See www.baylor.edu.

Lecture Series

Baylor University and the business school offer a number of lecture series, but none that are specifically dedicated to real estate.

International Programs

Baylor has numerous international study programs but none specifically dedicated to real estate.

Internship Placement Assistance

Internship assistance is provided by Baylor Career Services. Internships are not required for the real estate major, but are strongly encouraged. See www.baylor.edu/careerservices.

Job Placement Assistance

Job placement assistance is provided by Baylor Career Services, which schedules two on-campus job fairs each year and coordinates on-campus recruiting by firms and other organizations. See www.baylor.edu/careerservices.

Faculty

Charles J. Delaney, associate professor of real estate. MA, PhD, University of Florida; BA, University of Rhode Island. Real estate principles, appraisal, and finance.

Ludwig M. Dyson, Jr., associate professor of real estate. MS, PhD, University of Florida; BBA, Baylor University. Real estate principles, law of agency and contracts, investments, finance, management.

Bond University

Dr. Jim Smith, Head of School
Mirvac School of Sustainable Development
Business, Technology and Sustainable Development
Gold Coast, 4229
Australia
0011 61 7 5595 3374; fax 0011 61 7 5595 2209
Contact: Lynne Kirkland
Lkirkland@bond.edu.au
www.bond.edu.au

Degree	Year Program Began	Credit Hours	Years to Complete	Full-Time Students (2006–2007)	Part-Time Students (2006–2007)	Degrees Conferred (2006)
Bachelor of property and sustainable development	2006	240	2 (6 semesters)	2006: 10 2007: 218	2006: 1 2007: 29	1
Bachelor of urban design and planning	2008	240	2 (6 semesters)			
Master of property valuation	2007	120	1 (3 semesters)	3	2	
Master of urban planning	2007	120	1 (3 semesters)	4	4	

Degree	Application Deadline	Minimum High School GPA	Departmental Requirements
Bachelor of property and sustainable development	Accepted until orientation week	Unconditional offers: University ranking 85% Conditional offers: University ranking 63%	Evidence that candidate has completed year 12 or equivalent (copy of current high school results if not yet completed)
Bachelor of urban design and planning	Accepted until orientation week	Unconditional offers: University ranking 85% Conditional offers: University ranking 63%	Evidence that candidate has completed year 12 or equivalent (copy of current high school results if not yet completed)
Master of property valuation	Accepted until orientation week		Evidence that candidate has completed related undergraduate degree and/or has relevant qualifications and work experience
Master of urban planning	Accepted until orientation week		Evidence that candidate has completed related undergraduate degree and/or has relevant qualifications and work experience

Number of Faculty/FTE	Specialized Degree Accreditation	In-State Graduate Tuition	Out-of-State Graduate Tuition	In-State Undergraduate Tuition	Out-of-State Undergraduate Tuition
School of Sustainable Development: 11.45	RICS, AIPM, API, VRB, NSW Office of Fair Trading Department of Commerce	AUD $3,120 per subject*	AUD $3,120 per subject*	AUD $3,120 per subject*	AUD $3,120 per subject*

*Excludes study abroad.

Degree Specializations

The bachelor of property and sustainable development is a six-semester, full-time-equivalent, on-campus undergraduate degree. Bond University operates on a trimester schedule that permits full-time students taking the maximum number of subjects per trimester (four) to complete the degree in two academic years. The degree consists of 24 courses (four courses a semester for six semesters).

The degree in property valuation prepares graduates for challenging careers advising on the use, value, and potential of real property assets from an occupational, investment, and development perspective. Given the shortage of well-qualified people in this area, graduates have the opportunity to become industry leaders in Australia and internationally. The program provides the educational foundation for a range of positions, including property valuer, property manager, corporate real estate adviser, property finance and investment appraiser, and development manager.

The bachelor of urban design and planning provides a foundation for students intending to make their careers in a variety of planning professions. Planning is taught in the context of both historical and contemporary concerns, and studio- and project-based courses develop students' knowledge and skills in the practice of urban design and planning, and in planning communication. Students gain essential practical skills in managing development, and in basic research methods relevant to urban design and planning. In addition to the seven discipline-specific subjects, students gain knowledge of development and property by studying the specified relevant subjects from those areas.

The master of property valuation (MPV), a three-semester-equivalent, stand-alone program, provides a comprehensive route to an accredited graduate qualification. An alternative path to the MPV is by articulation from the graduate certificate/postgraduate diploma.

The master of urban planning provides a comprehensive foundation that allows graduates to undertake urban planning and development at a professional level. The program provides graduates with the tools and techniques that will allow them to obtain a wide range of planning-related jobs—in state and local government agencies, as private consultants, and in property development. This program incorporates the coursework of the Certificate and Postgraduate Diploma in Urban Planning and is intended to meet the professional accreditation requirements of the Planning Institute of Australia (currently under final review).

Program Description

The bachelor of property and sustainable development has four specializations: property valuation, urban development, construction management and quantity surveying, and asset and facilities management. The bachelor of urban design and planning was developed with close attention to the Property and Sustainability program, in order to facilitate a close connection between these related fields. Bachelor's programs, master's programs, and other graduate programs are offered within the Faculty of Business, Technology, and Sustainable Development.

Long-term sustainability is a core philosophy embedded in all programs offered by Bond University's Mirvac School of Sustainable Development. Our students learn firsthand about sustainability by living and studying within our six-star green-rated building. The concept of sustainability is embedded within each of the courses, and practical examples are demonstrated through the structure and functions of the building. Site visits, case studies, and research round out the students' understanding of property and sustainable development.

Core Curriculum

The first two semesters of the bachelor's in property and sustainable development and the bachelor's in urban planning and design consist of (1) core courses in business, humanities, and law and (2) four foundation courses. Core subjects include information technology or business applications of information technology; communication skills or public speaking; cultural and ethical values or contemporary issues in law and society; and strategic management or entrepreneurship. Foundation subjects include principles of sustainable property; understanding buildings (property program) or introducing urban design (planning program); and introduction to the economics of development and planning process.

Financial Aid

FEE-HELP loans, to help pay tuition for undergraduate and graduate coursework, are available to Australian citizens and to those holding permanent humanitarian visas. Financial support for other international citizens can be found at www.bond.edu.au/study/financing. Bond University offers a limited number of full and partial scholarships to students who demonstrate outstanding academic merit and other exceptional achievements. Industry scholarships—which require students to work two days per week—may also be available after completion of the second semester in the undergraduate program or after completion of the first semester in the graduate program. Postgraduate research assistants are selected according to area of study and faculty needs. For international inquiries, contact the Office of Admissions at 61 3 9627 4843 or international@bond.edu.au; for domestic inquiries, contact 1-800-074-074 or information@bond.edu.au.

Lecture Series

Bond University has established an extensive professional network through its faculty and through the School of Sustainable Development. For the duration of their studies, students benefit from firsthand contact with industry professionals—through guest lectures, field trips, case studies, and industry placements.

International Programs

Once each year, the School of Sustainable Development invites students to attend an international research tour focusing on course-related topics. Students may also study abroad for one or two semesters. Bond has many course offerings that complement studies abroad and add an international perspective to home degrees.

Online Program

Materials accessed online are supplementary to on-campus learning.

Program Advisory Group

Drawing on the academic and practical expertise of some of the best minds in the business, the School of Sustainable Development has selected an academic advisory panel to ensure that programs incorporate independent industry feedback on the curriculum, policies, and procedures. An industry advisory committee, a subcommittee of the academic advisory panel, helps maintain close industry connections to the program: committee members provide discipline-specific recommendations on the relevance of academic offerings. These committees meet three times a year and include over 40 industry representatives. In addition, external examiners—including academics and practitioners—have been appointed to ensure that the school meets the stringent accreditation standards of all five professional bodies that accredit the degrees.

Internship Placement Assistance

Fieldwork and workplace experience are incorporated progressively from semester two to semester six, culminating in the semester-long capstone project. The internship program is available to all students in the undergraduate program. Work-integrated learning is also fostered through internships within some courses. Melissa Hann, the career and professional development adviser, can assist students to arrange internships. Contact Melissa Hann at 61 7 5595 2267 or mhann@bond.edu.au.

Job Placement Assistance

According to the *Good Universities Guide*, Bond University graduates have Australia's best outcomes when it comes to getting a job, and Australia's highest starting salaries. Job placement assistance is managed through the Career Development Center, where many employers register interest in graduate placement and where the adviser seeks to match graduates to employers' needs. Contact Kirstie Mitchell, employment services specialist, at 61 7 5595 3388 or kimitche@bond.edu.au.

Clubs/Alumni Associations

Bond University's Alumni Network provides exclusive benefits to Bond graduates and helps them stay connected with classmates, teachers, and professional contacts, through Bond's many international events. Contact the Alumni Relations Office at alumni@bond.edu.au.

The Sustainable Development Student Association (SDSA) represents all students engaged in a property-related course of study, providing social events and networking opportunities. The SDSA also provides advice or support with academic affairs. Contact hsilvasi@student.bond.edu.au or info@bondbsa.com.

Other

Bond University is a private, not-for-profit university that emphasizes industry connections and support. Located on Australia's Gold Coast, in subtropical southeast Queensland, the university provides a balance of academic culture and social opportunities to local and overseas students within a secure, supportive environment. Modern, on-site residential accommodations are available for a large proportion of students.

Faculty

Dr. L. Armitage, associate professor of urban development. PhD, property market analysis, Queensland University of Technology; Master of Environmental Planning, Postgraduate Diploma in Urban Studies, Macquarie University; Diploma in Surveying, Oxford Polytechnic; General Practice Division examinations, RICS, UK. Principles of property valuation, property investment valuation, property agency and marketing, specialist valuation, statutory valuation.

Mr. S. Cooper, visiting teaching fellow. Master of Valuation, Master's Degree in Urban Development and Sustainability, Bond University; Postgraduate Diploma in Urban Development and Sustainability; Graduate Certificate in Urban Development and Sustainability. Principles of property valuation, sustainable construction.

Mr. B. McAuliffe, visiting teaching fellow. Bachelor of Applied Science in Property Economics, Queensland University of Technology; Master of Urban and Regional Planning, University of Queensland; Graduate Certificate in Design for Aged Environments; Master of Education; Graduate Diploma in Legal Studies. Principles of property valuation, property investment valuation.

Mr. S. McAuliffe, visiting teaching fellow. MEd, Graduate Diploma in legal studies, Queensland University of Technology; Graduate Certificate in Applied Finance, Australian Institute of Banking and Finance; BA, University of Queensland; BEc/BComm (current), real estate agent and auctioneer, Real Estate Institute of Queensland. Property agency and marketing, introduction to economics of development, property investment analysis, property finance and taxation, economics of sustainable development.

Affiliated Faculty

Mr. M. Baker, adjunct teaching fellow. Diploma in Architecture, Queensland Institute of Technology; Master of Social Planning and Development, University of Queensland; Graduate Diploma in Urban and Regional Planning, Queensland Institute of Technology; Local Government Town Planners Board Certificate. Planning process.

Dr. G. Earl, professor and dean. PhD, Queensland University of Technology; MSc, Postgraduate Diploma in Property Development, University of South Australia; Diploma in Quantity Surveying, Institute of Quantity Surveyors, UK. Capstone projects.

Dr. P. Kent, professor of accounting and associate academic dean. M Econ, Dip. Rur. Acc, B Econ, ASCPA5, PhD. Introduction to accounting.

Ms. T. Johnson, senior teaching fellow. LLB (Hons.). Property law.

Dr. C. Langston, professor of construction and facilities management. PhD, University of Technology, Sydney; Master of Applied Science, Bachelor of Applied Science (Hons./Medal), New South Wales Institute of Technology. Asset and facilities management.

Dr. D. O'Hare, associate professor of urban planning. PhD, philosophy, Joint Center for Urban Design, Oxford Brookes University; MA (coursework) (Urban Design), Joint Center for Urban Design, Oxford Polytechnic; Bachelor of Town Planning (1st Class Hons., University Medal), University of New South Wales. Research methods.

Dr. M. Shinn, assistant professor. MB, BS (1st Class Hons.) LLB (Hons.), University of Queensland. Business Law.

Dr. J. Smith, head of school and professor of urban development. PhD, MSc, University of Melbourne. Principles of sustainable property, understanding buildings, urban development, geographic information systems and property.

Dr. L. Tay, assistant professor of urban development. PhD, management, MPhil, land economy, University of Cambridge; MSc, real estate; BSc, estate management (1st Class Hons.), National University of Singapore; Diploma in Building with Merit, Singapore Polytechnic. Asset and facilities management, corporate real estate.

University of Cambridge

John Glascock, Grosvenor Professor of Real Estate Finance
Department of Land Economy
19 Silver Street
Cambridge, CB3 9EP
United Kingdom
44 1223 337129; fax 44 1223 337130
Landecon-pgadmissions@lists.cam.ac.uk
www.landecon.cam.ac.uk

Degree	Year Program Began	Years to Complete	Thesis or Final Product	Full-Time Students (2006–2007)
MPhil in real estate finance	2001	1	Yes	45

Degree	Application Deadline	Minimum Undergraduate GPA	Departmental Requirements
MPhil	March 31	3.5 or 2nd class Honors equivalent to division 1	Application form, personal statement, 2 letters of reference; when applicable for overseas students, proof of English-language proficiency

Number of Faculty	Specialized Degree Accreditation	In-State Graduate Tuition	Out-of-State Graduate Tuition
Faculty: 10 Affiliated Faculty: 11	RICS, IPF	£3,168 (university fee) £2,001 (college fee)	£8,832 (university fee) £2,001 (college fee)

Note: Tuition fees refer to the 2006–2007 financial year. All students must pay the college fee in addition to the university fee, and must be able to demonstrate that they can meet a total of £8,268 in living expenses for the duration of the course. In addition, students will need approximately £1,000 for field trips, textbooks, and related materials.

Degree Specialization

MPhil in real estate finance.

Program Description

The MPhil in real estate finance is a specialist graduate program offered by the Department of Land Economy. The typical student has a strong academic background and is usually 23 to 26 years of age. The department is an internationally recognized center for studies in real estate finance, urban and regional economics, and environmental law and policy. Cambridge has a long history of research and teaching in the field of land economics, with well-established undergraduate and graduate programs in the general area of land economy.

The real estate finance program aims to provide integrated theoretical and practical instruction in finance, investment, economics, and law as they relate to global commercial property markets. Students are provided with the analytical methods and techniques needed for commercial property financing, investment, and development. The program is designed to ensure that property specialists are able to interact with other professionals in corporate finance and related fields. To this end, particular emphasis is placed on ensuring that students are familiar with the latest concepts in mixed-asset portfolio analysis, risk management, financial engineering, and option-based valuation.

The Department of Land Economy also offers four other specialist MPhil programs: MPhil in planning, growth, and regeneration; MPhil in land economy research; MPhil in land economy; and MPhil in environmental policy.

Core Curriculum

The core curriculum consists of the following modules: introduction to real estate finance, research methods, real estate development, real estate finance and securitization, real estate investment and risk analysis, real estate finance and valuation (elective), and macroeconomy and housing (elective).

Financial Aid

No financial aid is offered through the Department of Land Economy; however, a large number of scholarships are available from trust funds, including the Cambridge Commonwealth Trust, the Cambridge Overseas Trust, the Cambridge Education Trust, and the Gates Cambridge Trust. Information about these awards is available at www.cam.ac.uk.

Lecture Series

Numerous lecture series in various departments are open to our students. In addition, the Department of Land Economy has a weekly seminar series. Speakers are typically from other academic or research institutions. Specific seminars of relevance to students in the real estate finance program are offered on an occasional basis; the speakers are drawn from the property industry. The real estate finance program is also a member of Cambridge Finance, whose weekly seminars are open to real estate finance students (see www.finance.group.cam.ac.uk).

International Programs

Students are expected to participate in field trips to Frankfurt, London, Manchester, and Liverpool (not all cities are visited every year). The trip schedule varies from time to time. Also, two-thirds of the intakes are usually non-UK students.

Program Advisory Group

The advisory group has 26 members, including senior executives and directors from leading property-related companies worldwide. The advisory group meets twice a year and provides strong strategic guidance for the real estate finance program. Members of the advisory group also act as mentors to the students. Companies represented include Bidwells Property Consultants, Cambridge Place Investment Management, Cyril Leonard, Equity International Properties, Grosvenor, Grupo Lar, ING Real Estate Capital Advisors, INVESCO, Investment Property Databank, Jones Lang LaSalle, JP Morgan, Kingdom Hotel Investments, Land Securities, Lehman Brothers, Meyer Bergman, Mitsui Fudosan, Olympic Delivery Authority, Orchard Investment Management LLP, SERGO plc, Slough Estates, Société Foncière Lyonnaise, and UBS Global Asset Management.

Internship Placement Assistance

Internships are available from companies in the UK and abroad; they are arranged individually.

Job Placement Assistance

Since the 2003–2004 academic year, the real estate finance program has published a resume book to assist graduates with job placement; the book is widely distributed through the advisory group and other industry contacts. Also, Cambridge University graduates are highly sought after in the job market: many international property service companies, management consulting firms, and investment banks recruit actively among Cambridge students. Program participants also have access to the University Careers Service, which offers a number of resources to assist students in their career search, including extensive information on European and international opportunities.

Clubs/Alumni Associations

Graduates of the real estate finance program can join the Cambridge University Land Society (CULS), an alumni group for land economy graduates. For more information about the CULS, see www.culandsoc.com/.

Other

The real estate finance program offers students mentoring opportunities with UK and global firms. An attempt is made to provide all students with this opportunity.

Awards

At the beginning of the 2006–2007 academic year, three awards were arranged for the MPhil in real estate finance: the Loizou Award, for the highest overall mark in the real estate finance MPhil; the Anastassiades Award, for the highest dissertation mark in the real estate finance MPhil; and the Douglas Blausten Award (given by the CULS), for the highest mark in the real estate development module.

Faculty

Phillip Arestis, director of research, Center for Economics and Public Policy. PhD, University of Surrey; MSc, University of London; BA, Athens. Professor, Levy Economics Institute, New York. Macroeconomy and housing.

Helen X. Bao, lecturer in real estate finance. PhD, City University, Hong Kong; MA, Dalian University, China. Research methods and development.

Shaun A. Bond, senior lecturer in real estate finance. PhD, MPhil, University of Cambridge; BEcon, University of Queensland. Real estate finance and securitization.

Martin Dixon, lecturer in law. PhD, University of Cambridge; MA, Oxford University. Legal issues in land use and finance.

Bernard Fingleton, reader; director, MPhil in land economy. PhD, MPhil, University of Cambridge; PhD, University of Wales. Research methods.

John Glascock, Grosvenor Professor of Real Estate Finance and program course director. PhD, University of North Texas; MA, Virginia Tech; MBA, Stetson University; MA, University of Cambridge; BSBA, Tennessee Tech University. Introduction to real estate finance.

Andreas Kontoleon, lecturer in environmental economics; director, MPhil in environmental policy. PhD, University College London; MPhil, University of Cambridge; BA, American College of Greece. Sustainability and international environmental policy.

Barry Moore, reader in economics. MA, University of Cambridge; MSc, BSc, University of London. Introduction to real estate finance.

Elisabete Silva, lecturer in planning; co-director, MPhil in planning, growth, and regeneration. PhD, regional planning, University of Massachusetts; Master in Regional Planning, New University of Lisbon; BA, geography and planning, University of Lisbon. Urban and environmental planning.

Peter Tyler, professor; co-director, MPhil in planning, growth and regeneration. PhD, University of Cambridge; MSc, University of Reading; BA, Lancaster University. Urban and environmental planning.

Affiliated Faculty

Jamie Alcock, visiting lecturer in finance, University of Queensland. PhD, mathematical finance; GCFM, finance; BA (Hons.), mathematical finance and statistics; BA, mathematics, University of Queensland. Research methods.

Andrew Baum, visiting professor, part-time professor of land management, University of Reading. Chairman of Property Funds Research. BSc, MPhil, PhD, University of Reading. Real estate development.

Natalie Bayfield, visiting lecturer. Director of Bayfield Training, UK; Director of BFM Ltd, City University. Financial modeling.

Mary G. Boss, visiting lecturer. Specialist in international career design, personal development, and cross-cultural communications, Boss International; career coach and trainer, INSEAD Business School, Fontainebleau (France) and Singapore. Career development.

John S. Howe, visiting professor, professor of finance and Missouri Bankers Chair, University of Missouri at Columbia. Masters, PhD, Purdue University. Corporate finance, corporate governance, financial contracting, real estate investment trusts.

Lei Feng, visiting scholar, associate professor of real estate economics, Renmin University, Beijing. Member, China Land Association. Land markets in China.

Mike Ford, visiting lecturer. BSc, MPhil, land economy, University of Cambridge. FRICS. Real estate development.

Johnnie Johnson, visiting professor; professor of decision and risk analysis; director, Center for Risk Research, University of Southampton. BSc, PhD, CMath, FIMA, ACII, AUMIST, University of Southampton. Real estate investment and risk analysis.

Chiuling Lu, visiting professor; professor of finance, National Chengchi University, Taiwan. PhD, finance, University of Connecticut. Director, Sinyi Real Estate Center. Investments and securitization.

Richard Peiser, visiting professor; professor of real estate development, Graduate School of Design, Harvard University; director, Real Estate Academic Initiative. PhD, University of Cambridge; MA, MBA, Harvard Business School. Real estate development.

Bing Wang, visiting scholar; lecturer, urban planning and design, Graduate School of Design, Harvard University. PhD, MArch, Harvard University; BA, architecture, Tsinghua University, Beijing. Founder and manager, HyperBina Inc., China; principal, China Real Estate Investment Company. Real estate development module.

Clemson University

J. Terrence Farris, Director
Department of Planning and Landscape Architecture
School of Design and Building
124 Lee Hall
Clemson, SC 29634
864-656-3926; fax 864-656-7519
curealestate-l@clemson.edu
www.clemson.edu/mred

Degree	Year Program Began	Credit Hours	Years to Complete	Thesis or Final Product	Part-Time Students (2008)	Degrees Conferred (2008)
MRED	Fall 2004	54	2	2 competititve and commercial master-planned community feasibility analyses in Atlanta, Charlotte, or South Carolina	20	20

Degree	Application Deadline	Minimum Undergraduate GPA	Minimum GRE or GMAT Score	Departmental Requirements
MRED	February 1—priority; possibly through May, until 20 students are accepted	3.0-4.0 preferred	Prefer GRE 1240-5.0 or GMAT 600-5.0; TOEFL 600	Resume, 2-page personal statement, 3 letters of reference, GRE or GMAT, TOEFL (for international students); some experience desired; site visit highly recommended

Number of Faculty/FTE	In-State Graduate Tuition	Out-of-State Graduate Tuition
13/5	$22,500 (includes Maymester/summer)	$22,500 (includes Maymester/summer)

Degree Specialization

The MRED, which is jointly offered by the College of Business and Behavioral Science and the College of Architecture, Arts, and Humanities, specializes in master-planned, mixed-use, infill, and destination/resort communities. We want our students to become great place makers—not just builders of projects.

Program Description

The complexities and dynamics of today's real estate industry demand professionals who view themselves as stewards of our world's fragile resources and as advocates of responsible land use. The MRED program recognizes that responsible development is not just a real estate industry fad. It is a way of life, and a way of work. Graduates enter the world with the building blocks to become champions of responsible development and sustainable growth, within the context of economic feasibility and value creation.

The Clemson MRED program closely follows the principles of the Urban Land Institute (ULI), which believes that development is a public/private partnership, and that quality development means integrating community, environment, and economics. We want each student to become a visionary—a craftsperson and a designer who recognizes the role of the developer in guiding the political, economic, physical, environmental, legal, and sociological aspects of creating the built environment.

This is the only graduate program in real estate development in the nation that offers a joint degree sponsored by an architectural college and a business college, with required classes in MBA/finance, law, construction science and management, architecture, city and regional planning, and real estate development. Our students have what MBA real estate specializations include—and so much more! Our blending of theory and real-world applications affords students the opportunity to mix with key players in the real estate industry on a regular basis. We are the proud recipients of the Hughes ULI Library Collection, which was donated by a ULI Foundation board member.

Our program emphasizes thorough knowledge of mixed-use, infill, and master-planned communities, of which there are premier examples in the region. Clemson is located on the I-85 corridor in a dynamic metro area of 1 million people (Greenville-Spartanburg), between the two major markets of Atlanta and Charlotte and within several hours' drive of an array of development types and issues, including coastal South Carolina, which includes Myrtle Beach, Charleston, and Hilton Head Island. Our location in the dynamic southeast serves as an excellent student laboratory.

We have extensive involvement with the development industry through roundtables, tours, and conferences. We are proud that all our students are members of the CNU, the ICSC, the NAIOP, and ULI (including active involvement in the ULI Young Leaders Group). The program is a founding sponsor of the South Carolina ULI District Council; and Dr. Farris, the program director, is the South Carolina Vice-Chair–Quality Growth and a member of the national Public-Private Partnership Council. All 40 students go to the fall ULI conference to visit leading-edge developments, expand their horizons, and network with real estate leaders. First-year students tour the South Carolina coast for 12 days in May to study some of the nation's premier resort, hotel, historic, mixed-use, golf, master-planned, and new urbanist communities. Weekly roundtables put students in touch with key executives in the real estate industry. There are also extended trips to Atlanta, Charlotte, Charleston, and Savannah.

We have a strict selection process that requires students to demonstrate exceptional track records in undergraduate study, work experience, or both. To maintain the personal scale of the program, entering classes are kept to fewer than 20 students per year. So far, students have come from over 18 states.

Core Curriculum

The MRED program is primarily a core program with required courses from MBA/finance, law, architecture, construction science and management, city and regional planning, and real estate development. Core courses include accounting and finance, real estate principles, development process, human settlement, site planning and infrastructure, building design and construction principles, investment, valuation, geographic information systems/technology, market analysis, law, real estate seminar roundtable, contractor role in the development process, personnel management and negotiations, public/private partnerships, a practicum in commercial development, and a practicum in master-planned/resort communities. All students must complete at least 54 credit hours. One elective is required; more may be allowed if the student is exempted from core courses because of prior completion. Two key electives are urban design, which emphasizes form-based zoning, and a seminar in destination recreation development communities, which features premier national experts from the resort/recreation industry.

Financial Aid

There are several research analyst (RA) positions in the Center for Real Estate Development (CRED) and several fellowships. All applicants are considered for an RA position; positions are awarded on the basis of CRED's needs and the applicant's experience. No graduate assistantships or tuition reductions are available for MRED students. Most second-year students have two-day-a-week paid professional internships.

MRED has an entrepreneurial tuition different from the rest of Clemson University, recognizing the value for the dollar commitment. Tuition covers memberships in ULI, NAIOP, ICSC, and CNU; a one-week ULI fall conference trip; a 12-day Maymester tour of coastal South Carolina (Myrtle Beach, Charleston, Hilton Head); two-day trips to Atlanta, Charlotte, Savannah; and other regional communities and conferences.

Standard federal loans are available. The program also receives funding from the Carolinas Chapter of SIOR, available to second-year students. The program also assists representative students to apply for fellowships. Contact Dr. J. Terrence Farris at 864-656-3903 or jfarris@clemson.edu.

Lecture Series

The CRED and the MRED program have numerous guest speakers from the real estate industry; lectures address best practices, finance, appraisal, brokerage, property management, design, environment, sustainability, land planning, market research, construction, regulatory approvals, management and organizational issues, entrepreneurship, and other leading issues.

The Charles Fraser Visiting Associates and Lecture Series honors the legacy of Charles Fraser, the developer of Hilton Head Island. Former Fraser associates share their knowledge of high-quality master-planned development and the real estate principles that Fraser espoused; offer advice and counsel; and participate actively in classes, studios, lectures, mentoring, and other activities.

The weekly Real Estate Seminar Roundtable brings students and approximately 30 premier real estate professionals together through two-hour on-site or videoconference sessions. Presentations and discussions explore cutting-edge projects and industry issues from around the country and internationally.

Clemson University's Restoration Institute provides opportunities for research and lectures on the restoration economy, with Charleston as a focus. Other lectures are sponsored by six departments within the program and elsewhere at the university.

International Programs

In place of the required ten-week summer internship, an international experience is allowed, with the approval of the director. The director of the CRED is past president of the International Real Estate Society, and the MRED program attracts internationally oriented lecturers.

Program Advisory Group

The broad-based, 23-member CRED Advancement Board, which has members from across the nation, meets quarterly to offer advice and counsel, discuss fundraising, share information on internships and permanent positions, and provide support. The program is honored to have Harry H. Frampton III, past chairman of ULI, alumnus and chairman of the Clemson University Foundation, and managing partner of East West Partners in Beaver Creek, Colorado, as a key adviser and supporter. See www.clemson.edu/mred for a list of premier members of the real estate community. The MRED program has numerous national and state ULI leaders in its network of advisers. A significant capital campaign is underway, and construction on a new building will begin in 2009, with MRED as its anchor.

Internship Placement Assistance

A minimum ten-week summer internship is required. The MRED program and the CRED assist students to find positions, often through the ULI network. Students have the opportunity to go anywhere they choose, subject to the program director's approval. A national executive search firm assists in placement. The goal is for all second-year students to work two days a week in paid internships with local private, public, and nonprofit entities. Positions are established primarily through the program. Assistance is also available through the Clemson Michelin Career Center. A new program coordinator will be hired in the spring of 2008 to assist with internship placement.

Job Placement Assistance

With the help of a national executive search firm specializing in real estate, the MRED program provides extensive placement assistance, including business protocol counseling, resume review, mock interviews, job-hunting strategies, contacts with firms, and direct consultation with the student during the offer and negotiation process. Networking at national and regional conferences and guidance from the Advancement Board provide further assistance. Students' resumes are posted on the program's Web site, and firms are invited to campus for interviews. Through brochures geared especially for employees, the MRED program constantly markets itself to key national development firms. Assistance is also available through the Clemson Michelin Career Center. A new program coordinator will be hired in the spring of 2008 to assist with job placement.

Clubs/Alumni Associations

The Clemson Student Real Estate Association sponsors student participation in state and national conferences and provides opportunities for exposure to real estate activities, networking with professionals from all disciplines, and learning about real estate and development trends. To build camaraderie and provide opportunities to interact with alumni, the association also sponsors social activities for MRED students.

MRED students have taken leadership roles with the Emerging Green Builders, the Carolinas Student Chapter of the CNU (the program is a founding sponsor), and the SC District Council of ULI Young Leaders, among other student groups.

Our growing MRED alumni association is evolving into an active organization that is closely linked to the program and provides mentoring for students, as well as job and internship opportunities.

Faculty

Robert Benedict, instructor, MRED program, and CRED research associate. Doctoral student in environmental design and planning, Clemson University; MBA, University of Georgia; MAHP, Goucher College; BA, University of North Carolina at Charlotte. Real estate development process, preservation economics, commercial practicum.

J. Terrence Farris, associate professor, MRED program director. AB, urban geography, St. Louis University; MUP, PhD, urban and regional planning, Michigan State University. CRE, AICP. Real estate development process, market and feasibility analysis, housing and community development, public/private partnerships.

Thomas Springer, professor of finance. PhD, real estate, University of Georgia; MBA, University of Georgia; BS, forestry, University of Florida. Real estate principles and real estate investment.

Neil G. Waller, professor of finance, Pulliam Fellow in Real Estate. PhD, finance and real estate, University of Texas; BS, MA, real estate and urban analysis, University of Florida. MAI. Real estate finance and real estate valuation.

Elaine Worzala, professor; director, CRED. PhD, real estate and urban land economics; MS, real estate appraisal and investment analysis, University of Wisconsin-Madison. Real estate principles, process and market analysis, valuation, technology, roundtables on the role of the architect and contractor, feasibility analysis, real estate finance and investments.

Affiliated Faculty

Dennis C. Bausman, assistant professor of construction science and management. PhD, construction management, Heriot-Watt University, Edinburgh; MCSM, Clemson University; BS, construction engineering, Iowa State University. Business strategic planning, financial management, business planning, project management.

Cliff Ellis, associate professor. PhD, University of California at Berkeley; MPCD, University of Colorado at Denver; BA, Colorado College. Land use planning, growth management, transportation planning, planning theory, urban design, metropolitan and regional planning, history of urban form, history of city planning, community development.

Robert E. Ellis, instructor. BArch, Clemson University. President and owner, the Ellis GroupArchitecture. AIA, NCARB. Building design and construction principles.

Judson R. Jahn, lecturer, School of Accounting and Legal Studies. JD, Mercer University; MBA, Clemson University. Partner, Merrill & Jahn, P.A. Real estate and construction law.

Roger W. Liska, professor, Department of Construction Science and Management. EdD, University of Georgia; MS, civil engineering, Wayne State University; BS, civil engineering, Michigan Technological University. Craftworker retention and total quality management.

Jeffrey J. McMillan, professor of accountancy. PhD, accounting, University of South Carolina. Financial accounting, behavioral, auditing, ethics, educational methods, market valuation.

Daniel J. Nadenicek, professor; chair, Department of Planning and Landscape Architecture. MLA, BLA, University of Minnesota; MS, BS, history, Mankato State University. Community design, human settlements, landscape and urban planning history.

Jeff Randolph, instructor, Department of Planning and Landscape Architecture. BA, political science; MCRP, Clemson University.

Cleveland State University

Dr. W. Dennis Keating, Professor
Department of Urban Studies
Levin College of Urban Affairs
2121 Euclid Avenue
Cleveland, OH 44115
216-687-2298; fax 216-687-9342
w.keating@csuohio.edu
http://urban.csuohio.edu/academics/mupdd.shtml

Degree	Year Program Began	Credit Hours	Years to Complete	Thesis or Final Product	Full-Time Students (2006–2007)	Part-Time Students (2006–2007)	Degrees Conferred (2006)
MUPDD	1992	48	2	Optional	40	27	34
Graduate certificate in urban real estate finance and development	1998	16	1–2	N/A	0	7	7

Degree	Minimum Undergraduate GPA	Minimum GRE or GMAT Score	Departmental Requirements
MUPPD	3.0	40% combined quantitative/verbal; 4.0 AW	2 letters of reference

Number of Faculty	Specialized Degree Accreditation	In-State Graduate Tuition	Out-of-State Graduate Tuition
10	PAB	$5,271/semester	$10,011/semester

Degree Specializations

MUPDD, with a specialization in urban real estate finance and development. Graduate certificate in urban real estate finance and development: four classes, two in the College of Urban Affairs and two in the College of Business.

Program Description

The planning program offers a strong core curriculum that includes a class in development and market analysis; additional electives in the real estate specialization strengthen applied skills and knowledge. The Levin College is nationally ranked as a school of public affairs. The university is located in a stimulating urban environment where niche opportunities in real estate development and a resurgent urban housing market offer students a laboratory for study and experience. A strong internship placement program allows students to work in public agencies and in local and regional real estate–related firms. The real estate specialization attracts students from across the nation. Students participate in the ULI Gerald D. Hines Student Urban Design competition annually.

Core Curriculum

The MUPDD has eight core courses and four electives. The real estate certificate program has four required courses, of which one is a MUPDD core course.

Financial Aid

Students with GPAs of 3.0 or above are eligible for a range of graduate assistantships/internships that include tuition and a stipend. Stipend-only internships are also available. Limited grants for certificate students are available. MUPDD students are eligible for several externally funded cash prizes and scholarships. Contact Fran Hunter at 216-687-2388 or fran@urban.csuohio.edu.

Lecture Series

Each real estate class has guest lecturers such as developers, lenders, representatives of nonprofit development organizations, and consultants. The degree program sponsors a lecture series on planning and development issues. The college has multiple lectures and other events relating to planning and real estate development each year.

Program Advisory Group

The MUPDD advisory committee meets at least once a year to advise on curriculum and practice issues.

Internship Placement Assistance

The college has a full-time staff person devoted to internship placement. An internship is not required, but is strongly suggested for students who are new to the field of planning and real estate. Internships may be for one semester, one year, or two years, and may be salaried or for tuition and a stipend. Contact Fran Hunter at 216-687-2388 or fran@urban.csuohio.edu.

Job Placement Assistance

A job board and Web site are available. The university provides a career services representative within the college. Faculty and research staff also assist students. An annual juried real estate paper and presentation program allows students to present to real estate practitioners.

Clubs/Alumni Associations

Student chapter of the American Planning Association.

Faculty

Robert A. Simons, professor of urban planning and real estate development. PhD, city and regional planning; MS, economics; MRP, University of North Carolina at Chapel Hill; BA, Colorado State University. Real estate development, market analysis and finance, public economics, environmental finance, brownfields redevelopment, urban redevelopment, environmental damage, housing policy.

James Webb, professor of real estate finance. PhD, James Nance College of Business, University of Illinois; MBA, BS, Northern Illinois University. Real estate finance, real estate investment, corporate finance and investments, decision theory for real estate investment, real estate management, impact of environmental hazards on property valuation.

University of Colorado

Byron Koste, Executive Director
CU Real Estate Center
Leeds School of Business, Koelbel Building
419 UCB
Boulder, CO 80309-0419
303-492-3258; fax 303-492-5507
byron.koste@cu.edu
http://leeds.colorado.edu/realestate

Degree	Years in Operation	Credit Hours	Years to Complete
BSBA with area of application	11	120	4
BSBA with certificate	11	120	4
MBA	11	55	2
JD/MBA	11	120	4

Number of Faculty/FTE	In-State Graduate Tuition	Out-of-State Graduate Tuition	In-State Undergraduate Tuition	Out-of-State Undergraduate Tuition	In-State Law Tuition	Out-of-State Law Tuition
9/6	$2,910/ semester	$10,816/ semester	$2,382/ semester	$10,816/ semester	$3,404/ semester	$10,972/ semester

Degree Specializations

BSBA with an area of application in real estate.
BSBA with a certificate in real estate.
MBA with a real estate and/or sustainable development track.
Joint law and MBA (JD/MBA) with a real estate track.

Program Description

In 2008, the University of Colorado (CU) Real Estate Center hired William Shutkin as director in Sustainable Development and Growth Management. This new appointment positions the center to be a leader in sustainable development issues nationwide. Shutkin is responsible for developing an interdisciplinary academic program focusing on growth management and sustainable development principles and practices. He is also teaching a survey course on sustainable development and growth management.

The CU Real Estate Center is a high-caliber academic program with strong ties to a group of leading industry professionals, the CU Real Estate Council. With the involvement of council members, the program offers coursework, internships, networking, and job placement assistance for both graduates and undergraduates. Graduate students also have the opportunity to be involved in the mentor program—through which, over a two-year period, industry professionals provide career advice, networking, and even internships. The active participation of council members has assisted the center to become involved in many activities that impact the university and community, and to work side by side with ULI, NAIOP, CREW, and other industry organizations and leaders. In 2002, the CU Real Estate Foundation was created to assist the university in the implementation of campus master plans, and to maximize financial returns to the university through the creation and management of a high-income-producing real estate portfolio.

Core Curriculum

Undergraduate: Principles of real estate practice, real estate law and financing instruments, real estate finance and investment analysis, real estate development, real estate case studies, real estate academic.

Graduate: real estate development, real estate finance and investment analysis, real estate law and contracts, real estate economics, real estate project competition, and a survey course in sustainable development and growth management.

Financial Aid

CU offers several types of financial aid, including student loans, grants, and work-study programs. A limited number of teaching assistantships, fellowships, and scholarships are available through the university and the Leeds School of Business. The Real Estate Center also offers fellowships and financial assistance through paid internships. For more information, contact the Office of Financial Aid at 303-492-5091.

Lecture Series

Interested students may participate in the Real Estate Projects and Case Studies Series. This lecture series provides an in-depth analysis of current real estate projects in the area and is taught by the industry professionals undertaking the projects.

International Programs

Study abroad programs are available for all students, although a study abroad program specifically related to real estate is not offered. Contact the Study Abroad Office at 303-492-7741.

Program Advisory Group

The CU Real Estate Council Education Committee is made up of industry representatives who advise the Real Estate Center on curriculum. The committee is crucial to the development of a program of study that offers students the skills they will need in the job market and the broad base of knowledge they will need to further their education.

Job Placement Assistance

Three different organizations assist in career development and job placement. The Real Estate Center works with the Real Estate Council to find internships and full-time employment for real estate students. The Career Services Office offers career planning, cooperative education, and internship programs; postgraduate employment opportunities; and on-campus interviewing. The Business Career Center of the Leeds School of Business provides assistance for all areas of the job search process. Contact the Real Estate Center at 303-492-3643; Career Services at 303-492-6541; or the Business Career Center at 303-492-1808.

Faculty

David Agnew, adjunct faculty of real estate. JD, Washington University. Real estate law and contracts.

John T. Ballantine, senior instructor. JD, University of Colorado at Boulder; MBA, Indiana University. Real estate law, business law, financial and managerial accounting.

Byron R. Koste, director, CU Real Estate Center. Executive Program graduate, Stanford University; MBA, Duquesne University. Real estate development, real estate investments, real estate project competition, undergraduate academic internships.

Adam Massey, adjunct faculty of real estate. MBA, University of Colorado at Boulder. Real estate case studies.

Liang Peng, assistant professor. PhD, Yale University. Principles of real estate practice, real estate finance and investment.

Curtis Sears, adjunct faculty of real estate. JD, University of Colorado at Boulder. Principles of real estate practice.

William A. Shutkin, director, Sustainable Development and Growth Management. JD, University of Virginia; MA, University of Virginia. Sustainable development and growth management.

Thomas G. Thibodeau, academic director, real estate program; chair, Real Estate Capital Markets. PhD, State University of New York at Stony Brook. Real estate fundamentals, real estate finance, real estate markets and valuation, general real estate, real estate economics and valuation.

Richard L. Woodruff, adjunct faculty of real estate. MBA, University of Colorado at Denver; BA, University of Colorado. Real estate development.

Columbia University

Lynne Sagalyn, Earle W. Kazis and Benjamin Schore Professor of Real Estate
Director, MBA Real Estate Program and the Paul Milstein Center for Real Estate
Columbia Business School
Uris 822; 3022 Broadway
New York, NY 10027
212-854-3380; fax 212-854-8776
lbs4@columbia.edu
www.gsb.columbia.edu/realestate

Degree	Years in Operation	Credit Hours	Years to Complete	Full-Time Students (2006–2007)	Degrees Conferred (2007)
MBA	30	60 (4 terms)	2	1,226	651

Number of Faculty	Specialized Degree Accreditation	In-State Graduate Tuition	Out-of-State Graduation Tuition
127 full time; 116 adjunct	AACSB	$43,436/year	$43,436/year

Degree Specializations

MBA with real estate concentration.
Joint degree programs are available in construction management (with the School of Engineering), planning (with the School of Architecture), and the School of International and Public Affairs.

Program Description

The MBA Real Estate Program offers a special focus on real estate finance and investment management. Its three-part foundation consists of a general analytical business education with an emphasis on finance, a specialized real estate curriculum, and strong links with industry professionals. Since 1978, the program has successfully turned out graduates with a strong understanding of real estate fundamentals, and the knowledge and skills needed to manage, lead, and remain ahead of the rapid changes in the real estate marketplace. Through a case-study approach, the curriculum stimulates critical thinking and helps students develop a talent for solving complex strategic, financial, and managerial problems.

A broad array of elective courses supports multiple career paths in real estate, including finance and investment banking, asset and portfolio management, entrepreneurial development, and public and nonprofit real estate management.

To meet the needs of tomorrow's entrepreneurs, the Business School's Entrepreneurship Program offers a wide range of courses and holds two business competitions geared to starting new ventures of all types. The MBA Real Estate Program also sponsors an annual business plan competition underwritten by the Seevak Family Foundation. The competition is combined with our Master Class in Real Estate Investment, which is designed to foster creative thinking and problem solving through research and teamwork and to cultivate effective communication skills. The competition, held in the spring term, awards monetary prizes for the winning business plans.

Core Curriculum

The MBA core consists of five full courses and eight half-courses, which make up approximately 45 percent of the overall requirement. Beginning in their second semester, real estate concentrators take their first real estate elective, Real Estate Finance. In the third semester, students can take Real Estate Capital Markets and/or Real Estate Transactions. Finally, in the fourth semester, students take the Advanced Real Estate Seminar and our culminating course, the Master Class in Real Estate Investment, in which students get priceless real-world experience working on a project with industry leaders from top companies such as Equity International, JP Morgan Chase, Lehman Brothers, Morgan Stanley, Starwood Capital, and Tishman Hotels; students also serve as consultants to, and learn from, approximately ten other projects.

Financial Aid

The Columbia Business School offers several scholarships for real estate entrants and second-year students. See www4.gsb.columbia.edu/realestate/ProspectiveStudents/scholarships; or contact the Financial Aid Office, Columbia Business School, 218 Uris Hall, 3022 Broadway, New York, NY 10027; or finaid@gsb.columbia.edu; 212-854-4057; fax 212-854-1809.

Lecture Series

The Real Estate Association organizes a speakers' series that keeps students abreast of current trends in the industry and the capital markets, helping them to explore the field before making a career decision and to establish a network with Columbia alumni and other industry leaders. Speakers are drawn from the development, finance, asset management, and investment advisory sectors.

International Programs

The Columbia Business School sponsors several international study tours each year. It also has an active and growing international business program for students and a special center—the Chazen Institute of International Business. The school has affiliations with many business schools abroad, and a significant proportion of its student body is from abroad, especially from Europe and East Asia.

Program Advisory Group

The MBA Real Estate Program Advisory Board is made up of senior executives from American Continental Properties Group; Apollo Real Estate Advisors; Capital Trust; Citigroup Property Investors; Credit Suisse First

Boston; Goldman Sachs & Company, Inc.; Janafsky & Walker LLP; JP Morgan; Lazard Frères & Co.; Lehman Brothers; Merrill Lynch & Co.; Milstein Properties; Morgan Stanley; NorthStar Capital Investment Corp.; Paul Hastings; Prudential Real Estate Investors; Simon Property Group; Taconic Investment Partners; the Time Group; Tishman Hotel Corporation; Tishman Realty Corporation; and Tishman Speyer Properties. The advisory board meets in the fall to discuss the overall direction of program activities and development, and in the spring to participate in the annual meeting of the Columbia Real Estate Forum, a group of 40 of the industry's most distinguished leaders that was formed in 1997 to stimulate candid discussion and debate regarding strategic issues facing the real estate industry today.

Job Placement Assistance

In addition to assistance from the Business School Career Resources and Placement Office, students receive personal advice and placement assistance from the staff of the Paul Milstein Center for Real Estate; from executive-in-residence; and from real estate industry leaders, who host a series of mentoring breakfasts. The Real Estate Association (REA) sponsors special functions, including a variety of job panels. Also available are ARGUS training and the Real Estate SuperCharger, a half-day session that gives students the chance to speak with alumni and industry representatives about real estate career tracks. The club also publishes a resume book that is distributed to companies for both full-time and summer placements.

Clubs/Alumni Associations

The Milstein Center works closely with the REA, a student group with over 200 members who are interested in real estate investment and management. Working together, the Milstein Center and the REA coordinate activities that leverage the educational and networking opportunities available to students. To enhance members' industry knowledge and career opportunities, the REA organizes industry orientation sessions and panels, site tours, local and international study trips, and social events. One of the largest and most active clubs at Columbia Business School, the REA makes an important contribution to students' total real estate experience. Alumni from the real estate program are active participants in the networking events, which include mentoring breakfasts, speaker lunches, evening speakers' events, and cocktail hours focused on different segments of the industry.

Columbia Business School's Real Estate Circle is a growing alumni community. Alumni join to broaden their professional and personal networks, participate in executive education, and contribute to student fellowships, helping to ensure that Columbia Business School continues to attract the brightest scholars, who will go on to enrich the alumni network. Throughout the year, the Real Estate Circle offers members the opportunity to attend networking and social events, including Circle Academy executive education sessions. These breakfasts bring alumni together with a leading academic or industry expert, who presents thought- and discussion-provoking content. Topics need not be focused on real estate, but are relevant to current practice.

Faculty

J. Daniel Adkinson, adjunct professor. BA, Williams College. Head of debt capital markets, J.P. Morgan Fleming, U.S. Real Estate Investments Group. Real estate capital markets and real estate finance.

Jeffrey Barclay, adjunct professor. MBA, BA, Columbia University. Managing director and head of acquisitions, ING Clarion Partners. Master class in real estate investment.

Camille Douglas, adjunct professor. MCP, Harvard University; BA, Smith College. Master class in real estate investment.

Michael Giliberto, adjunct professor. PhD, University of Washington; MA, University of Hartford; BA, Harvard University. Director of Portfolio Strategy within the Real Estate and Infrastructure Investment Group at JPMorgan Asset Management. Real estate capital markets.

Tomasz Piskorski, assistant professor. PhD, MS, New York University; MS, Catholic University, Leuven, Belgium; BA, Warsaw University. Real estate finance.

Jonah Rockoff, assistant professor. PhD, Harvard University; BA, Amherst College. Tax factors in business decisions.

Lynne Sagalyn, Earle W. Kazis and Benjamin Schore Professor of Real Estate; director, MBA Real Estate Program and the Paul Milstein Center for Real Estate. PhD, Massachusetts Institute of Technology; MCRP, Rutgers University; BS, Cornell University. Real estate transactions (law); advanced real estate seminar.

Catherine Thomas, assistant professor. PhD, Harvard University; MA, University of Edinburgh; AM, Harvard University. Managerial economics.

Neng Wang, Chong Khoon Lin Professor of Real Estate. PhD, Stanford; MA, University of California at San Diego; MS, California Institute of Technology; BS, Nanjing University. Real estate finance.

Cornell University

David L. Funk, Director
Program in Real Estate
114 W. Sibley Hall
Ithaca, NY 14853
607-255-7110; fax 607-255-0242
real_estate@cornell.edu
www.realestate.cornell.edu

Degree	Year Program Began	Credit Hours	Years to Complete	Thesis or Final Product	Full-Time Students (2006–2007)	Degrees Conferred (2006)
MPS	1996	62	2	Final project	46	15

Degree	Application Deadline	Minimum Undergraduate GPA	Minimum GRE or GMAT Score	Departmental Requirements
MPS	January 15/March 15/ June 1	No minimum	No minimum	Transcripts, statement of purpose, resume, 2 letters of reference, GMAT, online application

Number of Faculty	Specialized Degree Accreditation	In-State Graduate Tuition	Out-of-State Graduate Tuition
Full time: 17 Part time: 3	RICS	$34,600/year	$34,600/year

Degree Specialization

MPS in real estate.

Program Description

The MPS in real estate at Cornell University is a comprehensive two-year program. The primary focus is to provide an extensive foundation in real estate core courses, including finance and investment, economics, market analysis, real estate development, real estate law, transactions and deal structuring, planning, and construction planning and management. During the second year of the program, students select a specialization from among nine areas, including development, finance and development, and sustainable development.

The program also organizes conferences for professionals; brings industry leaders to campus to meet with students and others; fosters research on emerging issues in the field; initiates and coordinates public service efforts in areas such as affordable housing, industrial development, and land use planning; and works with the Cornell Real Estate Council. The *Cornell Real Estate Review*, a student-managed and edited publication, provides a hands-on connection to practice-oriented real estate research.

Cornell's program is carefully designed to provide a proper mix of academic and real-world exposures. Professors in key real estate courses have years of firsthand private sector experience upon which to base the classroom experience. The capstone project, performed by teams of students in their fourth semester, consists of a live case study, complete with on-site visits, of a current real estate development project. The hands-on experience of working with a real site provides an exceptional opportunity to apply knowledge gained throughout the program.

Core Curriculum

The 39 credits of required core courses include Construction Planning and Operations; Real Estate Development Process; Real Estate Seminar Series; Principles of Real Estate; Managerial Finance; Communication in Real Estate; Design in Real Estate; Real Estate Law; Residential Development; Real Estate Finance and Investments; Real Estate Marketing and Management; Real Estate Transactions and Deal Structuring; and the Capstone Project Workshop.

Financial Aid

Graduate teaching and research assistantships; scholarships; fellowships; and project and campus work are available.

Lecture Series

The Cornell Real Estate Industry seminar series brings industry leaders to campus weekly throughout each semester. Speakers provide background on their companies, their segment of the industry, current and anticipated critical issues, and their personal roles and responsibilities in their organizations. Guests and topics are carefully selected to provide broad exposure to the industry; its products, issues, and job opportunities; and leadership personalities and styles.

Each fall, the Cornell Real Estate Conference, which is entering its 26th year and is the longest-running university-based real estate conference in the country, brings together industry professionals, alumni, and students for two days of panel discussions, keynote presentations, industry updates, and networking.

International Programs

International students and alumni diversity are hallmarks of the Cornell Program in Real Estate: roughly 30 percent of each year's class is made up of students from Europe, Central and South America, and Asia. Beginning in 2009, students will be able to participate in an international real estate study tour as part of the program.

Program Advisory Group

The 45-member Cornell Real Estate Advisory Board is drawn from the Cornell Real Estate Council and from parallel professions in all areas of real estate; members are key decision makers and influential leaders in various areas of the real estate industry. The advisory board plays a major role in the continuing development of the program and in the program's relationship with the industry, and provides support for key initiatives. Advisory board members are central to the program and serve as mentors, speakers, employers, and advisers. The program's governing board reflects Cornell's unique interdisciplinary strengths in real estate: it consists of five deans (appointed by the provost) from the College of Architecture, Art and Planning; the College of Human Ecology; the Johnson School of Management; the School of Hotel Administration; and the Law School—all of which offer courses in the real estate degree program. The governing board oversees the program, guiding both its development and its relationships with other fields of study and research at Cornell.

Internship Placement Assistance

Summer internships with real estate companies are a key part of the Program in Real Estate experience. Typically, during the summer after their first year in the program, over 90 percent of students have internships, either in the United States or internationally. Contact the Coordinator of Career Management at 607-255-7110 or real_estate@cornell.edu.

Job Placement Assistance

Career management and placement are integral parts of the real estate program. Students work closely with their advisers throughout the program to design courses of study and career plans that suit their needs and interests. Cornell's Real Estate Career Services Office provides individual and workshop-based career management support to students and alumni; sponsors campus visits by corporate recruiters; produces the annual *Real Estate Recruiter Handbook*, which includes student profiles; and maintains real estate job databases. Contact the Coordinator of Career Management at 607-255-7110 or real_estate@cornell.edu.

Clubs/Alumni Associations

The Cornell Real Estate Council, which started with a small group of alumni in the 1970s, now has over 1,200 members worldwide and strongly supports the university's academic program. Members of the council participate in symposia, deliver lectures, meet with students to offer industry perspectives and case studies, and are active in Cornell's Real Estate Job Network for summer and permanent positions.

The Associate Real Estate Council (AREC) represents graduate students interested in the real estate industry. AREC's goal is to develop and promote Cornell's contact with the real estate industry by hosting guest lecturers, creating an annual resume book, promoting student research, and organizing trips to industry seminars, conferences, and current development projects.

Faculty

Robert H. Abrams, senior lecturer, city and regional planning. MBA, Harvard Business School; BS, Cornell University. Real estate development and management and real estate project workshop.

Franklin D. Becker, professor, design and environmental analysis; director, International Facility Management Program. PhD, University of California at Davis. Facility planning and management.

Richard S. Booth, professor, city and regional planning. JD, George Washington University. Environmental law, legal aspects of land use planning, environmental politics, resource management.

John (Jack) Corgel, professor, hotel administration. PhD, University of Georgia. Principles of real estate, real estate investment, real estate investments in the hospitality industry.

Milton Curry, associate professor, architecture. MArch, Harvard University; BArch, Cornell University. Urban real estate industry.

Jan deRoos, professor, hotel administration. PhD, Cornell University. Real estate investment and development.

David Funk, senior lecturer, city and regional planning; director, Program in Real Estate. PhD, University of Wisconsin. Real estate marketing and management, real estate transactions and deal structuring.

Jerome Hass, professor, finance and business strategy; Krause Faculty Fellow in Real Estate, Johnson School of Graduate Management. PhD, Carnegie Mellon University. Corporate and capital market finance, business strategy, the economics of energy and regulations.

Kenneth C. Hover, professor, civil and environmental engineering. PhD, Cornell University. Construction planning and operations.

Peng (Peter) Liu, assistant professor, hotel administration. PhD, University of California at Berkeley. Principles of real estate.

Vincent J. Mulcahy, associate professor, architecture. MArch, Harvard University. Architectural planning and design.

C. Bradley Olson, senior lecturer, city and regional planning; director, Program in Real Estate. MBA, University of California at Berkeley; BS, Cornell University. Real estate development process and residential development.

Rolf Pendall, assistant professor, city and regional planning. PhD, University of California at Berkeley. Land use planning; state, regional, and local growth management; zoning and subdivision regulation; affordable housing; domestic environmental planning and policy.

Daniel W.C. Quan, associate professor, real estate finance. PhD, University of California at Berkeley; PhD/MPhil, London School of Economics; MS, BS, University of British Columbia. Securitization and structured financial products, mortgage and asset-backed securities, hospitality real estate finance.

Henry W. Richardson, associate professor, architecture. MRP, BArch, Cornell University. Housing, urban design.

Michael Tomlan, associate professor, city and regional planning; director, Historic Preservation Planning Program. PhD, Cornell University; MSHP, Columbia University; BArch, University of Tennessee. Economics and finance of neighborhood rehabilitation.

Roger T. Trancik, professor, landscape architecture and city and regional planning. MLA, urban design, Harvard University. Landscape architecture, urban design and development.

Peter J. Trowbridge, professor, landscape architecture. MLA, Harvard University. Landscape architecture.

Affiliated Faculty

Mark Foerster, C. Bradley Olson Real Estate Faculty Fellow. JD, Syracuse University. Capstone project workshop.

Adam Klausner, adjunct assistant professor, hotel administration. JD, Cornell University. Real estate law.

Tom Samuels, Paul Rubacha Real Estate Faculty Fellow. MBA, Harvard Business School; MCP, Harvard Graduate School of Design. Real estate development.

University of Denver

Mark Lee Levine
Burns School of Real Estate and Construction Management
Daniels College of Business
2101 S. University Blvd., #380
Denver, CO 80208
303-871-3432; fax 303-871-2971
burnsevents@du.edu
www.daniels.du.edu/burns

Degree	Year Program Began	Credit Hours	Years to Complete	Full-Time Students (2006–2007)	Part-Time Students (2006–2007)	Degrees Conferred (2006)
BSBA	1938	185	4	283	N/A	85
MSRECM	1938	50	1	120	65	76
MSRECM Online	1988	50	2	N/A	152	13

Degree	Application Deadline	Average High School GPA	Departmental Requirements
BSBA	April 1	3.63	Academic achievement, grade point average, standardized test scores, whole-person assessment, Hyde interview results
MSRECM	Fall: May 15 Spring: December 15	N/A	Admission interview, professional resume, essay questions, letters of recommendation, undergraduate GPA, GMAT score
Executive MSRECM	Fall: May 15 Spring: December 15	N/A	Professional resume, essay questions, letters of recommendation, undergraduate GPA

Number of Faculty	In-State Graduate Tuition	In-State Undergraduate Tuition
BSBA: 7 MSRECM: 7 Executive MSRECM: 7	$873/credit	$873/credit

Degree Specializations

BSBA in real estate and finance.
BSBA in real estate and international business.
BSBA in real estate and marketing.
BSBA in real estate and accounting.
JD/MRECM.

Program Description

The Burns School of Real Estate and Construction Management is the oldest such program in the United States, dating back to 1938. It is a unique program that offers undergraduate, graduate, and executive master's degree programs in the areas of real estate and construction management, within a college of business. A joint JD/MCREM degree is also offered.

Core Curriculum

BSBA: Varies, depending on degree. See www.daniels.du.edu/burns-degreeoptions.aspx for current degree plans and for the most up-to-date program brochure.

MSRECM: Income property finance, income property investment, residential construction systems, commercial construction systems.

XMRECM: Income property finance, income property investment, residential construction systems, commercial construction systems.

Financial Aid

Federal Perkins loans, federal Stafford loans, federal Plus loans, private education loans, payment plans, and student employment are available. There are also federal grants, including Pell Grants, Supplemental Education Opportunity Grants, and ACG and SMART grants. Numerous state grants and scholarships are also available. Other options include University of Denver (DU) education grants, DU scholarships, private scholarships, and Burns School scholarships. Contact Jaz Edmonds, Financial Aid Adviser II, at 303-871-2330 or jaz.edmonds@du.edu.

Lecture Series

Each year, the Burns School hosts a nominated Visiting Scholar who participates in various events and visits classes. Topics vary within the RECM industry, depending on the scholar's particular area of expertise. Twice each year, the school also sponsors a Visiting Industry Expert who visits classes and participates in other on- and off-campus events. For a list of all past Visiting Scholars and Industry Experts, see http://daniels.du.edu/burns-visiting.aspx.

International Programs

The Burns School offers overseas inter-term sessions two to three times per year. Students can earn four to eight academic credits through these programs.

Online Program

The executive master's program and a distance learning certificate are both offered online.

Program Advisory Group

The Burns Advisory Board and its committees meet at least twice a year. The Curriculum Review Committee is represented on the Advisory Board.

Internship Placement Assistance

The Burns School works closely with the Daniels College of Business Career Placement Center to offer internships to students. In addition, Burns maintains a placement directory that holds information on all internships offered.

Job Placement Assistance

Along with the Burns School, the Daniels College of Business Career Placement Center offers job placement assistance. With a program that dates back 70 years, we pride ourselves on being able to draw on our alumni to place students all over the world.

Clubs/Alumni Associations

Burns students enjoy the benefits of a well-established real estate club that has both undergraduate and graduate members. For information on the DU RECM Club, see http://portfolio.du.edu/recmclub.

The RECM Recent Graduate Organization is an integral part of ongoing efforts to connect recent graduates to other alumni. The RECM Recent Graduate Organization coordinates annual social gatherings and works with the RECM Club to create a seamless transition for students from academia to the real world. Many members of the RECM Club are also very active in the DU Recent Graduate Organization. See http://daniels.du.edu/burns-alumnicouncil.aspx.

Other

There are many other activities for students, alumni, and members of the community, including the Women of Enterprise Conference, the Affordable Housing Conference, the Technology Construction Symposium, and the Real Estate Expo. For a complete listing of events offered by the Burns School of Real Estate and Construction Management, see www.daniels.du.edu/burns-events.aspx.

Students have the opportunity to participate in a residential or construction practicum, in which they form a home-building company with other students, choose a site, bid on the project, obtain permits, manage construction, and sell the property. To date, Daniels students have built more than 15 homes, priced from the $190s to the $400s, with profits benefiting the Burns School and charities.

Students also have the opportunity to participate in the annual NAIOP competition, where they work on a complex real estate problem, culminating in an internal competition with other student teams and an external competition with another university. The competition includes a written report and an oral presentation.

Faculty

Dr. Michael Crean, professor. JD candidate, University of Denver; PhD, finance and real estate, University of Colorado; MBA, real estate, University of Connecticut; BS, economics and finance, University of Pennsylvania (Wharton). MAI courses, the Appraisal Institute. Real estate law and practice, real estate finance, real estate appraisal, real estate investment, real estate concepts, income property finance, income property appraisal, income property investment.

Dr. Hazem Elzarka, associate professor. PhD, civil engineering, Clemson University; MS, civil engineering, BS, civil engineering, Ain Shams University, Cairo. Advanced estimating and scheduling, construction finance, value engineering and constructability analysis, project delivery systems, construction documents and quality control, project costing, construction simulation, computer applications in construction, soil mechanics, surveying.

Dr. Jeff Engelstad, clinical professor. PhD, urban geography, University of Denver; MRECM, real estate and construction management; BSBA, real estate and finance, Daniels College of Business, University of Denver. Microcomputer applications for real estate analysis, real estate concepts, income property investment, advanced real estate feasibility analysis, introduction to real estate, real estate finance and investment, real estate appraisal, commercial real estate practice and feasibility analysis, real estate investments seminar, income property finance.

Dr. Mark Levine, chair/professor. PhD, Business Century University; LLM, tax law, New York University; PAP, accounting, Graduate School of Management, Northwestern University; JD, School of Law, University of Denver; BS, business and economics, Colorado State University. Introduction to real estate, real estate taxation, ethics in real estate, real estate securities and syndications, global perspectives in real estate, commercial real estate practice and feasibility analysis, real estate appraisal, legal issues in real estate, introduction to the legal environment, risk management/insurance, ethics.

Dr. Glenn Mueller, professor. PhD, business administration, Georgia State University; MBA, marketing, Babson College; BSBA, finance, University of Denver. Real estate feasibility and development, real estate capital markets, advanced issues in real estate, real estate enterprise, real estate finance, managing the development process, real estate portfolio management and institutional real estate investment, corporate finance, managerial finance.

Stuart Stein, lecturer. MS, occupational education, cooperative education; BS, occupational education, Southern Illinois University at Carbondale; AAS, building construction technology, College of Lake County. Residential and commercial construction systems, residential practicums, codes and documents.

Dr. Ronald Throupe, assistant professor. PhD, business; MBA, finance and real estate, University of Georgia; BS, civil engineering, University of Connecticut; BA, Fairfield University. Real estate feasibility and development, real estate finance, income property investments.

Adjunct Faculty

Kyle Cascioli, president, Real Estate Services, Barrett Associates. MBA.

Walter S. Clements, president, Green Leaf Properties, Inc. MRCM, CCIM, CRS, GRI.

Bruce Cousins, president, Architechnic, Ltd. AIA.

Jeff Engebretson, partner, DRS Engineering Contractors. BS, CPA.

Philip Feigin, partner, Rothgerber Johnson & Lyons, LLP.

Iris Foster, asset manager. MSRCM.

Edward L. Fronapfel, owner and principal, Professional Investigative Engineers. MSCE, CPE.

Joel Glover, partner, Rothgerber Johnson & Lyons, LLP.

Kyle Holtan-Brown, estimator, Haseldon Resort Constructors, LLC. MSRECM, CPE.

William M. James, president, James Real Estate Services, Inc.. MBA, MAI, CCIM.

Elizabeth Kraft, New Providence Company.

Steve Laposa, director, PriceWaterhouseCoopers. PhD.

Libbi Levine, attorney, Isaacson Rosenbaum, P.C. MSRCM, JD, LLM.

Andrew Lonegran, manager, Deman Construction Services, Inc. AACE, PSP.

Dan Metzger, assistant vice president, Lowe Enterprises Real Estate Group.

James Meurer, partner, Asset Valuation Advisors, LLP. EdD, MAI, SRA.

Ryan Oliver, owner/consultant, Dividend Realty Group, LLC.

Jessica Quinn, owner/project manager/consultant, BuilderChix, LLC/Genesis Homes. JD.

Gary M. Ralston, president, Florida Retail Development, LLC. CCIM, SIOR, CPM, CRE, CLS.

Gerald Rome, Colorado Deputy Commissioner of Securities, Colorado Department of Regulatory Agencies.

Steven Sessions, president and chief executive officer, management Services, Fuller Real Estate. JD, RPA.

Michael Sunoo, real estate broker associate, Levine Ltd. Realtors. MSRCM, JD.

Brad Weiman, managing director, Integra Realty Resources–Denver. MAI.

Fred Wood, Appraiser, Vectra Bank Colorado. MAI.

Dublin Institute of Technology

Martin Hanratty, Head
Department of Real Estate
School of Real Estate and Construction Economics
Bolton Street
Dublin, Ireland
353 1 4023675; fax 353 1 4023994
martin.hanratty@dit.ie
www.dit.ie

Degree	Years in Operation	Credit Hours	Years to Complete	Full-Time Students (2006–2007)	Part-Time Students (2006–2007)	Degrees Conferred (2007)
BSc in property economics	40	4,800 hours; 240 ECTS credits	4	218	40	42
MSc in real estate	3	1,800 hours; 90 ECTS credits	2.5			

Number of Faculty	Specialized Degree Accreditation	Application Deadline	Undergraduate Tuition, European Union (EU) Citizens	Undergraduate Tuition, Non-EU Citizens
17	RICS, SCS, IAVI	BSc in property economics: January 31 preceding September start MSc in real estate: last week in April preceding September start	No fees	€10,000/academic year

Degree Specializations

BSc in property economics.
MSc in real estate.

Program Description

The BSc in property economics is a full-time, four-year honors degree program. The program is vocationally oriented and is intended to educate students for a range of careers in the property industry and related industries in Ireland and overseas. The broad aim of the program is to develop professionals who are capable of operating in dynamic and competitive environments. The program therefore seeks to foster graduates who are both literate and numerate; have good analytical, interpersonal, and communication skills; and are adaptable, practical, critical, responsible, and environmentally sensitive. There is a particular emphasis on property valuation that, together with the core subjects of economics, investment, and planning, gives the program its orientation. Property valuation requires a broad knowledge of a wide range of subjects and a fundamental understanding of the economic, physical, and legal frameworks within which buildings are used and the property market operates. Thus, the program is generalist in the sense that its scope is wide, but specific in that it seeks to apply knowledge to a particular sector of the economy in a manner that will give the graduate a foundation to pursue a career as a property valuer. The educational approach develops students' ability to evaluate and integrate information from diverse sources to arrive at a conclusion.

The MSc in real estate program is part time, delivered over two and a half years (five semesters). The program is both practically oriented and theoretically rigorous, and is intended to provide an opportunity for graduates who do not have a background in property to prepare themselves for a range of careers in real estate and related industries. The need for competitiveness and efficiency in both the private and public sectors has resulted in a growing awareness of the role of real estate as an economic and business resource. This, together with an increased emphasis on urban economic policy and major infrastructural development, has created an enhanced demand for those with professional qualifications in real estate and training in the methods and techniques of real estate appraisal. The content of the program includes subjects pertinent to the practice of valuation surveyors and real estate professionals. The program is strongly oriented to real estate valuation, appraisal, and investment.

Core Curriculum
BSc in property economics

Year 1: Valuation, Professional Development, Economics, Finance, Law, Construction Studies and Cartography, Quantitative Methods, Integrating Project.
Year 2: Valuation, Property Management and Marketing, Economics, Planning, Law, Construction Technology, Quantitative Analysis.
Year 3, Final Part I: Valuation, Urban Economics, Investment Portfolio Analysis, Taxation, Planning, Building, Integrated Project, Architecture and Urban Sociology.
Year 4, Final Part I: Valuation I, Investment, Valuations and Taxation, Urban Economics, Finance and Funding, Planning.

MSc in Real Estate

Semester 1: Valuations 1, Building Appraisal, Real Estate Law
Semester 2: Real Estate Investment Appraisal, Planning, Valuations 2
Semester 3: Real Estate Development Appraisal, Urban Economics, Investment Portfolio Analysis
Semester 4: Integrating Project, Real Estate Finance, Corporate Real Estate Management or Research Themes in Real Estate
Semester 5: Research Methods and Dissertation

Financial Aid

There are no fees for undergraduate European Union citizens.

Lecture Series

Lectures are offered over two 15-week semesters, from September until May, principally by faculty.

Job Placement Assistance

The school and the Dublin Institute of Technology Careers Service have strong links with industry and the professions, and assist graduates with job placement.

Faculty

Emer Byrne, lecturer. BSc, physics, chemistry, and math, University College Dublin; Dip. AVEA, Dublin Institute of Technology. MIAVI, ARICS. Valuation, property management.

Frank Corcoran, lecturer. BCL, University College Dublin. Solicitor. Property and environmental law.

Thomas Dunne, head of school. FRICS. Valuations, professional development.

Emer Fallon, lecturer; committee chair, MSc real estate program. MPhil, Dublin Institute of Technology; BSc (Surv), Dublin Institute of Technology and Trinity College Dublin. Real estate finance and valuations.

Martin Hanratty, committee chair, BSc property economics program; head of department. MSc, planning and development economics, Dublin Institute of Technology. FRICS, FIAVI. Tender documentation, planning and development.

Brian Hughes, lecturer. Diploma in Environmental Economics, Dublin Institute of Technology. FRICS. Urban and land economics, valuation.

Myles Keaveney, lecturer. MSc, construction and project management, University of Ulster. Building construction.

Helen McGrath. PhD, Dublin City University; BSc (Surv); Dip. AVEA, Dublin Institute of Technology. Valuation, property management.

Declan McKeown, lecturer. BSc (Surv), Dublin Institute of Technology and Trinity College Dublin. Property management, marketing, investment analysis.

John Molloy, lecturer. Diploma in Environmental Economics; MA, Dublin Institute of Technology. FRICS. Valuation.

Cornelius O'Shea, lecturer. BSc, math and science, University College Dublin; BArch, Dublin Institute of Technology. Construction, building maintenance.

Tracy Pickerill, lecturer. MSc, building and urban conservation, University College Dublin; BSc (Surv), Dublin Institute of Technology and Trinity College Dublin. Valuation, economics.

Thomas Power, lecturer. BA, MSc, business studies, University College Dublin. Economics, investment, financial analysis.

Terry Prendergast, lecturer. MPhil, urban design and regional planning, University of Edinburgh; BSc (Surv), Dublin Institute of Technology and Trinity College Dublin. Planning.

Anne Russell, lecturer. MSC, Trinity College Dublin; BComm, University College Dublin. Taxation.

Lorcan Sirr, lecturer; faculty head of research. PhD, planning and development; MA, urban design and regeneration, University of Manchester; BSc (Hons.) estate management, University of Greenwich; BA (OU); Dip. AVEA, Dublin Institute of Technology. MIAVI. Valuation, urban economics.

Stephen Walsh, lecturer. MA, University College Dublin; BA, Trinity College Dublin. Quantitative methods, economics, investment analysis.

Florida State University

Dean Gatzlaff, Chair and Mark Bane Professor of Real Estate
Department of Risk Management/Insurance, Real Estate and Business Law
College of Business
313 Rovetta Business Building
Tallahassee, FL 32306-1110
850-644-4070; fax 850-644-4077
dgatzlaff@fsu.edu
www.ree.fsu.edu

Degree	Year Program Began	Credit Hours	Years to Complete	Thesis or Final Product	Full-Time Students (2006–2007)	Degrees Conferred (2006)
BS	1958	120	4	None	425	203
MBA, real estate concentration	2004	42	2	None	45	25

Degree	Application Deadline	Minimum High School or Undergraduate GPA	Minimum GRE or GMAT Score	Departmental Requirements
BS		2.9		
MBA, real estate concentration	June 1	3.0	500	Undergraduate transcripts, GMAT scores, resume/experience, 2 letters of reference, personal statement

Degree	Number of Faculty/FTE	Specialized Degree Accreditation	In-State Graduate Tuition	Out-of-State Graduate Tuition	In-State Undergraduate Tuition	Out-of-State Undergraduate Tuition
BS: 8/6	8/6	BA: AACSB			$104.23/credit	$541.95/credit
MBA (on campus)			$248.18/credit	$879.58/credit		
MBA (online)			$423.53/credit	$1,054.23/credit		

Degree Specializations

BS with a major in real estate, with a dual major in finance or marketing encouraged.
MBA with a concentration in real estate.

Program Description

The real estate program at Florida State University (FSU) is housed in the Department of Risk Management/Insurance, Real Estate, and Business Law in the College of Business. The program currently enrolls about 300 majors (including a number of double majors in finance, management, and marketing). The goal of the program is to produce broadly trained real estate analysts who are able to enter a wide variety of real estate–related fields (e.g., brokerage/leasing/property management; consulting/appraisal; lending/underwriting; acquisitions/development/construction; institutional investment; and government). Throughout the course of study, students are routinely assigned project work on actual commercial and residential projects. In addition, students acquire hands-on experience with software designed to assist real estate professionals.

Core Curriculum

BS with a major in real estate: in addition to the College of Business requirements, students are required to complete courses in real estate principles, real estate law, real estate appraisal, market analysis, real estate finance, and real estate investment. MBA with a concentration in real estate: in addition to the MBA core requirements, students are required to complete advanced coursework in real estate law, real estate finance, real estate valuation, and real estate investment.

Financial Aid

A wide variety of financial aid sources are available through the university, college, and department. To obtain information on financial aid, visit www.finaid.fsu.edu/. Information is also available through the Express Telephone System from 8:00 a.m. to 6:00 a.m. (22 hours a day), at 850-644-0539. The hours of operation for the Office of Financial Aid are 8:30 a.m. to 5:00 p.m., Monday through Friday. Counseling is available by phone or at the information center Monday through Friday, 8:30 a.m. to 5:00 p.m.

Lecture Series

The Center for Real Estate Education and Research, the Real Estate Society, and the Real Estate Alumni Network co-sponsor the Real Estate Trends and Networking Conference each fall semester. Speakers have included Governor Jeb Bush; Jim Seneff, chief executive officer, CNL Financial Group, Inc.; and Peter Rummell, chief executive officer, the St. Joe Company. The conference is typically a sold-out event. See www.fsurealestate.com.

Each spring, the Evan Jennings Executive Speaker Series in Real Estate brings several top executives to speak to students in the program.

International Programs

Opportunities are available for undergraduates and graduate students in real estate to study overseas through the FSU Study Abroad Program. The university operates international study centers in Panama, Italy, Spain, and the UK. In addition, it offers programs in other regions throughout the world.

Program Advisory Group

The real estate faculty meet at least twice a year with the program's Executive Advisory Board and the board's Conference Committee. The board is made up of 40 senior-level executives—20 directors and 20 Conference Committee members—who advise the faculty on broad-based program initiatives.

Internship Placement Assistance

Internships are available through the alumni network, departmental job listings and announcements, and the College of Business Placement Office.

Job Placement Assistance

Job placement occurs through the alumni network, departmental job listings and announcements, internship opportunities, and the College of Business Placement Office.

Clubs/Alumni Associations

The FSU Real Estate Society provides opportunities for members to enhance their knowledge of the real estate industry through professional activities and contacts with practitioners. See www.cob.fsu.edu/rmi/ree/ree_society.asp.

Online Program

Designed with the busy working professional in mind, the online MBA with a concentration in real estate can be completed in a little more than two years. Thanks to a high-quality distance-learning structure that features a 100-percent online interface with the same standards, core courses, and professors as the on-campus, face-to-face MBA program, online program students can attend class from anywhere in the world.

Faculty

Stephen Bailey, assistant in real estate and business law. JD, BS, Florida State University. Real estate law and appraisal.

Richard Benton, adjunct professor. Principal, Benton Associates. Real estate law.

H. Glenn Boggs, professor of real estate and business law and Nardozza Scholars Program Fellow. JD, Florida State University College of Law; BS, U.S. Naval Academy. Real estate law.

Barry A. Diskin, professor of real estate and Nardozza Scholars Program Fellow. PhD, MBA, BA, Georgia State University. Real estate valuation and market analysis.

Dean H. Gatzlaff, chair and Mark Bane Professor of Real Estate. PhD, University of Florida; MBA, University of Wisconsin at LaCrosse; BArch, University of Minnesota. Real estate feasibility and investment.

Steve Griffith, adjunct professor. President, Bell Griffith Associates, Inc. Real estate appraisal.

G. Stacy Sirmans, Kenneth G. Bacheller Professor of Real Estate. PhD, University of Georgia; MBA, BBA, Valdosta State College. Real estate finance and investment.

William Woodyard, assistant in real estate and business law. JD, West Virginia University; BA, Marshall University.

University of Florida

David C. Ling, William D. Hussey Professor of Real Estate
Department of Finance, Insurance, and Real Estate
Warrington College of Business Administration
University of Florida
P.O. Box 117168
Gainesville, FL 32611
352-273-0313; fax 352-392-0301
Contact: Pam DeMichele
demichpl@ufl.edu
www.realestate.ufl.edu

Degree	Years in Operation	Credit Hours	Years to Complete	Full-Time Students (2006–2007)	Degrees Conferred (2007)
MBA	58	30-58	1-2	10	10
MS	58	34	1	21	21
MS/JD	58			7	7
PHD	58	110	4	2	0

Number of Faculty/FTE	Specialized Degree Accreditation	In-State Graduate Tuition	Out-of-State Graduate Tuition	In-State Undergraduate Tuition	Out-of-State Undergraduate Tuition
9/5	AASCB, EQUIS	$284/credit	$915/credit	$112.73/credit	$571.66/credit

Degree Specializations

MBA with a concentration in real estate MSRE.
PhD in finance with real estate emphasis.

Program Description

The MSRE program at the University of Florida offers students many opportunities for professional interaction, through the University of Florida Friends and Alumni of Real Estate (UF-FARE) and the Real Estate Advisory Board. Each student selects three board members who serve as personal mentors and provide career guidance and counseling throughout the program.

Under an agreement with the CCIM Institute, the University of Florida's MSRE program counts as 75 percent of the coursework required for the CCIM designation; it is considered part of the "qualified experience" requirement. The CCIM designation, in turn, counts as four of the 34 hours required for the master's degree.

Core Curriculum

Introduction to real estate, investment property analysis, real estate portfolios and securities, secondary mortgage markets and institutions, real estate market and transaction analysis, quantitative analysis, geographic information systems (GIS)/location analysis, real estate development, capstone seminar, and applied project.

Financial Aid

Approximately $46,000 in private scholarship money was awarded to MSRE applicants in 2006–2007, and we expect that amount to grow each year. All MSRE applicants are considered, and the most highly qualified receive scholarships.

Lecture Series

Each year, the Alfred A. Ring Distinguished Speaker Series brings 12 to 14 high-profile industry professionals to campus to speak to and interact with students and faculty.

Program Advisory Group

The Bergstrom Center for Real Estate Studies facilitates the University of Florida Real Estate Advisory Board, which is made up of almost 150 prominent industry professionals.

Job Placement Assistance

Job placement assistance is offered by the MSRE program staff, the Warrington College of Business Administration Graduate Career Services, and the University of Florida Career Resource Center. Contact Pam DeMichele at 352-273-0310.

Faculty

Wayne Archer, professor. PhD, Indiana University; MS, Wichita State University; BA, Westmar College. Housing markets analysis, mortgage valuation, securitization, GIS.

David T. Brown, associate professor. PhD, Washington University in St. Louis; BS, Tulane University. Bankruptcy and financial distress, real estate workouts, fixed-income valuation, interest-rate risk management.

David C. Ling, William D. Hussey Professor of Real Estate. PhD, Ohio State University; BS, Central Michigan University. Real estate finance and investment, housing economics, federal income taxation, real estate securities.

Edgar J. McDougall, adjunct professor. PhD, BS, University of Florida. Development, transactions, real estate capital markets.

Georgia Institute of Technology

Roozbeh Kangari, Director
Building Construction Program
College of Architecture
280 Ferst Drive, 1st Floor
Atlanta, GA 30332-0680
404-894-4875; fax 404-894-1641
Contact: Brenda Morris
brenda.morris@coa.gatech.edu
bc@coa.gatech.edu
www.bcprogram.com

Degree	Year Program Began	Credit Hours	Years to Complete	Thesis or Final Product	Full-Time Students (2006–2007)	Part-Time Students (2006–2007)	Degrees Conferred (2006)
MS in building construction and integrated facility management	2000	36	Full-time students: 1 year Part-time students: 2 years	Optional	18	82	25

Degree	Application Deadline	Departmental Requirements
MS in building construction and integrated facility management	Fall semester: March 15 for international applicants; July 15 for U.S. citizens	Resume, GRE or GMAT score, 3 letters of recommendation, transcripts from previous academic institutions

Number of Faculty/FTE	In-State Graduate Tuition	Out-of-State Graduate Tuition
12/7	$443/semester	$1,335/semester

Degree Specialization

MS in building construction and integrated facility management.

Program Description

The graduate program in building construction and integrated facility management is a management-oriented master's program that combines construction and management skills. The program has three specialized industry tracks: (1) integrated facility management, (2) integrated project delivery systems, and (3) residential construction development. Georgia Tech offers students cutting-edge research, excellent faculty, an exciting educational environment, and close ties with industry associations and companies.

Integrated Facility Management

The integrated facility and property management track focuses on developing and fine-tuning the management skills necessary for success in the facility and property management industry. Courses explore the many facets of integrated facility management, including asset management, project management, facility operations and maintenance, energy management, workplace design and consulting, facility technology integration, design and construction, and real estate development. The program is endorsed by the IFMA.

Integrated Project Delivery Systems

In the integrated project delivery systems track, students learn to analyze and select the most appropriate and effective project delivery systems for constructing a facility. The curriculum emphasizes integrated problem solving through state-of-the-art technical and management techniques. Students examine, and learn to manage, a variety of project delivery systems, which can be used independently or integrated. Methods include the design-build system, the construction management/agent method, the hybrid bridging and partnering system, the negotiated select team method, and the traditional delivery method.

Residential Construction Development

The residential construction development track focuses on the largest and fastest-growing area of the construction industry. Students study all segments of the housing industry, including single-family, multifamily, mixed-use, and affordable housing; housing for seniors; and renovation. Students are provided with a comprehensive view of relevant public policy, development, design, and construction issues, and gain a realistic understanding of the current business environment and prospects for the future.

Core Curriculum

The core curriculum varies, depending on the chosen track.

Integrated Facility Management

Core courses (18 semester hours): BC 6100, Professional Trends in Facility Management; BC 6200, Maintenance Management of Built Assets; BC 6300, Safety and Environmental Issues; BC 6400,

Facility Planning, Project Management, and Benchmarking; BC 6500, Real Estate Asset and Income Property Management; BC 6600, Facilities Management Financial Analysis.

Integrated Project Delivery Systems

Core courses (18 semester hours): BC 6150, Design-Build Organization and Management; BC 6250, Value Management for Integrated Facility Design and Construction; BC 6350, Design and Construction Law; BC 6400, Integrated Facility Planning, Project Management, and Benchmarking; BC 6550, Design and Construction Processes; BC 6650, Advanced Project Management.

Residential Construction Development

Core courses (18 semester hours): Real Estate Development and Construction; Trends and Policies for Residential Construction; Residential Design and Construction; Business and Finance in Residential Construction; Facility Planning, Project Management and Benchmarking; Community Design and Construction; or Livable Communities: Design and Implementation.

Financial Aid

Students can apply for financial aid through the Georgia Tech office of Financial Services: www.finaid.gatech.edu/.

Lecture Series

The College of Architecture sponsors two lecture series. See www.coa.gatech.edu/symposium/ or www.coa.gatech.edu/news/lectures.php.

International Programs

Through the Building Construction Study Abroad Program, students can visit international construction and architectural firms, as well as various construction sites. The program allows students to experience global partnership firsthand, while developing a greater appreciation for international practices, culture, and technology. Students spend one summer semester in Paris, taking three required courses and one professional elective course and earning 12 semester hours of credit toward their degree. For more information, contact the Building Construction Program Office at 404-894-4875 or bc@coa.gatech.edu.

Program Advisory Group

The Industry Advisory Group meets annually to review the curriculum and to discuss new trends or topics to add to the program.

Internship Placement Assistance

Students interested in internships meet with their academic adviser, who will assist with placement. Internships are not required for graduate students. See www.coa.gatech.edu/bc/undergrad/bc4680Spring2007.pdf.

Job Placement Assistance

The Building Construction Program hosts an annual career fair that is attended by representatives from over 45 companies. In addition, representatives from these companies visit campus throughout the year, host social events, and invite students to industry events. Students are offered many networking activities throughout the academic year.

Clubs/Alumni Associations

For information on the Student Construction Association, see http://cyberbuzz.gatech.edu/sca/. In addition, the following organizations have student chapters: ABC (Associated Builders and Contractors); AGC (Associated General Contractors); CMAA (Construction Management Association of America); DBIA (Design Build Institute of America); MCAA (Mechanical Contractors Association of America); and NAHB (National Association of Home Builders). The Alumni Board meets four times per year.

Faculty

W.J. Blane, assistant professor. BCE; MS, management, Georgia Institute of Technology. Real estate and construction finance, law and development.

Dr. Daniel Castro, assistant professor. PhD, civil engineering, Purdue University; MS, construction management, University of Reading; BS, civil engineering, Universidad de Los Andes, Colombia. Sustainability, energy, and technology.

Dr. Roozbeh Kangari, director, Building Construction Program. PhD, civil engineering, University of Illinois at Urbana-Champaign; MS, civil engineering, Syracuse University; BS, civil engineering, University of Tehran. Risk management, automation, robotics.

Dr. Linda Thomas Mobley, associate professor and associate director. PhD, building construction, College of Architecture, Georgia Institute of Technology; JD, University of Miami; MS, civil engineering, University of Florida; BS, civil engineering, University of Florida. Construction law, contracting, risk management, integrated facility management, building mold, indoor air-quality evaluation.

Kathy Roper, assistant professor. Master of Communications; BA, journalism and management, Georgia State University. Integrated facility management.

Dr. Saeid Sadri, associate professor. PhD, construction management, School of Civil Engineering, Georgia Institute of Technology; MS, BA, architecture, College of Fine Arts, University of Tehran. Project management and residential building.

Maureen Weidner, instructor. Master of Building Construction, Bachelor of Environmental Design, Texas A&M University. Real estate development and structures.

Affiliated Faculty

April Atkins, instructor. Community planning, policy, development.

Jim Butler, instructor. Construction law.

Mark Collins, instructor. Construction marketing, entrepreneurship.

Thom Keel, instructor. Project management, facility management, marketing.

Debbie Phillips, instructor. Residential property management.

Soheil Rouhi, instructor. Structural engineering, construction technology.

Jack Wexler, instructor. Construction contracts.

University of Georgia

Henry J. Munneke, Associate Professor
Department of Insurance, Legal Studies, and Real Estate
Terry College of Business
206 Brooks Hall
Athens, GA 30602-6255
706-542-4290; fax 706-542-4295
hmunneke@terry.uga.edu
www.terry.uga.edu/realestate/

Degree	Year Program Began	Credit Hours	Time to Complete	Thesis or Final Product	Full-Time Students (2006–2007)	Degrees Conferred (2006)
BBA	1958	121	4 years	No	210	76
MBA (11 months)	1976	42	11 months	No	14	14
MBA (2-year)	1976	65	2 years[a]	No	13	13
PhD	1968	40–57	3–4 years[b]	Yes	4	0

a. Students who do not have a BBA from an AACSB-accredited school must take 65 semester hours (two years, full time).
b. A PhD requires one to one-and-one-half years of coursework beyond that for the MBA, written and oral exams, and a dissertation.

Degree	Application Deadline	Minimum High School or Undergraduate GPA	Minimum GRE or GMAT Score	Departmental Requirements
BBA	January 20/ September 1	2.60		Only students who have completed 60+ credit hours and have completed the BBA core curriculum may apply to the College of Business; applicants must also submit a statement of purpose (see www.terry.uga.edu/undergraduate).
MBA (11 months)	February 15 (domestic); April 15 (international)[a]		540–760	A 4-year bachelor's degree in business administration from an AACSB-International accredited institution, 2 years of professional experience, essays, resume, interview, 3 letters of reference (see www.terry.uga.edu/fulltime/requirements.html).
MBA (2-year)	March 3 (domestic); May 12 (international)[a]		540–760	A 4-year bachelor's degree in business administration from an AACSB-International accredited institution, 2 years of professional experience, essays, resume, interview, 3 letters of reference (see www.terry.uga.edu/fulltime/requirements.html).
PhD	July 1 (domestic); April 15 (international)[a]			See www.terry.uga/edu/phd.

a. The program features rolling admissions. The admissions committee begins reviewing applications in November. To receive priority consideration for assistantship awards, application materials should be completed by January 1.

Number of Faculty/FTE	Specialized Degree Accreditation	In-State Graduate Tuition	Out-of-State Graduate Tuition	In-State Undergraduate Tuition	Out-of-State Undergraduate Tuition
4/4	AACSB	$3,085/semester	$10,712/semester	$2,607/semester	$9,471/semester

Degree Specializations

BBA in real estate.
MBA with a concentration in real estate.
PhD with a major in real estate.

Program Description

The BBA in real estate provides the student with an analytical foundation and a firm understanding of real estate finance, investment, and valuation. The major in real estate is designed for students who are planning a career in real estate brokerage, leasing, mortgage lending, investments, management, appraising, or development.

The MBA with a real estate concentration is geared toward students who want a focused plan of study in real estate, along with a general background in all aspects of business. This program focuses on advanced concepts and methodology that will be useful for the business professional.

The PhD program is designed to prepare students for teaching and research at universities and colleges and for positions in government and business. By supplementing the program with courses from other areas within the College of Business Administration, students can choose the direction and concentration within their specialty (e.g., a major in real estate and a minor in finance or law). This flexibility gives students wide latitude in choosing a program that corresponds with a specific career path.

Core Curriculum

The BBA in real estate requires courses in real estate principles, investments, finance, and appraisal, in addition to the courses in accounting, statistics, computer science, marketing, finance, management, production, economics, and business policy that are required for all BBA students. Electives include real estate development and real estate law.

The MBA with a concentration in real estate includes courses in real estate investment, finance, and advanced valuation theories. Electives include real estate development, real estate law, city planning, retail site selection, and geographic information systems. An additional concentration in finance or marketing is recommended.

The core courses for the PhD in real estate are designed to build a strong foundation in economics, finance theory, and research methodology, and to provide intensive training in real estate investments, finance, and appraisal.

Financial Aid

Approximately 25 scholarships, ranging from $50 to $500, are awarded each semester to undergraduates in their final two years of study. The MBA program offers assistantships to at least 50 percent of the MBA students. For information, contact the MBA program director at 706-542-5671. Four graduate assistantships with varying stipends are available to PhD students. Several other sources of financial aid are also available to PhD students. For information, contact Dr. James B. Kau at 706-542-4290.

Lecture Series

The Real Estate Society holds meetings at which real estate practitioners discuss current industry issues and career opportunities, providing students with an opportunity to interact with practitioners from a variety of areas within the industry.

Internship Placement Assistance

The internship placement program is a joint effort on the part of the Terry College of Business Real Estate Program, real estate industry leaders, and leading firms, working together to provide a unique educational experience that combines academic work with practical experience. Students are especially encouraged to enroll during the summer between their junior and senior years, and can receive up to two classes' worth of credit.

Job Placement Assistance

The university provides a career counseling and placement service to undergraduates. The Terry MBA program offers a placement service for graduate students. The real estate program compiles a resume book semi-annually; the book includes both graduate and undergraduate resumes.

Clubs/Alumni Associations

The Real Estate Society is an undergraduate student organization that allows students to interact with other real estate majors and with other students who are interested in real estate as a career. Each semester, meetings are held at which practitioners from many areas of the real estate industry provide insight into their particular jobs, careers, development, and the real estate industry as a whole.

Faculty

Carolyn A. Dehring, assistant professor of real estate. PhD, finance, University of Illinois at Urbana-Champaign. Real estate investments and analysis.

James B. Kau, professor of real estate and holder of the C. Herman and Mary Virginia Terry Chair of Business Administration. PhD, economics, University of Washington. Real estate finance and housing economics.

Richard W. Martin, associate professor of real estate. PhD, economics, University of Illinois at Urbana-Champaign. Real estate development, market analysis, urban economics.

Henry J. Munneke, professor of real estate. PhD, economics, University of Illinois at Urbana-Champaign. Real estate appraisal, market analysis, land economics.

Harvard University

Daniel Schodek, Director of MDesS
Antonine Picon, Director of DDes
Richard Peiser, Adviser
Real Estate Development
Advanced Studies Program
Harvard Design School
48 Quincy Street
Cambridge, MA 02138
617-495-2337; fax 617-495-2943
belfman@gsd.harvard.edu
www.gsd.harvard.edu

Degree	Year Program Began	Credit Hours	Years to Complete	Thesis or Final Product	Full-Time Students (2007–2008)	Degrees Conferred (2007–2008)
MDesS	1986	48	1.5	Thesis/scholarly paper	60	32
DDes	1986	16	3	Thesis	34	12

Degree	Application Deadline	Departmental Requirements
MDesS	January 18	
DDes	January 18	Research statement, resume, 3 letters of recommendation, GRE or GMAT for RE/PM concentration, portfolio, TOEFL (international students)

Degree Specializations

The MDesS is a cross-discipline program centered on real estate development and project management in a design environment. Students do not need a design background to apply.

The DDes features concentrations in real estate, project management, or urban design and planning.

Program Description

The MDesS is a three-semester program with four areas of concentration, one of which is real estate development and project management.

Normally a three-year program, the DDes offers advanced study and research in design and real estate disciplines. The program focuses on applied research. Students must have a master's degree to apply to the DDes program.

Core Curriculum

The MDesS has required courses, but students may take other courses at the Graduate School of Design (GSD) besides real estate and project management; they may also take courses at other professional schools within Harvard University and at the Massachusetts Institute of Technology.

The DDes has a required pro-seminar course, but all other coursework is geared toward individual research.

Financial Aid

GSD grants are available for MDesS and DDes students. International students may apply for international grants. See www.gsd.harvard.edu/admissions or call 617-496-1241.

Lecture Series

The Harvard Design School offers many lectures, to which all students are invited. These are arranged by each department: architecture, landscape architecture, and urban planning.

Program Advisory Group

The Advanced Studies Program Committee is made up of five faculty members for the DDes and seven faculty members for the MDesS. It formally governs the program and answers to the faculty of design.

Job Placement Assistance

The GSD provides advice on real estate careers through faculty and through career services, which sponsors networking events, seminars, and career panels. Upon graduation, DDes students obtain teaching, consulting, and administrative positions. See www.gsd.harvard.edu/career.

Clubs/Alumni Associations

There are several student groups at the GSD for students interested in real estate: the Real Estate Development Club, the Harvard Urban Planning Organization, and Housing GSD. See www.gsd.harvard.edu/people/students/student_forum/groups.

Faculty

Alan A. Altshuler, Ruth and Frank Stanton Professor in Urban Policy. PhD, MA, University of Chicago. Urban politics, land use policy, transportation.

Joan Busquets, Martin Bucksbaum Professor in Practice of Urban Planning and Design. PhD, MArch, University of Barcelona. Courses and studios in urbanism.

Margaret Crawford, professor of urban design and planning theory. Diploma, Architectural Association; PhD, University of California at Los Angeles. History and theory of urban development, planning, design.

Susan Fainstein, professor of urban planning and design. AB, Harvard University; PhD, political science, Massachusetts Institute of Technology. Politics and economics of urban redevelopment; tourism, comparative urban and social policy, planning theory, gender and planning.

José A. Gómez-Ibáñez, professor of urban planning and public policy in the field of transportation. PhD, Harvard University. Economics, infrastructure.

Jerrold S. Kayden, associate professor of urban planning. JD, MCRP, Harvard University. Planning and environmental law, public and private development, law, design.

Niall G. Kirkwood, associate professor of landscape architecture. MLA, University of Pennsylvania; BArch, University of Manchester. Land reclamation, contaminated sites, innovative landscape construction technologies.

James Kostaras. MAUD, Harvard Design School; BArch, Rhode Island School of Design. Urban planning and development.

Alex Krieger, professor in practice of urban design. MCPUD, Harvard Design School; BArch, Cornell University. Design studio; design of the American city.

Richard B. Peiser, Michael D. Spear Professor of Real Estate Development. PhD, land economy, University of Cambridge; MBA, Harvard Business School. Real estate finance and development; research seminar on securitization; development studio.

Spiro N. Pollalis, professor of design technology and management. PhD, MBA, Massachusetts Institute of Technology. Information and building technology, privatization of public projects.

Nicolas P. Retsinas, lecturer in housing studies. MCP, Harvard University. Researches issues critical to U.S. housing and community development.

Peter G. Rowe, Raymond Garbe Professor of Architecture and Urban Design. MAUD, Rice University; BArch, Melbourne University. Cultural interpretation in architecture and urban design.

Antoine Hashim Sarkis, assistant professor of architecture. PhD, architecture, Harvard University; MArch, Harvard Design School; BArch, Rhode Island School of Design. Design studio, post–World War II American architecture, urbanism in representation.

Daniel L. Schodek, Kumagai Professor of Architectural Technology. PhD, civil engineering, Massachusetts Institute of Technology; BS, MS, architectural engineering, University of Texas at Austin. Recent developments in computer-aided design and computer-aided manufacturing, design for assembly, smart materials, automation.

James Stockward, lecturer in housing studies. MCP, Harvard Design School. Housing policy.

Affiliated Faculty

Faculty of Design of the Graduate School of Design.

Indiana University

Jeffrey D. Fisher, Professor
Department of Finance
Kelley School of Business, Suite 746
1309 East 10th Street
Bloomington, IN 47405
812-855-7794; fax 812-855-9006
cres@indiana.edu; fisher@indiana.edu
www.indiana.edu/~cres

Degree	Years in Operation	Credit Hours	Years to Complete
BS	81	124	4
MBA	54	54	2

Number of Faculty	In-State Graduate Tuition	Out-of-State Graduate Tuition	In-State Undergraduate Tuition	Out-of-State Undergraduate Tuition
BS: 4			$3,499.80/ semester	$10,739.40/ semester
MBA: 1	$8,398/ semester	$16,707/ semester		

Degree Specializations

BS in finance with a concentration in real estate.
MBA in finance with a concentration in real estate.

Program Description

Indiana University students can major in real estate at either the undergraduate or graduate level. Because real estate is part of the Department of Finance, students must complete a minimum number of finance classes. However, marketing, economics, and other electives can be added to round out the overall education. Real estate courses integrate computer analysis with theory and practical appli-cations in order to develop the students' decision-making ability.

Undergraduate students are admitted to the Kelley School of Business after they have successfully passed two years of general classes, usually with a final GPA of 3.0 or higher. Graduate students also complete a business core, with classes such as finance, marketing, production, computer, and statistical analysis. Further education can be obtained through applied research in independent study classes. The Center for Real Estate Studies offers seminars and conferences that are free to students, to provide contact with local and national companies.

Core Curriculum

Required undergraduate courses: real estate practice and principles, appraisal, finance, and investment. Optional courses: real estate principles, law, urban economics, and independent studies. Required graduate courses: real estate finance and investment analysis. Optional courses: independent study in real estate and land economics.

Financial Aid

Graduate research assistantships are offered each semester. Various private companies offer scholarships, and various national organizations offer scholarships and internships. Work-study opportunities are available for undergraduates.

Program Advisory Group

The Center for Real Estate Studies has an advisory board made up of leading real estate practitioners from around the country.

Internship Placement Assistance

The department assists with internships when available.

Job Placement Assistance

The Placement Office at the Kelley School of Business offers on-site interviewing with more than 500 companies, with an average of more than ten interviews per student. Real estate resume books are mailed to over 100 interested companies throughout the United States, and faculty and staff provide additional referrals. Contact the Center for Real Estate Studies at 812-855-7794.

Clubs/Alumni Associations

Indiana University Real Estate Club.

Faculty

Thomas Battle, ABD, MS, Indiana University. Real estate principles and appraisal.

Jeffrey D. Fisher, professor. PhD, Ohio State University. Real estate finance, investment analysis, appraisals.

Douglas McCoy, adjunct professor. MBA/JD, Indiana University. Real estate finance, investment analysis, appraisals.

The Johns Hopkins University

Carey Business School
Michael A. Anikeeff, Professor and Chair
Edward St. John Department of Real Estate
10 North Charles Street
Baltimore, MD 21201
410-516-0772; fax 410-659-8440
Contact: Marie Moineau
Mcmoineau@jhu.edu
www.carey.jhu.edu

Degree	Year Program Began	Credit Hours	Years to Complete	Thesis or Final Product	Full-Time Students (2006–2007)	Part-Time Students (2006–2007)	Degrees Conferred (2006)
MSRE	1989	40	Full-time: 1 Part-time: 3–5	Practicum/thesis	10	256	53

Degree	Application Deadline	Minimum Undergraduate GPA	Departmental Requirements
MSRE	Full-time: March 15 Part-time: July 1; November 1	3.0	Resume, personal statement, GMAT (full-time only), 2 letters of professional recommendation, official transcript

Number of Faculty	In-State Graduate Tuition	Out-of-State Graduate Tuition
48	Full-time: $36,000 Part-time: $735/credit	Full-time: $36,000 Part-time: $735/credit

Degree Specialization

MSRE.

Program Description

The Edward St. John Department of Real Estate is an endowed department within the Carey Business School. The program is based on the concept pioneered by Richard Ely, professor of Economics at Johns Hopkins, 1882–1883. Considered the father of urban land economics, Ely championed the multidisciplinary approach that has been incorporated into the department. The Urban Land Institute (ULI) and the honorary organization Lambda Alpha International are also based in this tradition. The degree program is accredited by RICS.

Core Curriculum

The MSRE is a 40-credit degree program that provides students with a comprehensive understanding of real estate development, investment, and management. The core curriculum integrates the study of market analysis, law, design, construction, investment, finance, and land use regulation. Students are prepared for a broad range of careers, from developer to commercial broker, investment analyst, and real estate asset manager.

Core requirements include real estate enterprise, legal issues in real estate, real estate construction, market analysis and site selection, design issues, regulation of real estate, real estate finance, urban land economics, real estate investments, analytical techniques in real estate development, and capital markets.

Electives for the part-time program include urban planning, real estate appraisal, asset management, international real estate development, housing and public policy, environmental issues in real estate, sustainable development, insurance/risk management, and commercial marketing and leasing.

There are five tracks for the part-time program: general development, institutional real estate investment management, real estate valuation and appraisal (meets MAI requirements of the Appraisal Institute), community development, and international real estate. The requirements may be completed in two-and-a-half years, but must be completed within five years.

In 2005, the department established a full-time accelerated MSRE program. This cohort-based program is designed for individuals entering the real estate industry. This cohort is scheduled in a 12-month concentrated format. The course of study includes a full-time internship/practicum in which students apply what they have learned in the classroom. Because of the concentrated format, specialization is provided through the internship/practicum rather than through electives.

Financial Aid

A number of scholarships and other sources of financial aid are available. Contact the Office of Financial Aid at 410-516-9808 or onestop.finaid@jhu.edu.

Lecture Series

The real estate program co-sponsors lectures with organizations such as ULI, RICS, the Baltimore Architecture Foundation, Commercial Real Estate Women, the International Real Estate Federation American Chapter, and the Association of Foreign Investors in Real Estate. Speakers are leaders in the real estate industry. The JHU Real Estate Forum is an association of students, alumni, faculty, and members of the advisory board that meets for lectures, seminars, and conferences and sponsors other industry-related activities.

International Programs

In addition to its track in international real estate, the program participates in the European Challenge, a case competition sponsored by universities in the Economic Union.

Program Advisory Group

The advisory board consists of top professionals in the Baltimore/Washington region, representing all sectors of the development industry: law, architecture, finance, public policy, construction, etc. Traditionally, the board meets three times each year. Activities include development and fundraising, discussions of the research agenda, curriculum development, and student advising.

Job Placement Assistance

The school provides placement through the Professional Career Services Office, 410-516-9730 or careerservices@jhu.edu. The department also maintains an employment book for real estate–related jobs.

Faculty

Michael A. Anikeeff, PhD. Professor and chair.

Isaac F. Megbolugbe, PhD, associate professor and director, Urban Planning and Development Programs.

Practitioner Faculty

Gary D. Anderson, PhD. Dewberry.

Sharon L. Anderson, MBA. ALT Advisors, LLC.

Alfred Barry III, AB Associates.

Anirban Basu, JD. Sage Policy Group, Inc.

M.J. (Jay) Brodie, MA. Baltimore Development Corporation.

Robert Cannon, LLB. Saul, Ewing, Weinberg & Green.

J. Joseph Clarke, MAS, MLA. J.J. Clarke Enterprises.

Lisa M. Decker, MS. The Whiting-Turner Contracting Company.

Nazir G. Dossani, PhD. Carey Business School.

Gretchen M. Dudney, MBA. Consultant.

Charles B. Duff, Jr., MCP. Jubilee Baltimore, Inc.

Terry R. Dunkin, MS. Colliers Pinkard Company.

Edward Ely, Ely Development Services, LLC.

Stephen J. Ferrandi, MS. NAI KLNB.

Michael Furbish, MBA. Furbish Company.

Donald A. Gabriel, JD. Baltimore County.

Elena Garrison, MS. Comstock Homebuilding Companies, Inc.

Gordon Godat, MS. BCT Architects.

Jay Gouline, MBA. Springlake Corporation.

Oliver Harris, MS. US Bank.

Diane L. Hartley, MBA. Clark Education.

Mark Hassinger, MCP. WestDulles Properties, LLC.

Thomas Hauser, JD. Ballard, Spahr, Andrews & Ingersoll.

Julian A. Josephs, MBA. Chain Links Retail Advisors.

Demetri Koutrouvelis, MS. Studley, Inc.

M. Shawn Krantz, MBA. Brownstone Capital, LLC.

Gary Lachman, JD. Liberty International Real Estate Funds.

Jon M. Laria, JD. Ballard, Spahr, Andrews & Ingersoll.

Robert A. Manekin, JD. The Staubach Company.

Gene C. Parker, Jr., MS. Continental Realty Company.

Patrick Phillips, MPA, MLA. Economic Research Associates.

Douglas Porter, MCP. Growth Management Institute.

Robert T. Rajewski, MS. McCrary Development.

Coleman G. Rector, MS. The Rector Companies.

Scott Rosenberg, MS. Rosenberg A+I.

Tara A. Scanlon, JD. Holland & Knight, LLP.

Scott Sherman, JD. U.S. Environmental Protection Agency.

Harvey Singer, MBA. REDMARK Economics for Real Estate Development & Market Research.

David Sislen, MBA. Bristol Capital Corporation.

J. Eric Smart, MCP. Bolan Smart Associates, Inc.

Roger P. Staiger III. Consultant.

Jeffrey Turner, MS. Brailsford & Dunlavey.

Emily Vaias, JD. Linowes & Blocher, LLP.

Alan P. Vollmann, JD. Holland & Knight, LLP.

Robert Wertheimer, MLA. Insurance Services Group, Inc.

The John Marshall Law School

Celeste M. Hammond, Professor
Center for Real Estate Law
315 South Plymouth Court
Chicago, IL 60604
312-427-2737
6estate@jmls.edu
www.jmls.edu

Degree	Year Program Began	Credit Hours	Years to Complete	Full-Time Students (2006–2007)	Part-Time Students (2006–2007)	Degrees Conferred (2006)
LLM in real estate law	1995	24	5	9	32	15

Degree	Application Deadline	Minimum GPA	Departmental Requirements
LLM in real estate law	For spring: December 15 For fall: August 1	3.0 for those just completing a JD program	Resume, personal statement, names of 2 references; applicants are expected to have taken courses in real estate transactions and federal income tax while earning their JD degree.

Number of Adjuncts/FTE	In-State Graduate Tuition	Out-of-State Graduate Tuition
39/8	$1,120/credit	$1,120/credit

Degree Specialization

LLM in real estate law.

Program Description

The LLM in Real Estate Law Program began admitting students in 1995. Students must have earned a JD degree to be admitted, except for JD students at the John Marshall Law School, who may enroll in a joint JD/LLM program while still earning their JD degree.

Core Curriculum

The 24 credit hours for the degree include both required and elective courses. Required courses total 16 credit hours, and are given once each academic year, to enable students to earn their LLM in two semesters. The courses include Commercial Real Estate Transactions, Real Estate Finance, Federal Income Tax Aspects of Real Estate, Leasing Environmental Law, and Construction Law, and a workshop in Drafting and Negotiation Skills. Electives are given periodically and cover topics such as insurance, affordable housing, real estate taxes, land use and zoning, condominiums, alternative dispute resolution, bankruptcy, fair housing/fair lending, real estate litigation, and securitization.

Financial Aid

Student loans, work-study opportunities, and research assistantships (depending on faculty needs) are available. Students occasionally find and apply for scholarships given by real estate organizations.

Lecture Series

The annual Kratovil Conference addresses topics related to real estate law and practice. With continuing education now mandatory in Illinois, the Center for Real Estate Law, along with other John Marshall centers, is sponsoring several CLE programs each semester, which are open to all students without charge. In addition, each semester the Center for Real Estate Law and the Real Estate Law Student Chapter of Lambda Alpha International jointly present a series of programs featuring a real estate attorney or real estate professional.

International Programs

International travel is sometimes offered as part of an elective course on international real estate transactions.

Program Advisory Group

The Advisory Board, which is made up of attorneys, academics, and real estate professionals, meets annually before the Kratovil Conference or another real estate program.

Internship Placement Assistance

Students who are completing the requirements for their LLM in two semesters and who have no practical experience are able to take a practicum for two credit hours. Placements are made by the Center for Real Estate Law.

Job Placement Assistance

Students have access to all programs and staff of the Career Services Office, which works with current JD and LLM students and with alumni. The Center for Real Estate Law serves as a program resource for the Career Services Office, and gives career advice to students and alumni.

Clubs/Alumni Associations

The Real Estate Law Student Chapter of Lambda Alpha International is the student organization for real estate students.

Faculty

F. Willis Caruso, clinical professor. Fair housing/fair lending.

Professor Celeste M. Hammond, director of the Center for Real Estate Law. Alternative dispute resolution.

Professor Debra Stark. Commercial real estate transactions.

Adjunct Faculty

Ben Applegate, JD. Affordable housing.

Michelle Bella, MS, real estate. Real estate industry.

Paul Carman, JD. Federal income tax aspects of real estate.

David S. Chernoff, JD. Drafting and negotiation skills workshop.

Paul Davis, JD. Affordable housing.

Karen Ercoli, JD. Leasing, ownership, and management.

James Hagy, JD. International aspects of real estate.

Harold Hicks, JD, LLM. State, local, and transfer taxes.

Thomas Jaconetty, JD. State, local and transfer taxes.

Evan McKenzie, JD. Condominiums, cooperatives, and other common-ownership communities.

Art Pape, JD. Insurance aspects of real estate transactions.

Jordan Peters, JD. Real estate finance.

Stanley Sklar, JD. Construction law.

Lorence Slutsky, JD. Construction law.

Sanford Stein, JD. Environmental controls and concerns affecting real estate.

Marquette University

Mark Eppli, Professor and Bell Chair in Real Estate
Department of Finance
College of Business Administration
Marquette University
P.O. Box 1881
Milwaukee, WI 53201
414-288-8041; fax 414-288-1668
Contact: Nicole Truog
nicole.truog@marquette.edu
www.busadm.mu.edu

Degree	Year Program Began	Credit Hours	Years to Complete	Thesis or Final Product	Full-Time Students (2006–2007)	Part-Time Students (2006–2007)	Degrees Conferred (2006)
BSBA	2004	129	4		124		28
MSAE	1983	30	1–2	Noncredit master's essay	29	6	18

Degree	Application Deadline	Minimum High School or Undergraduate GPA	Minimum SAT, ACT, GRE, or GMAT Score	Departmental Requirements
BBA	December 1	3.40 (average)	SAT: 1160 ACT: 26	Application, personal essays, 3 letters of recommendation
MSAE	Rolling	3.00	GMAT: 610 (average) GRE: 650 (average)	Application, personal essays, resume or job profile, 3 letters of recommendation

Number of Faculty/FTE	Specialized Degree Accreditation	In-State Graduate Tuition	Out-of-State Graduate Tuition	In-State Undergraduate Tuition	Out-of-State Undergraduate Tuition
5/3	BSBA: AACSB MSAE: AACSB	$800/credit	$800/credit	$26,270/year	$26,270/year

Degree Specializations

BSBA with a major in real estate.
MSAE (master of science in applied economics; jointly sponsored by the Real Estate Program and the Department of Economics in the College of Business).

Program Description

The BSBA with a major in real estate educates applied decision makers in the development, financing, valuation, and servicing of income-producing real estate. The program prepares students for careers in commercial real estate development, finance, and management. The real estate major builds on the strength of the university and college's mission of training ethical, effective, and educated managers.

Core Curriculum

REAL 150, Principles of Commercial Real Estate Development; REAL 151, Commercial Real Estate Finance; three courses selected from the following (including either REAL 156 or REAL 157): REAL 105, Internship in Real Estate; REAL 156, Commercial Real Estate Valuation; REAL 157, Cases in Commercial Real Estate; REAL 159, Issues in Real Estate; FINA 181, Investment Analysis; FINA 183, Advanced Financial Management; ENTP 151, New Venture Creation; MANA 154, Negotiations and New Ventures; ECON 146, Urban Economics; MARK 142, Marketing Research; ACCO 140, Financial Statement Analysis.

Financial Aid

Undergraduate financial aid is provided in a variety of forms by the College of Business Administration and the university. Graduate financial aid provided annually by the College of Business Administration includes four graduate assistantships (nine credits per year plus a stipend); four tuition-support awards (nine credits per year); and numerous other tuition scholarships.

Lecture Series

Quarterly lectures are co-sponsored by the Marquette University Real Estate Program, the Commercial Association of Realtors—Wisconsin, the *Business Journal*, and the *Small Business Times*. Presentations have been made by ULI Resident Fellows (William Hudnut and Maureen McAvey); Fortune 400 corporate real estate professionals; and local, regional, and national government officials and real estate professionals.

International Programs

Numerous study abroad programs are available to College of Business students; however, none are specifically offered by the Real Estate Program.

Program Advisory Group

The Bell Chair Advisors is a loosely knit group of 180 real estate and related professionals who meet semi-annually and assist with curriculum, placement, financial, and teaching support of the program. The Bell Chair Advisors are guided by a nine-member board that includes area developers, financial institutions, law firms, construction firms, not-for-profits, architects, and urban planners.

Internship Placement Assistance

Internship placement assistance is provided through the director of career development and placement, the Bell Chair, and the Bell Chair Advisors. Contact Marq Stankowski, College of Business Administration Director of Career Development, at 414-288-7394 or marq.stankowski@marquette.edu.

Job Placement Assistance

Job placement assistance is provided through the Career Services Center, the Bell Chair, and the Bell Chair Advisors. Contact the Career Services Center at 414-288-7423.

Clubs/Alumni Associations

With over 65 members, the undergraduate Real Estate Club (reclub@marquette.edu) is the largest student organization in the College of Business Administration. Activities include site visits, meetings with industry leaders, networking, and community service.

CIRCLES is an innovative business networking program that connects Marquette alumni and friends doing business in, or providing services to, the following areas: real estate and construction, financial services, manufacturing and distribution, and engineering. At CIRCLES events held throughout the country, Marquette alumni and friends of the university have the opportunity to network; find employees, mentors, and business associations; and develop business leads and contacts.

Faculty

Sherryl Andrus, adjunct professor of finance. BA, Utah State University. NSREA.

David E. Clark, associate professor of economics; chair, Department of Economics. PhD, MS, State University of New York at Binghamton; BS, State University of New York at Oswego.

Mark J. Eppli, professor of finance and Robert B. Bell, Sr., Chair in Real Estate. PhD, MS, BBA, University of Wisconsin–Madison.

David Krill, adjunct professor of finance. MS, University of Wisconsin–Madison; BA, Marquette University.

Anthony Pennington-Cross, associate professor of finance. PhD, George Washington University; BA, Oberlin College.

Nicole M. Truog, lecturer; associate director, Real Estate Programs. MA, Loyola University Chicago; BS, Marquette University.

University of Maryland

Margaret McFarland, Director
School of Architecture, Planning, and Preservation
University of Maryland
Architecture Building, Room 1243
College Park, MD 20912
301-405-6790; fax 301-314-9583
mmcf@umd.edu
www.arch.umd.edu/real_estate_development

Degree	Year Program Began	Credit Hours	Years to Complete	Thesis or Final Product	Full-Time Students (2006–2007)	Part-Time Students (2006–2007)	Degrees Conferred (2006)
MRED	2006	33	1	Capstone project	6	65	0
Graduate certificate of real estate development	2006	12	0.75			5	1

Degree	Application Deadline	Minimum Undergraduate GPA	Minimum GRE or GMAT Score	Departmental Requirements
MRED	March 1	3.0	TBD	Resume, statement of experience and interest, 3 letters of recommendation
Graduate certificate	May 15	3.0	N/A	Resume

Number of Faculty/FTE	In-State Graduate Tuition	Out-of-State Graduate Tuition
MRED: 15/1.5	$733/credit hour	$927/credit hour

Degree Specializations

MRED.
Graduate certificate of real estate development.

Program Description

The MRED program at the University of Maryland was established in 2006 as a multidisciplinary approach to real estate development education, with a focus on collaborative, professional education in preparation for a sustainable future. It is committed to preparing students to engage in development that meets a quadruple bottom line: financially viable, environmentally sensitive, socially responsible, and beautifully designed. We have a deep interest in sustainable design and development, affordable housing, and public/private finance models. We have a large full-time faculty and a long history of Maryland-based industry expertise. Finally, we have an unparalleled location for the study of adaptive use and redevelopment.

The program is not cohort based; classes form in both fall and spring, and students may take one to four courses per term, proceeding at their own pace. The degree can take anywhere from 12 months to five years to complete; the average is two years. Part-time and full-time students are in the same classes, most of which meet after 4:00 in the afternoon—except for studios, capstones, and site visits. Students are encouraged to stay abreast of industry developments by participating in trade and professional associations, many of which have their national headquarters in the Baltimore/Washington area. Mentored trips to the ICSC and other industry events, both local and national, are offered periodically.

In early 2008, the Colvin Institute of Real Estate Development was established to support enrichment activities for students, and to serve as the home of research and publications related to real estate development. The Colvin Institute undertakes joint ventures with the National Center for Smart Growth Research and Education, engaging in educational outreach and research in the areas of land use policy; infrastructure finance; and development finance, design, construction, and management.

Core Curriculum

Required classes offered by the MRED program: RDEV 688A, Development Law Process and Ethics; RDEV 688B, Finance I; RDEV 688C, Design and Construction Management; RDEV 688D, Residential Property Management for Developers; RDEV 688E, Negotiations and Conflict Resolution; RDEV 688G, Planning Policy and Practice for Developers; RDEV 688J, Design Principles and Practices for Developers; RDEV 688I, Capstone Project.

Upon the request of the student, courses from other departments may be substituted for the core requirements. In addition, required courses may be waived or other courses substituted when the student has an advanced degree in or knowledge of a field such as architecture, law, business, or planning.

Financial Aid

Two graduate assistantships, at a maximum of 20 hours per week, are available. There are three industry-supported scholarships. Through a memorandum of understanding between the MRED program and the Office of the Secretary of Defense, full-time scholarships are available for civilians who are working in the real estate privatization arena for one of the military services.

Lecture Series

Most Wednesday evenings in the spring and fall semesters, there are lectures on planning, real estate, design, historic preservation, and their interrelationships. Each May, the MRED Annual Symposium—a weekend event—features speakers from government, industry, and academia on a topic of leading interest to real estate development students. Two to four times per year, gallery talks are offered to introduce and elucidate exhibits in the Kibel Gallery.

International Programs

Two international programs are under development: a two-week study tour of the Pacific Rim, and a three- to six-week new town development studio in Northeast India.

Program Advisory Group

The MRED Council of Advisors, which meets twice a year, includes developers; lenders; investors; accounting, legal, and environmental consultants; market analysts; civil engineers; construction contractors; and property management companies. The group provides networking opportunities for students and feedback on curriculum and programming; council members also promote the MRED program to the real estate development industry and serve as mentors for students. Finally, the council provides a forum for networking and the exchange of ideas among members.

Internship Placement Assistance

At this time, only informal internship placements are available. There is no internship requirement.

Job Placement Assistance

There is currently no formal job placement program, although industry contacts do lead to connections between students and job opportunities.

Clubs/Alumni Associations

Clubs and associations are under development but not yet active.

Other

A team made up of three MRED students, one MBA student, and two community planning students fielded and mentored by MRED faculty took the championship prize of $15,000 at the national REIDO competition in the spring of 2008, which proposed a redevelopment of a dense and challenging urban mixed-use site in northern Virginia.

Faculty

John Colvin, founder, Colvin Institute of Real Estate Development. BA, business, University of Maryland. President, Questar Inc.

Michael Daugard, adjunct professor. MBA, finance and investments, University of Maryland.

Maria Day-Marshall, adjunct professor. LLM, Georgetown University Law Center; JD, Columbus School of Law; Catholic University of America; BA, Fisk University. Senior business manager, Fannie Mae. Public finance, tax-exempt public housing, infrastructure, tax-increment financing.

Robert Kenison, adjunct professor. BA, St. Anselm College; LLB, Harvard University. Federal housing-assistance programs, equity, ethics, faith-based action as a vehicle for community empowerment.

Mary J. Konsoulis, adjunct professor; senior editor, *Real Estate Review*. MA, city and regional planning, Harvard University. Planning practice, historic preservation, adaptive use.

Robert M. Lefenfeld, adjunct professor. MURP, George Washington University; BA, Northeastern University. Managing partner and founder, Real Property Research Group. Market analysis, land economics.

Margaret McFarland, director, Colvin Institute of Real Estate Development; editor-in-chief, *Real Estate Review*. JD, University of Michigan; AM, urban studies, University of Chicago; BA, Andrews University. Real estate development law, process and ethics, affordable-housing finance, tax-exempt financing, public housing management and operations, accessible housing, appellate litigation.

Robert Rosenfeld, adjunct faculty, real estate development. MBA, Harvard Business School; BS, Wharton School of Finance, University of Pennsylvania. President, JBGRosenfeld Retail. Retail development and finance.

Steven Shapiro, adjunct faculty. BA, business, Georgetown University; JD, LLM, Georgetown University Law Center; MA, engineering, University of Maryland. Project management and strategic planning, Whiting-Turner. Design and construction management, sustainable development, development process.

Julie Smith, adjunct faculty. BS, business administration, State University of New York at Oswego. President, Bozzuto Management Company; partner, Bozzuto Group.

John Stainback, adjunct faculty. BA, architecture and urban sociology, and Master's of City Planning and Architecture, University of Pennsylvania. President, Stainback Public/Private Real Estate. Public/private finance, downtown redevelopment, transit-oriented development, new town centers.

Affiliate Faculty

Carl Bovill, associate professor of architecture. BSME, University of California, Santa Barbara; MSME, University of California at Berkeley; MArch, University of Hawaii. Materials and methods of construction, environmental control systems.

John I. Carruthers, adjunct professor, Urban and Regional Studies Program. PhD, University of Washington; MS, University of Arizona; BA, Hunter College. Urban economics, land use governance, public finance.

James R. Cohen, lecturer, Urban and Regional Studies Program. MRP, PhD, Cornell University. Associate editor, *Housing Policy Debate*. Land use planning, growth management, planning history and theory.

Karl F.G. DuPuy, professor of architecture. AB, Dartmouth College; MArch, University of Pennsylvania; MArch, Delft University of Technology, the Netherlands. AIA. Urban design theory, practice, and history.

David Falk, Senior Fellow, School of Public Policy. BA, Harvard College; JD, Harvard Law School. Real estate finance and development process, affordable housing, state and local tax policy.

Charles Field, senior research fellow, School of Public Policy. PhD, city and regional planning, Harvard University; JD, Georgetown University Law Center; MUP, New York University; BA, government, Cornell University. Theory and practice of negotiation and conflict resolution.

Marie Howland, professor; director of the doctoral program in urban and regional planning and design. BA, economics; MCP, city and regional planning, University of California at Berkeley; PhD, urban studies and planning, Massachusetts Institute of Technology. Urban and regional economic planning, economic development, suburban office development, telecommunications and urban form.

Massachusetts Institute of Technology

David Geltner, Director
MIT Center for Real Estate
77 Massachusetts Avenue, Building W31-310
Cambridge, MA 02139
617-253-4373; fax 617-258-6991
mit-cre@mit.edu
http://web.mit.edu/cre

Degree	Year Program Began	Credit Hours	Years to Complete	Thesis or Final Product	Full-Time Students (2006–2007)	Degrees Conferred (2006)
MSRED	1984	93	1	Thesis	36	34

Degree	Application Deadline	Minimum GPA	Departmental Requirements
MSRED	February 15	GMAT required	MIT graduate admissions application, resume, personal statement, 3 letters of reference, GMAT

Number of Faculty/FTE	In-State Graduate Tuition	Out-of-State Graduate Tuition
13/6	$50,000	$50,000

Degree Specialization

MSRED.

Program Description

Intensive, one-year interdisciplinary program for students with significant work experience in real estate. The emphasis is on the case-study method, with group projects. The thesis work integrates the student's skills in finance, design, economics, planning, management, and development. The Center for Real Estate of the Massachusetts Institute of Technology (MIT) is supported by partner firms and individuals from throughout the United States and abroad, many of whom act as guest speakers, provide research opportunities, and help recruit and place students.

Core Curriculum

Real estate investment and finance, economics, legal issues in the development process, capital markets, real estate development, leadership in real estate, entrepreneurship, real estate sustainability.

Financial Aid

Grants are available to minority students and to students who are committed to public sector work. General grants are given on the basis of need.

Lecture Series

The Center for Real Estate has a vibrant series of lectures that are incorporated into the classroom structure and also offered outside the classroom. The leadership course features a number of prominent leaders in the real estate industry; the real estate development and real estate investment and finance courses invite practitioners into the classroom to critique case studies and provide technical assistance to student groups; and the professional development program features Leaders in Real Estate—alumni and others from all facets of the industry who offer one-on-one interactions with students.

International Programs

Students may enroll in courses that focus on international development and markets, which include travel to various countries.

Program Advisory Group

The curriculum faculty committee includes faculty who teach core curriculum and one student representative.

Job Placement Assistance

Career services at the MIT Center for Real Estate does not focus on getting students jobs but on giving them the skills, information, and opportunity necessary to achieve their career goals. The objective is to maximize students' ability to present themselves effectively and to pursue the job they desire. Workshops on resume writing, interviewing, and networking are offered during the fall, and workshops on job search and negotiation skills are offered during the spring.

Clubs/Alumni Associations

The Alumni Association of the Center for Real Estate.

Faculty

Brian (Tony) Ciochetti, professor of the practice of real estate. PhD, MS, University of Wisconsin-Madison; BA, finance, University of Oregon. Real estate development, finance.

Lynn Fisher, assistant professor of real estate. PhD, MS, BA, Pennsylvania State University. Real estate finance, law, economics.

Dennis Frenchman, professor of the practice of real estate. MCP, MArch/AS, MIT; BArch, University of Cincinnati. Urban design, real estate development.

David Geltner, professor of real estate. PhD, MIT; MS, Carnegie Mellon University; BGS, University of Michigan. Real estate finance and investment.

W. Todd McGram, lecturer. MBA, finance; BA, Columbia University. Real estate investment and finance.

Peter Roth, lecturer. MS, MArch, MIT; BS, University of Texas. Real estate development.

Gloria Schuck, lecturer. EdD, managerial education; EdM, Harvard University; MA, BA, University of Northern Iowa. Management, leadership.

William Wheaton, professor. PhD, economics, University of Pennsylvania; BA, Princeton University. Real estate economics.

University of Michigan

Dennis R. Capozza, Department Chair
Department of Finance/Real Estate
Stephen M. Ross School of Business
701 Tappan Street
Ann Arbor, MI 48109-1234
734-764-1269; fax 734 936-8715
capozza@umich.edu
www.bus.umich.edu

Degree	Year Program Began	Credit Hours	Years to Complete	Full-Time Students (2006–2007)	Part-Time Students (2006–2007)	Degrees Conferred (2006)
BBA	1943	120	3	1,069		351
MBA (full-time)	1925	57	2 (unless dual degree)	834		502
MBA (evening)		60	Varies		762	178
MAcc		33	1	60		54

Degree	Application Deadline	Departmental Requirements
BBA	March 31	Students enter the 3-year, full-time BBA program in the fall of their sophomore year; entering students must have a minimum of 27 transferable credits (with a maximum of 45 credits brought in), and must submit transcripts, essays, and other information as outlined in the application. For specific requirements, see www.bus.umich.edu/admissions/bba.
MBA (full-time)		See www.bus.umich.edu/admissions/mba.
MBA (eveniing)	October 1	See www.bus.umich.educ/admissions/evenmba.
MAcc		See www.bus.umich.edu/admissions/macc.

Specialized Degree Accreditation	In-State Graduate Tuition	Out-of-State Graduate Tuition	In-State Undergraduate Tuition	Out-of-State Undergraduate Tuition
AACSB for all programs	$19,050/semester	$21,550/semester	$6,198/semester	$16,900/semester

Program Description

See www.bus.umich.edu/.

Core Curriculum

Finance. Real estate investment: This course assumes familiarity with the basic institutions of real estate and covers fundamental issues in real estate, including mortgage analysis, renting versus buying, valuation and appraisal, taxation, commercial property markets, and investment analysis. For more detailed information by degree, see www.bus.umich.edu/academics/curriculum/.

Financial Aid

Scholarships are available. Contact 734-764-5139 or umbsfinaid@umich.edu, or visit www.bus.umich.edu/admissions/financialaid/.

Lecture Series

The annual two-day real estate forum held in November provides an opportunity for alumni, students, and friends to explore problems and opportunities facing the industry.

International Programs

See www.umich.edu/~cibe/students/studyabroad.html.

Internship Placement Assistance

Internship placement assistance is available; see www.bus.umich.edu/studentcareerservices.

Job Placement Assistance

Job placement assistance is available. See www.bus.umich.edu/studentcareerservices.

Clubs/Alumni Associations

For information on the Real Estate Club, see www.bus.umich.edu/organizations/clubs.

Faculty

Peter Allen, adjunct professor of real estate. MBA, University of Michigan; BA, DePaul University. Real estate development.

Dennis R. Capozza, professor of finance and real estate; Dale L. Dykema Professorship in Business Administration. PhD, Johns Hopkins University; BA, University of Pennsylvania. Real estate finance, urban growth and development.

Lynda Oswald, professor of business law. JD, MBA, BA, University of Michigan.

George Siedel, professor of business law. JD, University of Michigan; BBA, College of Wooster. Real estate law.

Robert Van Order, adjunct lecturer of finance. MBA, University of Michigan; BS, Oakland University.

National University of Singapore

Yu Shi Ming, Head of Department
Associate Professor, Department of Real Estate
School of Design and Environment
4 Architecture Drive
Singapore 117566
65-6516-3469; fax 65-6774-8684
rsthead@nus.edu.sg
www.rst.nus.edu.sg

Degree	Year Program Began	Credit Hours	Years to Complete	Thesis or Final Product	Full-Time Students (2006–2007)	Part-Time Students (2006–2007)	Degrees Conferred (2006)
BSc (full-time)	1969	160 modular	3.5–4	Dissertation	528	0	
BSc (part-time	1999	160 modular	3.5–4	Dissertation	0	76	
MSc in real estate	1992	40 modular	1–3	Dissertation	7	32	
MSc in estate mgmt.	1969	N/A	2–3	Thesis	20		3
PhD	1977	N/A	3–5	Thesis	13		2

Degree	Application Deadline	Minimum High School or Undergraduate GPA	Minimum SAT, GRE, or GMAT Score	Departmental Requirements
BSc (full-time)	April 1		1800	Good GCE A-level results; diploma, relevant work experience; TOEFL/IELTS score (for applicants whose previous instruction was not in English)
BSc (part-time)	March 15			
MSc in real state	March 15			
MSc in estate management	December 15; May 15	80	1200–1400 (verbal and quantitative); 3.5–4.0 (analytical)	Research proposal, 2 letters of reference, TOEFL score (for applicants whose undergraduate instruction was not in English)
PhD	December 15; May 15	80	1200–1400 (verbal and quantitative); 3.5–4.0 (analytical)	Research proposal, 2 letters of reference, TOEFL score (for applicants whose undergraduate instruction was not in English)

Degree	Specialized Degree Accreditation	In-State Graduate Tuition (2007-2008)	Out-of-State Graduate Tuition (2007-2008)	In-State Undergraduate Tuition (2008-2009)	Out-of-State Undergraduate Tuition (2008-2009)
BSc (full-time)	RICS, SISV			S$6,360/year	S$9,540/year
BSc (part-time)	RICS, SISV			S$900/module	S$900/module
MSc in real estate		S$5,450/year	S$6,000/year		
MSc in estate mgmt.		S$4,350/year	S$4,790/year		
PhD		S$4,350/year	S$4,790/year		

Degree Specializations

BSc in real estate (honors).
MSc in real estate.
MSc in estate management.
PhD.

Undergraduate Program

The BSc in real estate program at NUS trains students to create and manage wealth in the context of the built environment. This program recognizes that "Real estate is space and money over time"; it is unique in providing an explicit link between the spatial features and financial attributes of real estate. Graduates from the Department of Real Estate (DRE) play key roles in the development of the built environment and in the advancement of the quality of urban living through the transformation and management of real estate resources. The advantages of a comprehensive NUS education also allow graduates to diversify into other areas, securing managerial positions in organizations like banks, fund and asset management companies, insurance companies, and training establishments.

Graduate Programs

The MSc in real estate offers a broad-based professional education at the graduate level. Designed to prepare candidates for advanced real estate careers in business, consultancy, research, or public service, the program is offered on a one-year full-time basis or a one-and-a-half-year part-time basis. The part-time program is open only to students who reside in Singapore.

The MBA with a specialization in real estate, a joint program offered by the Department of Real Estate and the NUS Business School, prepares students to face new challenges and create opportunities in the real estate sector. The program is distinctive in that it applies the best of real estate and business techniques in a uniquely Asian setting.

The DRE offers two research programs: an MSc in estate management and a PhD. Both are designed to equip candidates with cutting-edge analytical techniques and expertise. Students apply technical knowledge to real-world problems and undertake research that will make significant contributions to the real estate industry. These programs prepare students for academic careers in leading universities or institutions of higher education in the Asia-Pacific region. Potential research topics include housing, corporate and securitized real estate, and institutional and spatial analysis of real estate.

Program Description

The DRE offers one of the largest undergraduate real estate programs in Asia. This is a professional honors degree designed to be completed in four years by students proceeding at a normal pace. Students who are able to progress at a faster pace can complete the course in three-and-a-half years. The program is fully recognized by renowned local and foreign professional institutions, and is accredited by the RICS and the Singapore Institute of Surveyors and Valuers. Graduates of the program are exempt from all examinations required for professional membership in these institutions.

The BSc in real estate has several special features:
- The University Scholars Program (USP): an interdisciplinary program that provides advanced students with greater challenges (see www.usp.nus.edu.sg/ aboutusp/index.html).
- A broad-based curriculum: General Education Module (GEM), Singapore Studies (SS), and Unrestricted Electives (UE) are introduced to encourage students from various facilities to interact.
- Real-life learning: Throughout their course of study, through site visits, integrated projects, professional practice, and internships, students have the opportunity to apply the knowledge gained from their studies to real-life situations.
- A global outlook: Students are given opportunities to live and study abroad through the Student Exchange Program and NUS Overseas Colleges. Summer programs are also organized to give students an exposure to regional real estate markets.

Core Curriculum

BSc in real estate: Real estate finance and investment, urban planning, urban economics, real estate development and management. MSc in real estate: Real estate investment and portfolio analysis, real estate marketing and negotiation, corporate law, real estate development, planning, appraisal.

Financial Aid

Scholarships are available for both undergraduate and graduate students. See www.nus.edu.sg/registrar/sfau.html. For overseas field trips that will broaden their understanding of overseas real estate markets, students can apply for Travelling Loan Funds through the School of Design and Environment.

Lecture Series

The DRE organizes Public Talks covering current topics in the real estate industry. Speakers share knowledge and market updates with students, alumni, and the general public. See www.rst.nus.edu.sg/industry/index.asp?d=publictalk.

International Programs

NUS has three international programs: the Student Exchange Program, the Summer Program, and the NUS Overseas Colleges.

Student Exchange Program

Through the Student Exchange Program (SEP), students can spend one semester (preferably during the third year of study) at an approved overseas university that offers a similar course of study. Subject to approval, credits earned in overseas universities can be transferred to relevant NUS modules, and will count toward graduation. The grades obtained from overseas modules, however, will not be counted in the cumulative average points. The SEP allows students to widen their outlook and establish networks early in their professional lives. See www.rst.nus.edu.sg/programme/sep/index.htm.

Summer Program

Through the Summer Program, third-year undergraduates have the opportunity to participate in field trips to overseas real estate markets. Students attend lectures and seminars at NUS, and at partner universities in the country they are visiting; the focus is on country-specific issues and on socioeconomic, demographic, and political dimensions underlying real estate processes. Visits to projects and organizations are an integral part of the program. Each students completes a project requiring in-depth study of selected aspects of the real estate industry in the country. Past summer programs involved trips to major cities in China, including Beijing, Hangzhou, Nanjing, Shanghai, Suzhou, and Tianjin.

NUS Overseas Colleges

The NUS Overseas Colleges program is a highly innovative program that provides students with education and experience in leading entrepreneurial and academic hubs around the world. Students can intern with start-up companies for up to a year, while taking entrepreneurship-related courses at renowned partner universities such as Stanford University, the University of Pennsylvania, and Fudan University. See www.overseas.nus.edu.sg/noc/.

Program Advisory Group

As noted earlier, the DRE undergraduate real estate programs are accredited by the RICS and by the Singapore Institute of Surveyors and Valuers. The DRE has also set up a Department Consultative Committee, made up of industry leaders, to advise on program-related matters. A Visiting Committee, made up of renowned academics and industry representatives from overseas, also provides valuable counsel on course development.

Internship Placement Assistance

The Real Estate Internship Program, a partnership between industry and academia, provides opportunities for internship training in mainstream private property companies as well as in public institutions that serve the industry. Contact associate professor David Ho at rsthkhd@nus.edu.sg.

Job Placement Assistance

Upon request, organizations and firms can post job vacancies. Contact Rebecca Er at rstehhr@nus.edu.sg.

Clubs/Alumni Associations

For information on the Building and Estate Management Alumni club, call (65) 6516-6504; (65) 6516-3440; or e-mail secretariat1@bema.org.sg.

Faculty

Kwame Addae-Dapaah, senior lecturer. PhD, MSc, BSc (Hons.). Property development and valuation.

Muhammad Faishal Bin Ibrahim, assistant professor. PhD; MSc, real estate; BSc (Hons.), estate management. Property development and valuation.

Cheng Fook Jam, lecturer. MSc; Dipl., urban valuation. Property development and valuation.

Lawrence Chin Kein Hoong, senior lecturer. PhD; BSc (Hons.), estate management. Urban planning and management.

Chow Yuen Leng, senior tutor. MSc; BSc (Hons.). Real estate finance and asset market.

Alice Christudason, associate professor. PhD; LLM; LLB (Hons.). Property development and valuation.

Fu Yuming, associate professor. PhD, MSc, BEng. Real estate finance and asset market.

David Ho Kim Hin, associate professor. PhD, MPhil. Real estate finance and asset market.

Lim Lan Yuan, associate professor. MBA; MSc, construction management; BSc, estate management; LLB. Urban planning and management.

Liow Kim Hiang, associate professor. PhD; MSc, property and maintenance management; BSc (Hons.), estate management. Real estate finance and asset markets.

Liow Wen-Chi, assistant professor. PhD.

Lum Sau Kim, associate professor. PhD; MSc, land economy; BSc (Hons.), estate management. Real estate finance and asset market.

Malone-Lee Lai Choo, senior lecturer. PhD; Master, town and country planning; BSc. Urban planning and management.

Ong Seow Eng, professor. PhD; MBus, finance; BSc (Hons.), estate management. Real estate finance and asset market.

Joseph Ooi Thian Leong, associate professor. PhD; MSc, real estate; BSc (Hons.), estate management. Real estate finance and asset market.

Sim Loo Lee, associate professor. PhD; MSc; BA (Hons.); LLB (Hons.). Property development and valuation.

Sing Tien Foo, associate professor. PhD; MPhil, land economics; BSc (Hons.), estate management; Dipl., building management. Real estate finance and asset market.

Harold Tan Hock Chye, senior lecturer. MA, business administration; BSc (Hons.), estate management.

Tu Yong, associate professor. PhD; MSc, statistics and economics; BSc, computing. Real estate finance and asset market.

Grace Wong Khei Mie, senior lecturer. PhD; MPhil, land economics; MSc, property and maintenance management; BSc (Hons.), estate management. Urban planning and management.

Yu Shi Ming, associate professor. PhD; MSc, urban land appraisal; Dipl. (Hons.), urban valuation. Property development and valuation.

Belinda Yuen, associate professor. PhD; MA, town and regional planning; BA (Hons.). Urban planning and management.

Zhu Jieming, associate professor. PhD; MUPD; BA, urban planning and development. Urban planning and management.

University of Nebraska at Omaha

Dr. Donald Baum, Chair
Department of Economics and Real Estate
College of Business Administration
6001 Dodge Street
Omaha, NE 68182
402-554-2538; fax 402-554-3747
Contact: Dr. Roger Sindt
rsindt@mail.unomaha.edu
http://cba.unomaha.edu/econ/

Degree	Year Program Began	Credit Hours	Years to Complete	Full-Time Students (2006–2007)	Part-Time Students (2006–2007)	Degrees Conferred (2006)
BSBA	1950	125	4	45	15	15

Degree	Application Deadline	Minimum High School GPA	Minimum SAT
BSBA	Rolling applications	2.5	950

Number of Faculty/FTE	Specialized Degree Accreditation	In-State Graduate Tuition	Out-of-State Graduate Tuition	In-State Undergraduate Tuition	Out-of-State Undergraduate Tuition
5/2.5	AACSB	$192.75/semester	$507.25/semester	$154.75/semester	$456/semester

Degree Specialization

BSBA with a major in real estate and land use economics.

Program Description

The BSBA degree with a major in real estate and land use economics is designed to help develop skills in critical thinking and reasoning; the approach is based on applying concepts and theory to real estate and real estate–related business problems.

Core Curriculum

Real estate principles and practices, residential finance, commercial finance, fundamentals of appraisal, real estate law.

Financial Aid

The College of Business Administration and the real estate program offer competitive scholarships.

Program Advisory Group

The Advisory Council is convened as needed to advise on program issues.

Internship Placement Assistance

Internship placement is through the assistance of department faculty. An internship is an elective part of the coursework.

Job Placement Assistance

Job placement is provided through the assistance of department faculty.

Clubs/Alumni Associations

The Rho Epsilon Real Estate Club has both active and alumni chapters. The active chapter adviser can be reached at rsindt@mail.unomaha.edu.

Faculty

Steven Shultz, associate professor. PhD, University of Arizona.

Roger Sindt, professor. PhD, Texas A&M University.

University of Nevada, Las Vegas

Debra March, Executive Director
Lied Institute for Real Estate Studies
Finance Department
College of Business
Box 456025
Las Vegas, NV 89154-6025
702-895-4492; fax 702-895-4650
debra.march@unlv.edu
www.liedinstitute.com

Degree	Year Program Began	Credit Hours	Years to Complete	Thesis or Final Product	Full-Time Students (2006–2007)	Part-Time Students (2006–2007)	Degrees Conferred (2006)
BSBA in real estate	1975	120–130	4	Yes	95	23	12

Degree	Application Deadline	Minimum High School GPA
BSBA in real estate	See www.univ.edu/admissions/edu	2.75

Number of Faculty	Specialized Degree Accreditation	In-State Graduate Tuition	Out-of-State Graduate Tuition	In-State Undergraduate Tuition	Out-of-State Undergraduate Tuition
Full-time: 3 Part-time: 3	AACSB	$149.00/credit	$4,955.50/credit	$105.25/credit	$4,955.50/credit

Degree Specializations

BSBA with a major in real estate.
BSBA with a minor in real estate.

Program Description

A major in real estate gives the student a unique background in urban planning and land use regulation, real estate law, real estate finance, real estate investments, and appraisal. Since Las Vegas is the fastest-growing urban center in the Western Hemisphere, real estate development in this environment requires a dynamic application of business principles. Advanced courses in real estate law, property and liability insurance, real estate brokerage, securities and syndications, income-property appraisal, and construction technologies are available as upper-division electives. Interaction with the School of Architecture, community governments, trade organizations, contractors, and developers is facilitated and encouraged by the Lied Institute for Real Estate Studies.

Core Curriculum

BSBA, real estate, 2006–2008, required major courses: BLW 331, Real Estate Law I; FIN 308, International Financial Management; FIN 432, Real Estate Finance; FIN 434, Real Estate Investment; FIN 436, Income Property Valuation.

Required major courses (select four): AAL 446, Land Use Planning and Controls; BLW 431, Real Estate Law II; ECON 470, Urban and Regional Economics; GEY 430, Geographic Information Systems: Theory and Application; FIN 303, Intermediate Managerial Finance; FIN 307, Investments; FIN 312, Capital Markets; FIN 321, Corporate Risk Management; FIN 322, Insurance and Risk Management; FIN 433, Residential Property Appraisal; FIN 481, Finance Internship; FIN 490, Independent Study.

Required business core: BLW 302, Legal Environment; BUS 395, Current Issues in Business; FIN 301, Principles of Managerial Finance; MGT 301, Principles of Management and Organizational Behavior; SCM 352, Operations Management; IS 301, Introduction to Information Systems; MKT 301, Marketing Management.

Financial Aid

Twenty individual real estate scholarships are available, each for $20,000 per academic year. Millennium Scholarships are also available, and there is a CCIM-sponsored scholarship for UNLV real estate students that includes a $1,000 cash award and a complimentary introduction class.

Lecture Series

Monthly speakers are featured in conjunction with student organization meetings. Other sources of lectures include the Mentor Program; internships; seminars on Plans Reading/with BOMA; and the Seminar on Public Lands.

Program Advisory Group

The Lied Institute Board of Governors provides financial and program oversight. The committee is made up of corporate, foundation, and UNLV leaders. The Lied Institute Executive Committee provides oversight of the volunteer advisory board and its committees. The Lied Institute Advisory Board is made up of leaders in the real estate, development, finance, and construction industries.

Internship Placement Assistance

Internship opportunities are available to all real estate majors and minors. A mentor program is available each semester. Program assistance is provided by faculty, the College of Business Advising Center, and Lied Institute staff. Student organizations also provide information on internship opportunities.

Job Placement Assistance

Job placement assistance is provided through the Lied Institute and the UNLV Career Placement Center. Other sources of assistance are the annual Career Explorations Forum and student organizations, which post and disseminate job opportunities.

Clubs/Alumni Associations

The Real Estate and Business Society is a student professional organization that partners with alumni. A number of trade organizations sponsor student memberships, including the NAIOP, BOMA, and CCIM.

Other

The Lied Institute offers a dynamic executive-education program, including the Commercial Real Estate Certification, the BOMA Education Partnership; Online Mortgage Lending Coursework; the Annual Real Estate Roundtable Series; and the annual Lieder Awards.

The Lied Institute will be launching a master's degree in real estate development in 2009.

Faculty

Robert Aalberts, professor of real estate and business law. JD, Loyola University; MA, geography, University of Missouri-Columbia. Editor-in-chief, *Real Estate Law Journal.* Real estate property law and business law.

Dr. Terrence "Mike" Clauretie, professor of real estate. PhD, economics, Washington State University; CPA, Sheperd State College; BA, economics, Stonehill College. Real estate finance and investments.

Dr. Richard Hoyt, professor of real estate. PhD, finance, economics, management, marketing, University of Arkansas; MBA, BA, California State University, Long Beach. Real estate finance, investments, appraisal, and valuation.

Dr. Percy Poon, finance chair; professor of finance. PhD, finance, Louisiana State University; MBA, Texas State University; Honors Diploma with Distinction, economics, Hong Kong Baptist University. Financial management and investments.

New York University

(Construction Management)
Tom G. Geurts, Director of Academic Affairs
NYU Schack Institute of Real Estate
School of Continuing and Professional Studies
145 Fourth Avenue, Room 219
New York, NY 10003
212-998-7100; fax 212-995-4674
Contact: Marcie Burros
marcie.burros@nyu.edu
scps.gradadmissions@nyu.edu
www.scps.nyu.edu/realestate

Degree	Year Program Began	Credit Hours	Years to Complete	Thesis or Final Product	Full-Time Students (2006–2007)	Part-Time Students (2006–2007)	Degrees Conferred (2006)
MSCM	2002	42	1.5–5	Capstone project	7	51	32

Degree	Minimum Undergraduate GPA	Minimum GRE or GMAT Score	Departmental Requirements
MSCM	3.0	1100/550	2 letters of recommendation, personal statement, resume, 1–2 years progressive work experience

Number of Faculty	Specialized Degree Accreditation	In-State Graduate Tuition	Out-of-State Graduate Tuition
Full-time: 4 Part-time: 24	RICS	$4,489/course	$4,489/course

Degree Specialization

MSCM with two concentrations: Construction Management for the Development Process or Construction Project Management.

Program Description

The NYU Schack Institute of Real Estate is New York University's home for applied research, graduate study, and continuing professional education in real estate, construction management, and related fields. Founded as the Real Estate Institute in 1967—as part of what is now the NYU School of Continuing and Professional Studies—the Schack Institute is named in honor of the Schack family, three generations of New York real estate owners and developers, and donors of a transformative gift that has helped create a permanent endowment to fund faculty, students, research, and facilities enhancements. The institute is recognized as an unmatched resource for the education and career development of real estate leaders. Our students benefit from a close-knit relationship with the real estate and construction industries that spans four decades. Because our curriculum undergoes constant evaluation, our faculty members are empowered to address current issues in their courses, keeping students abreast of today's most critical industry developments.

Our MSCM program began in 2002. The curriculum incorporates all the components of managing a construction project and solidifies proficiency in estimating, scheduling, cost control, project planning, negotiation, and labor relations. Studies explore the various types of contractual relationships governing the owner, the contractor, the designers, and the subcontractors of a project. Bidding, handling disputes and claims, devising and implementing strategic business plans, and an understanding of real estate development round out the area of study.

Core Curriculum

Please note that all tier and concentration courses are required.

Tier Courses

Tier I: Principles of Real Estate Accounting and Taxation; Legal Principles and Practices; Construction Cost Estimating; Construction Methods and Technology.

Tier II: Construction Financial and Cost Control; Project Management: Planning, Scheduling, and Control; the Development Process; Construction Safety Management.

Tier III: Advanced Construction Scheduling and Control; Operating and Managing the Construction Organization.

Concentrations

Students choose one area of concentration.

Construction Management for the Development Process: Business Development and Management; Negotiation and Dispute Resolution; Capstone: Applied Project in Finance and Development.

Construction Project Management: Labor Relations in Construction; Managing On-Site Construction Operations; Capstone: Applied Project in Planning, Control, and Completion Strategies.

Electives

Students select one course from a list of elective courses or from another concentration in this program—or, with permission from the program director, from the MSRE program.

Financial Aid

New students are eligible for need-based scholarships ranging from $1,000 to $2,000 per year. Contact financial.aid@nyu.edu.

Lecture Series

We frequently offer breakfast seminars and symposiums on current real estate–related issues. These are in addition to required courses. Workshops in ARGUS and Advanced EXCEL are also offered to augment coursework.

The student association of the NYU Schack Institute of Real Estate offers an impressive roster of guest industry speakers. Faculty frequently sponsor ad hoc programs or guest speakers as well.

Program Advisory Group

The NYU Schack Institute of Real Estate Advisory Board, which is made up of over 100 industry leaders drawn from both the real estate and construction management arenas, is instrumental in charting the direction of the institute and in supporting and assuring the achievement of the faculty and staff. The advisory board meets at regular intervals, and its members are often called on to advise on particular matters, especially curriculum and faculty development. In addition, the board serves as a resource for hiring referrals for students and alumni, supports our special programs and conferences, and contributes to our learning community.

Internship Placement Assistance

Internships for credit are not part of our required coursework.

Job Placement Assistance

All students have unlimited access to the School of Continuing and Professional Studies Office of Career Management, which is geared to students pursuing master's degrees. Students may also access the services of the main University Office of Career Management (the Wasserman Center for Career Development). With the support of our alumni association, we hold a major career information event every fall. Our Industry Career Fair, one of the largest of its kind, is held in the spring. In addition, students have numerous opportunities, in the course of their studies, to explore the job market.

The NYU Schack Institute of Real Estate sponsors two major conferences: the Annual Capital Markets conference in the fall and the Annual REIT Conference in the spring. All students are encouraged to attend these events. Both the student association and the alumni association of the NYU Schack Institute of Real Estate administer mentor programs. Students are also offered preferential access to our major social fundraisers: the Evening of Monopoly in the fall, and the Urban Leadership Award dinner in the spring.

Contact Fran Brooks at 212-992-3237, or fb228@nyu.edu.

Clubs/Alumni Associations

The student association is a vibrant, integral part of the NYU Schack Institute of Real Estate community. The student association includes a number of "special interest" subgroups (e.g., WREN [Women's Real Estate Network], the Entrepreneur & Investor Group, and the Building Tour Group), and schedules a frequent and impressive roster of guest speakers covering all aspects of the industry. The student association also administers a much-sought-after peer-to-peer mentoring program.

The alumni association of the NYU Schack Institute of Real Estate, which has close to 2,000 members, is equally engaged with our graduate students. Every fall, the alumni association sponsors the Evening of Monopoly, a major fundraising event that draws well over 500 attendees. Funds raised at Monopoly help the alumni association fund four student scholarships in the fall and spring semesters. The alumni association also works with the graduate program to offer two career events for students and recent grads: Information Night in the fall and the Industry Career Fair in the spring. The alumni association also sponsors an alumni/student mentoring program, geared for students who are closer to graduation. Finally, the alumni association sponsors topical panel discussions each fall and spring.

Contact Fran Brooks (fb228@nyu.edu) for additional information about the student association or the alumni association.

Other

The NYU Schack Institute of Real Estate is located in New York City, at the heart of the world's most closely watched real estate market, and its programs capture the expertise and energy that drive our region's place on the global stage. It is a hub for industry activity and special events—including a speaker series, breakfast programs, lectures, and panel discussions. Our graduate students have the opportunity to make use of NYU's carefully maintained relationships with the industry, and to experience New York City as a living laboratory where they can hone their skills.

Faculty

John Eschemuller, clinical associate professor. BCE, City College of New York; MBA, Pace University. PE. Applied project in planning, control, and completion strategies; operating and managing a construction organization.

Tom G. Geurts, director of academic affairs and clinical associate professor. BS, Higher Technical College, Zwolle, Netherlands; MS, University of Amsterdam; PhD, Penn State University. Corporate finance; risk and portfolio management.

Richard Lambeck, clinical assistant professor. BSCE, Lafayette College; MSCE, New York University. PE. Managing on-site construction operations; construction methods and technology.

D. Kenneth Patton, divisional dean; Klara and Larry Silverstein Chair of Real Estate. BS, U.S. Merchant Marine Academy; MS, Northwestern University.

Adjunct Faculty

There are 24 adjunct faculty members in the MSCM program; their names are included in the faculty listing at the back of the book.

New York University

(Real Estate)
Tom G. Geurts, Director of Academic Affairs
NYU Schack Institute of Real Estate
School of Continuing and Professional Studies
145 Fourth Avenue, Room 219
New York, NY 10003
212-998-7100; fax 212-995-4674
Contact: Marcie Burros
marcie.burros@nyu.edu
scps.gradadmissions@nyu.edu
www.scps.nyu.edu/realestate

Degree	Year Program Began	Credit Hours	Years to Complete	Thesis or Final Product	Full-Time Students (2006–2007)	Part-Time Students (2006–2007)	Degrees Conferred (2006)
MSRE	1988	42	1.5–5	Capstone project	59	463	192

Degree	Minimum Undergraduate GPA	Minimum GRE or GMAT Score	Departmental Requirements
MSRE	3.0	1100/550	2 letters of recommendation, personal statement, resume, 2 years progressive work experience

Number of Faculty/FTE	Specialized Degree Accreditation	In-State Graduate Tuition	Out-of-State Graduate Tuition
Full-time: 11 Part-time: 73	RICS	$4,489/course $14,186/semester	$4,489/course $14,186/semester

Degree Specialization

MSRE.

Program Description

The NYU Schack Institute of Real Estate is New York University's home for applied research, graduate study, and continuing professional education in real estate, construction management, and related fields. Founded as the Real Estate Institute in 1967—as part of what is now the NYU School of Continuing and Professional Studies—the Schack Institute is named in honor of the Schack family, three generations of New York real estate owners and developers, and donors of a transformative gift that has helped create a permanent endowment to fund faculty, students, research, and facilities enhancements. The institute is recognized as an unmatched resource for the education and career development of real estate leaders. Our students benefit from a close-knit relationship with the real estate and construction industries that spans four decades. Because our curriculum undergoes constant evaluation, our faculty members are empowered to address current issues in their courses, keeping students abreast of today's most critical industry developments.

Our master of science in real estate program began in 1988. The curriculum provides students with the fundamental knowledge and advanced analytical skills necessary for success in the real estate industry and prepares students for success in a profession practiced across borders with respect to development, ownership, management, and finance. The program integrates theory with real-world application in all phases of the real estate deal—from initiating and negotiating to financing and closing the transaction. Students master the fundamentals through a required core curriculum and choose the remainder of their courses from concentration areas and electives that match their career goals.

Core Curriculum

Please note that all tier and concentration courses are required.

Tier Courses

Tier I: Principles of Real Estate Accounting and Taxation; Legal Principles and Practices; Real Estate Economics; Real Estate Valuation and Analysis.

Tier II: Market and Feasibility Analysis; Real Estate Finance; the Development Process; Negotiation and Dispute Resolution.

Tier III: Corporate Finance; Real Estate Capital Markets.

Concentrations

Students choose one area of concentration.
Finance and Investment: Real Estate Finance and Investment Analysis; Risk and Portfolio Management; Capstone Course.
Development: Planning and Design Issues in Development; Land Use and Environmental Regulation; Capstone Course.
Asset Management: Managing Building Systems and Operations; Real Estate Asset Management; Capstone Course.

Electives

Students select one course from a list of elective courses or from another concentration in this program—or, with permission from the program director, from the MSCM program.

Financial Aid

New students are eligible for need-based scholarships ranging from $1,000 to $2,000 per year. Contact financial.aid@nyu.edu.

Lecture Series

We frequently offer breakfast seminars and symposiums on current real estate–related issues. These are in addition to required courses. Workshops in ARGUS and Advanced EXCEL are also offered to augment coursework.

The student association of the NYU Schack Institute of Real Estate offers an impressive roster of guest industry speakers. Faculty frequently sponsor ad hoc programs or guest speakers as well.

Program Advisory Group

The NYU Schack Institute of Real Estate Advisory Board, which is made up of over 100 industry leaders drawn from both the real estate and construction management arenas, is instrumental in charting the direction of the institute and in supporting and assuring the achievement of the faculty and staff. The advisory board meets at regular intervals, and its members are often called on to advise on particular matters, especially curriculum and faculty development. In addition, the board serves as a resource for hiring referrals for students and alumni, supports our special programs and conferences, and contributes to our learning community.

Internship Placement Assistance

Internships for credit are not part of our required coursework.

Job Placement Assistance

All students have unlimited access to the School of Continuing and Professional Studies Office of Career Management, which is geared to students pursuing master's degrees. Students may also access the services of the main University Office of Career Management (the Wasserman Center for Career Development). With the support of our alumni association, we hold a major career information event every fall. Our Industry Career Fair, one of the largest of its kind, is held in the spring. In addition, students have numerous opportunities, in the course of their studies, to explore the job market.

The NYU Schack Institute of Real Estate sponsors two major conferences: the Annual Capital Markets conference in the fall and the Annual REIT Conference in the spring. All students are encouraged to attend these events. Both the student association and the alumni association of the NYU Schack Institute of Real Estate administer mentor programs. Students are also offered preferential access to our major social fundraisers: the Evening of Monopoly in the fall, and the Urban Leadership Award dinner in the spring.

Contact Fran Brooks at 212-992-3237, or fb228@nyu.edu.

Clubs/Alumni Associations

The student association is a vibrant, integral part of the NYU Schack Institute of Real Estate community. The student association includes a number of "special interest" subgroups (e.g., WREN [Women's Real Estate Network], the Entrepreneur & Investor Group, and the Building Tour Group), and schedules a frequent and impressive roster of guest speakers covering all aspects of the industry. The student association also administers a much-sought-after peer-to-peer mentoring program.

The alumni association of the NYU Schack Institute of Real Estate, which has close to 2,000 members, is equally engaged with our graduate students. Every fall, the alumni association sponsors the Evening of Monopoly, a major fundraising event that draws well over 500 attendees. Funds raised at Monopoly help the alumni association fund four student scholarships in the fall and spring semesters. The alumni association also works with

the graduate program to offer two career events for students and recent grads: Information Night in the fall and the Industry Career Fair in the spring. The alumni association also sponsors an alumni/student mentoring program, geared for students who are closer to graduation. Finally, the alumni association sponsors topical panel discussions each fall and spring.

Contact Fran Brooks (fb228@nyu.edu) for additional information about the student association or the alumni association.

Other

The NYU Schack Institute of Real Estate is located in New York City, at the heart of the world's most closely watched real estate market, and its programs capture the expertise and energy that drive our region's place on the global stage. It is a hub for industry activity and special events—including a speaker series, breakfast programs, lectures, and panel discussions. Our graduate students have the opportunity to make use of NYU's carefully maintained relationships with the industry, and to experience New York City as a living laboratory where they can hone their skills.

Faculty

Faculty whose names are marked with an asterisk also teach in the MSCM program.

Tom G. Geurts, clinical associate professor; Director of Academic Affairs. BS, Higher Technical College, Zwolle, Netherlands; MS, University of Amsterdam; PhD, Penn State University. Corporate finance; risk and portfolio management.

Pamela Hannigan, clinical assistant professor. BS, Massachusetts Institute of Technology; MS, PhD (ABD), New York University. Research Fellow, Harvard Institute of Economic Research. Real estate economics.

*Barry Hersh, clinical associate professor. BA, City University of New York; MUP, New York University. AICP. Development process; green building and sustainable development.

Hugh F. Kelly, clinical associate professor. BA, Cathedral College; PhD (ABD), University of Ulster. CRE. Risk and portfolio management; real estate economics.

*Constantine Kontokosta. BSE, University of Pennsylvania; MS, New York University; MSUP, MPhil, PhD (ABD), Columbia University. AICP, PE. Development process; land use and environmental regulation.

*Gerald M. Levy, clinical associate professor. BA, Columbia University; MA, Harvard University. MAI, CRE, FRICS. Negotiation and dispute resolution.

Lawrence Longua, clinical associate professor. BSS, Fairfield University; MBA, Dowling College. Real estate capital markets.

Michael Moynihan, clinical assistant professor. AB, Columbia University; MPA, Harvard University. Real estate economics.

D. Kenneth Patton, divisional dean; Klara and Larry Silverstein Chair of Real Estate. BS, U.S. Merchant Marine Academy; MS, Northwestern University.

Michael J. Rushman, clinical associate professor. BA, Hamilton College; MRP, Cornell University; JD, Georgetown University; PhD, Arizona State University. Capstone in development; seminar in community development.

Rosemary Scanlon, clinical associate professor. BA, St. Francis Xavier University, Nova Scotia; MA, University of New Brunswick; PMD, Harvard Business School. Real estate economics.

Adjunct Faculty

There are 74 adjunct faculty members in the MSRE program; their names are included in the faculty listing at the back of the book.

University of North Carolina at Chapel Hill

Emil E. Malizia, Professor and Chairman
Department of City and Regional Planning
CB #3140
Chapel Hill, NC 27599-3140
919-962-4759; fax 919-962-5206
malizia@email.unc.edu
www.planning.unc.edu/

Degree	Years in Operation	Credit Hours	Years to Complete	Full-Time Students (2006–2007)	Degrees Conferred (2007)
MCRP	61	51	2	83	45
PhD	36	MS+36	5	23	5

Number of Faculty/FTE	Specialized Degree Accreditation	In-State Graduate Tuition	Out-of-State Graduate Tuition
16/12.25	MCRP: PAB	$2,056.50	$9,055.50

Degree Specializations

MCRP with a specialization in real estate development.
PhD with a focus on real estate investment, finance, and development.

Program Description

The objectives of the MCRP program are to prepare you for your first professional job and for a long-term career in planning. The program is structured to provide (1) a core of planning theory, urban theory, and planning methods; (2) in-depth coverage of substantive knowledge, methods, techniques, and institutions in an area of specialization; (3) elective courses to broaden or deepen knowledge and skills in particular areas of interest; and (4) application of knowledge and skills in a problem-solving workshop and master's project.

Satisfactory completion of the MCRP degree requires you to pass a minimum of 51 credit hours. Although the department has no internship requirement, we strongly recommend that students get professional work experience in the summer following the first year in the program.

Financial Aid

All applicants for aid will automatically be considered for all sources of aid for which they qualify; the student does not have to apply separately for each. Applicants may compete for several types of fellowships and assistantships: (1) awards made by the department; (2) university awards for which applicants to the department are considered; and (3) awards made by outside agencies for which applicants to the department are considered. Forms and additional information can be obtained from the Office of Scholarships and Student Aid, Campus Box 2300, Vance Hall, UNC–Chapel Hill, Chapel Hill, NC 27599-2300.

Lecture Series

The Center for Real Estate Development at the Kenan-Flagler Business School offers career panels and a lecture series featuring distinguished speakers. These programs allow students to interact with prominent real estate developers and other development professionals.

Job Placement Assistance

An extensive computerized database is maintained for access to career search information and contacts.

Clubs/Alumni Associations

Planners Forum; DCRP Alumni Association.

Faculty

David Godschalk. PhD, MRP, University of North Carolina; BArch, University of Florida; BA, Dartmouth College. Negotiation, site planning, growth management, geographic information systems.

David Hartzell, professor of finance; Steven D. Bell and Leonard W. Wood Distinguished Professor in Real Estate. PhD, UNC–Chapel Hill; MA, BS, University of Delaware.

Emil Malizia. PhD, MRP, Cornell University; BA, Rutgers University. Market analysis, feasibility, co-development.

Roberto Quercia, director, Center for Community Capital. PhD, UNC–Chapel Hill; MA, University of Hawaii at Manoa.

University of North Carolina at Chapel Hill

David Hartzell, Professor and Director
Center for Real Estate Development
Kenan-Flagler School of Business
CB #3490
Chapel Hill, NC 27599-3490
919-962-3160
dave_hartzell@unc.edu
www.kenan-flagler.unc.edu

Degree	Years in Operation	Credit Hours	Years to Complete	Full-Time Students (2006–2007)	Degrees Conferred (2007)
MBA	32	60	2	100	45

Number of Faculty/FTE	Specialized Degree Accreditation	In-State Graduate Tuition	Out-of-State Graduate Tuition
9/4	AACSB	$18,375	$36,749

Degree Specialization

MBA with a specialization in real estate development.

Program Description

MBA students who concentrate in real estate development take background courses in general business management during the first year of the program. In the second semester of the first year, a real estate elective is offered to introduce students to real estate finance and investments and to prepare them for summer internships. In the second year, students pursue additional electives in specialized programs designed to help them meet their career goals. The highlight of the real estate program is a comprehensive capstone development course in which students work in teams on local projects. This course integrates students' work in the areas of finance, design and planning, capital budgeting, and investment analysis in a real-world setting. Of the top 20 MBA programs ranked by *BusinessWeek*, Kenan-Flagler is the only one with a focus on real estate development. UNC's Center for Real Estate Development (CRED) is supported by numerous firms and individuals throughout the United States; these firms and individuals are a source of distinguished guest lecturers, research opportunities, and assistance with recruitment and placement.

CRED offers an intensive interdisciplinary real estate program with Kenan-Flagler, and students can broaden their education by taking classes offered by the Department of City and Regional Planning, the UNC School of Law, and the Institute for the Environment.

A three-year joint program with the Department of City and Regional Planning (DCRP) is also offered. Students take core courses in the DCRP in the first year, core courses in Kenan-Flagler Business School in the second year, and electives in the third year, according to their career interests.

Core Curriculum

In the first year of the MBA program, students take core general business classes across all functional areas. In the second semester of the first year and in the second year of the MBA program, real estate concentrators take the following required courses: the Real Estate Process, Project and Site Planning, Real Estate Capital Markets, and the Development Process. For many students, practicums provide additional exposure to real estate decision making. Second-year students take a broad range of electives within the Kenan-Flagler Business School, the DCRP, the School of Law, and the Institute for the Environment. For details on the Real Estate Concentration, see www.kenan-flagler.unc.edu/assets/documents/mba_realestate.pdf.

Financial Aid

For information on financial aid, contact the Kenan-Flagler Business School Financial Aid Office at 919-962-3236 or mba.info@unc.edu.

Lecture Series

The CRED hosts an annual conference with attendees and speakers from around the country. It also offers career panels and a distinguished lecturer series. These programs allow students to interact with prominent real estate executives.

International Programs

MBA students have opportunities for exchanges with top business schools worldwide. Within the MBA program, an intensive Real Estate Global Immersion Elective (GIE) is offered in which students travel to different countries to learn about global real estate practices and opportunities. In spring 2008, the GIE was held in Dubai and Istanbul; previous GIEs have been held in Australia, New Zealand, China, and Thailand.

Program Advisory Group

The CRED advisory board is made up of real estate practitioners who advise on curriculum and career services, and serve as advisers and mentors to students in the program.

Job Placement Assistance

Full placement services are available through the Career Management Center and through an extensive alumni database. An annual resume book is compiled, and on-campus interviews are conducted.

Clubs/Alumni Associations

The active MBA Real Estate Club sponsors the annual UNC Real Estate Development Invitational Case Competition, with participation by teams from the top MBA programs in the United Sates.

Faculty

Wally Boudry. PhD, New York University; BS, Queensland University. Capital markets, finance.

Stephen Cumbie. MBA, University of North Carolina. Real estate development process.

David Godschalk. PhD, MRP, University of North Carolina; BArch, University of Florida; BA, Dartmouth College. Negotiation, site planning, growth management, geographic information systems.

Clay Hamner. DBA, Indiana University; MS, BS, University of Georgia. Entrepreneurship, private equity.

David Hartzell. PhD, University of North Carolina; MA, BS, University of Delaware. Capital markets, investments, development.

Tom Harvey. MBA, BS, University of North Carolina. Real estate development process.

Mike Miles. PhD, University of Texas; MBA, Stanford University; BA, Washington and Lee University. Real estate development process.

University of North Carolina at Charlotte

Steven Ott, John Crosland, Sr., Distinguished Professor of Real Estate and Development
Department of Finance and Business Law
Belk College of Business
9201 University City Boulevard
Charlotte, NC 28223
704-687-7571; fax 704-687-6987
dcread@uncc.edu
www.realestate.uncc.edu

Degree	Year Program Began	Credit Hours	Years to Complete	Thesis or Final Product	Full-Time Students (2006–2007)	Part-Time Students (2006–2007)	Degrees Conferred (2006)
MBA with a concentration in real estate finance and development	2002	37	2	Project	60	240	147

Degree	Application Deadline	Minimum Undergraduate GPA	Minimum GRE or GMAT Score	Departmental Requirements
MBA	Varies	3.0	530	At least 3 evaluations from people who are familiar with the applicant's academic and professional qualifications; an essay describing the applicant's experience and objectives in undertaking graduate study; a resume or a description of work experience; 2 official copies of the applicant's transcripts; official GMAT scores.

Number of Faculty	Specialized Degree Accreditation	In-State Graduate Tuition	Out-of-State Graduate Tuition
56	AACSB	$5,000/semester	$9,000/semester

Degree Specialization

MBA with a concentration in real estate finance and development.

Program Description

Because of the major presence and sophistication of the real estate and financial service industries in Charlotte, there is a growing regional demand for employees with graduate-level education in real estate finance and development. Specifically, highly trained employees are needed for positions in appraisal, brokerage, lending, investment advice, consulting, market research, development, financial analysis, and capital markets.

To meet these needs, UNC Charlotte and the Charlotte real estate and financial services community have established a real estate finance and development concentration at the MBA level. The concentration combines the graduate-level business education provided by the MBA program with courses that specialize in real estate. Real estate courses are designed to develop students' analytical and technical competence and to provide them with a solid understanding of the real estate process. The goal of the program is to provide students with the educational foundation and skills necessary to become managers and leaders within the real estate industry.

Core Curriculum

Preparatory courses: MBAD 5112, Foundations of Microeconomics; MBAD 5113, Foundations of Macroeconomics; MBAD 5131, Fundamentals of Financial Accounting and Financial Management; MBAD 5141, Business Statistics; MBAD 5142, Quantitative Analysis in Business; MBAD 5191, Legal Environment in Business.

Core curriculum: MBAD 6100, Leadership and Ethics; MBAD 6112, the Economics of Business Decisions; MBAD 6121, Business Information Systems; MBAD 6131, Management Accounting; MBAD 6141, Operations Management; MBAD 6152, Financial Management; MBAD 6161, Organizational Leadership; MBAD 6171, Marketing Management; MBAD 6193, International Business; MBAD 6194, Management Strategy.

Real estate curriculum: MBAD 6158, Real Estate Finance and Investment, and MBAD 6159, Real Estate Development, plus one of the following courses: MBAD 6160, Real Estate Capital Markets; MBAD 6258, Site Feasibility Analysis; MBAD 6259, Applied Real Estate Development.

Financial Aid

Loans are available for graduate students through the Financial Aid Office. Other funds are also available:

- The MBA office has one Non-Resident Tuition Differential Grant available for a nonresident graduate assistant. This award is made in May for the following year and is based on academic qualifications.
- The Graduate School has limited funds available for in-state tuition grants, which are awarded on the basis of academic achievement and financial need.
- A limited number of graduate assistantships are available for MBA students in the Belk College of Business Administration each academic year. Graduate assistants work 20 hours per week assisting faculty with class preparation and research. They must be enrolled in at least six credit hours; maintain a 3.0 GPA; may not be employed elsewhere during their appointment as graduate assistants; and are expected to join the MBA Association and support its activities.

Lecture Series

Two or three lectures are presented each semester covering various real estate development topics. The MBA program also hosts two additional lectures each semester by regional business leaders.

International Programs

There are four international opportunities: (1) a double MBA program at EGADE, the graduate business school of Tec de Monterrey; (2) joint course projects with universities in Europe and Latin America; (3) international exchanges with numerous universities; (4) an annual international real estate study tour.

Program Advisory Group

The Belk College of Business has established an advisory board for the real estate program that meets twice a year to provide broad-based guidance on program goals and development and on student recruitment and placement. To enhance our students' educational experience and to provide networking and contact opportunities, advisory board members participate in the program in many ways, including (1) serving as guest lecturers; (2) speaking to students on real estate–related topics and issues; (3) offering internship opportunities to provide hands-on experience to students; (4) providing topics, questions, and guidance for students who do independent research as part of their coursework; (5) serving as members of committees that evaluate student presentations and research; and (6) providing potential employment opportunities for program graduates.

Internship Placement Assistance

Both undergraduate and graduate business students have opportunities for supervised and paid employment experiences in public agencies and private companies in the community. These opportunities are offered through a variety of experiential learning programs, including cooperative education, directed study, and internships.

Job Placement Assistance

UNC Charlotte and the Belk College of Business offer career assistance for both graduate and undergraduate students. The University Career Center maintains numerous resources to assist students in employment searches, including job postings and recruiting schedules. Students can also benefit from a variety of services and workshops designed to build skills in resume writing, interviewing, and networking.

Clubs/Alumni Associations

For information on the MBA Association, contact Danielle Stevens at mbaasoc@email.uncc.edu. For information on the Real Estate Alumni Association, contact Dustin Read at dcread@uncc.edu.

MBA Alumni Association.

Faculty

Richard Buttimer, professor of finance and real estate. PhD, BBA, University of Georgia. Real estate capital markets.

Bill Graves, associate professor of geography. PhD, MA, University of Georgia; BA, University of North Carolina at Chapel Hill. Site and market feasibility analysis.

Steven Ott, John Crosland, Sr., Distinguished Professor of Real Estate and Development. PhD, MS, University of Wisconsin-Madison; BBA, University of Wisconsin-Whitewater. Real estate finance, development, and investment.

Dustin Read, instructor of finance and business law. JD, University of Missouri; MA, University of Florida; BBA, Truman State University. Real estate investment and land use policy.

University of Northern Iowa

Arthur Cox, Director, Real Estate Education Program
College of Business Administration
Curris Business Building 317
Cedar Falls, IA 50614-0124
319-273-6986; fax 319-273-2922
arthur.cox@uni.edu
www.cba.uni.edu/dbweb/pages/programs/under-majors-real-est.cfm

Degree	Year Program Began	Credit Hours	Years to Complete	Full-Time Students (2006–2007)	Degrees Conferred (2007)
BA	1990	120	4	220	59

Degree	Minimum High School GPA
BA	2.50

Number of Faculty/FTE	Specialized Degree Accreditation	In-State Graduate Tuition	Out-of-State Graduate Tuition	In-State Undergraduate Tuition	Out-of-State Undergraduate Tuition
4/2	AACSB	$3,542/semester	$7,696/semester	$3,095/semester	$7,141/semester

Degree Specialization

BA with a major in real estate.

Program Description

In 1988, the Iowa Association of Realtors approached the University of Northern Iowa (UNI) to explore the university's willingness to create a real estate education program. Subsequently, as the result of joint efforts on the part of the UNI and the Iowa Real Estate Commission, the UNI Real Estate Education Program was created by legislation and an agreement between UNI and the Iowa Department of Commerce. The UNI Real Estate Education Program is the only four-year degree program leading to a major in real estate in the state of Iowa.

The program's mission is multifaceted. One goal is to enhance the general level of competence and professionalism of real estate professionals in the state of Iowa. A second goal is to provide a high-quality educational experience that will prepare students for careers in the real estate industry. A third goal is to facilitate economic development in Iowa.

The primary vehicle for accomplishing the program's objectives is education, with the main focus on undergraduates. Four courses in real estate are required for all real estate majors: Principles of Real Estate, Real Estate Appraisal and Investment, Real Estate Law and Brokerage, and Real Estate Finance. The balance of the curriculum includes the UNI liberal arts core, required core courses in the College of Business Administration, and electives. Industry relations have been and continue to be important aspects of the program's activities.

The director has traveled extensively speaking to industry groups. One of the primary purposes is to inform the industry of the potential to hire top-quality employees from the UNI Real Estate Education Program. Employers of graduates range from local firms to large multinationals.

The program trains students for a wide variety of careers in real estate. Real estate is broadly defined to include all aspects of decision making associated with land development, real asset management, finance, and brokerage, as well as the management of relevant business activities. Such careers encompass real estate appraisal, valuation, and investment analysis; land use decisions; mortgage banking, including loan origination, underwriting, and secondary market activities; real property leasing and management; real estate law; and brokerage.

The UNI Real Estate Education Program prides itself on its close ties with the real estate industry, which open many doors for students with respect to scholarships, research opportunities, and career choices. In addition, all faculty have had work experience in the real estate industry.

Core Curriculum

Core courses: Principles of Real Estate, Real Estate Finance, Real Estate Appraisal and Investment, Real Estate Law and Brokerage, Intermediate Financial Management, Advanced Financial Management.

Financial Aid

The University of Northern Iowa, the College of Business Administration, and the Real Estate Education Program all offer extensive scholarships. Approximately $30,000 in scholarships are awarded annually, specifically for real estate majors and real estate minors. Contact Denise Parks at 319-273-2720 or denise.parks@uni.edu; or Arthur Cox at 319-273-6986 or cox@uni.edu.

Lecture Series

Several times each semester, the UNI Real Estate Education Program cooperates with several professional associations to offer seminars that students may attend, usually at no cost. Topics encompass all aspects of real estate, including residential and commercial brokerage, appraisal, valuation and investment analysis, property management, and technology. The seminars are offered in conjunction with the Iowa Chapter of the Appraisal Institute, the Iowa Chapter of CCIM, the Mid-Continent Chapter of SIOR, the Iowa Association of Realtors, the Iowa Chapter of the Institute of Real Estate Management, and the Iowa Commercial Real Estate Association.

International Programs

A number of international study and exchange programs in Europe and Asia are available through the college and university.

Program Advisory Group

The UNI Real Estate Education Program has a very active Advisory Council that meets once each semester. Groups and associations with representation on the council include the Iowa Association of Realtors, the Appraisal Institute, CCIM, SIOR, the Institute of Real Estate Management, the Mortgage Bankers Association, Counselors of Real Estate, the Iowa Commercial Real Estate Association, the Iowa Real Estate Commission, and the Iowa Association of Realtors Foundation.

Internship Placement Assistance

Approximately half of UNI real estate students have an internship experience. Internship placement assistance is offered, and participation is highly recommended, though not required. Many students have more than one internship experience during their undergraduate careers; many are full-time placements running for eight or nine months—that is, a semester and a summer. The director of the real estate program has an extensive network of internship and employment contacts. In addition, the members of the real estate program assist students in securing internship experience.

Student research opportunities are available through both the Real Estate Education Program and the College of Business Administration. The real estate program has established relationships with several industry groups for research purposes. Students are able to participate in some of these projects and may be compensated for their endeavors. Recent projects have been completed for the Iowa Association of Realtors, the Des Moines Home Builders Association, and Homeward, Inc.

Contact Laura Wilson at 319-273-3821 or laura.wilson@uniedu; or Julie Grosse at 319-273-6041 or julie.grosse@uni.edu.

Job Placement Assistance

Job placement assistance is offered at all levels. The University Career Office maintains a staff in the Curris Business Building so that students can easily take advantage of its services. The university maintains an online search and resume service for both students and employers, and the director of the Real Estate Education Program has an extensive network of employer contacts. In addition, the members of the Real Estate Advisory Council assist students in securing career opportunities. Contact Laura Wilson at 319-273-3821 or laura.wilson@uniedu.

Clubs/Alumni Associations

The student real estate club is the Rho Epsilon Real Estate Club. Contact Arthur Cox at 319-273-6986 or cox@uni.edu. The alumni network is known as the Real Estate Education Program Friends Network. Contact Kurt Mumm at 515-224-8794 or Kmumm@ gemidamericapacific.com; or Dan Dickman at 515-248-9664 or dickman.dan@principal.com.

Faculty

Arthur Cox, associate professor of finance; director, UNI Real Estate Education Program. PhD, insurance; MA, finance; BBA, finance, University of Iowa. Principles of real estate, real estate finance, real estate appraisal and investment.

Richard Followill, professor of finance. PhD, MBA, finance, University of Alabama; BS, industrial engineering, University of Alabama.

Patrick Galles, adjunct instructor of real estate. JD, Creighton University; BBA, University of Iowa.

Robert Himschoot, adjunct instructor of real estate. JD, University of Iowa; BA, University of Northern Iowa. Principles of real estate.

Eric Johnson, adjunct instructor of real estate. JD, MBA, BA, University of Iowa. Real estate law and brokerage.

Keith Jones, adjunct instructor of real estate. BA, University of Northern Iowa. Real estate appraisal and investment.

Old Dominion University

Jon R. Crunkleton, Associate Professor
College of Business and Public Administration
Department of Finance
2060 Constant Hall
Norfolk, VA 23529
757-683-3584
jcrunkle@odu.edu
http://bpa.odu.edu/bpa/departments/finance.shtml
www.odu.edu/bpa/creed

Degree	Credit Hours	Years to Complete	Full-Time Students (2006–2007)	Degrees Conferred (2007)
BS	120	4	23	16

Number of Faculty/FTE	In-State Undergraduate Tuition	Out-of-State Undergraduate Tuition
2/1	$211/credit hour	$585/credit hour

Degree Specialization

BSBA in finance, real estate track.

Program Description

Finance majors in the real estate track take courses exploring real estate finance, appraisal, investment analysis, and market analysis. Students complete a group of core business courses offered in the College of Business and Public Administration and selected general education courses required by the university. Finance majors may also minor in numerous subjects throughout the university. The program prepares students for entry-level positions in real estate by tying theory to practical applications in appraisal, finance, and real estate investments.

Core Curriculum

In addition to General Education, College, and Common Body of Knowledge course requirements, finance majors in the real estate track may take the following courses: Principles of Real Estate, International Financial Management, Real Estate Finance, Real Estate Appraisal, Real Estate Investment Analysis, Urban Economics, and Investments. Students have a wide variety of other course options, such as construction management (School of Engineering), urban economics (Economics Department), and salesmanship (Marketing Department).

Financial Aid

The Office of Student Financial Aid (757-683-3683) supports the mission of the university by enabling students and families to reduce or eliminate financial barriers that might prevent them from participating in the programs offered by Old Dominion University. The office administers need-based aid funded by federal, state, university, and private sources; aid is awarded in the form of grants, federal Direct Subsidized Loans, Perkins Loans, employment, and scholarships. Merit-based scholarships are also available.

The office also administers federal loan programs that are not based on need (Direct Unsubsidized, parent PLUS), and provides information and support to students interested in alternative loan options. Through the department, specific scholarships are available to qualified real estate track students.

Program Advisory Group

The advisory group gives advice on curriculum, research, and student affairs. Groups and industry segments represented include appraisers, commercial sales and leasing, residential sales, mortgage banking, commercial finance, construction lending, public assessors, economic developers, residential and commercial developers, real estate lawyers, and property managers.

Internship Placement Assistance

In conjunction with the Old Dominion Career Advantage Program, numerous local companies offer internships. In addition to gaining valuable career preparation experience, students are encouraged to earn academic credit for their participation in these programs.

Job Placement Assistance

Graduates of the real estate track are employed in positions as real estate appraisers, real estate sales and leasing agents, property managers, developers, and lending officers. The Career Management Center offers the Career Advantage Program to students, the Alumni Advantage Program to graduates, and Recruiting Advantage Partnerships to employers. All consist of a full array of career programs and services. The Career Management Center has a satellite office in the College of Business and Public Administration; contact 757-683-5777.

Clubs/Alumni Associations

The Finance Club is open to all finance majors (financial management, real estate, and insurance).

Other

The E.V. Williams Center for Real Estate and Economic Development provides information and resources for the Hampton Roads real estate and economic development communities in their quest to improve the regional economy through job creation and investment. The center fosters relationships with the development community by hosting seminars on key development issues affecting the region and works closely with all related professional service organizations. The center maintains a comprehensive collection of information, including detailed demographic and real estate data, and employs the latest in geographic information and mapping software. Students have the opportunity to work as assistants in the center.

Once a year, the E.V. Williams Center presents and publishes the Hampton Roads Real Estate Market Review and Forecast to the regional real estate industry. The survey topics include the office, industrial, retail, single-family, multifamily, and investment real estate markets.

Faculty

Jon Crunkleton, associate professor. PhD, University of South Carolina. Real estate principles, finance, investments, and appraisal.

John Lombard, associate professor. PhD, economic geography, State University of New York at Buffalo. Economic development and research methods.

Penn State University

Austin J. Jaffe, Chair
Insurance and Real Estate
Smeal College of Business
355 Business
University Park, PA 16802
814-865-4172; fax 814-865-6284
ajj@psu.edu

Degree	Year Program Began	Credit Hours	Years to Complete	Thesis or Final Product	Full-Time Students (2006–2007)	Part-Time Students (2006–2007)	Degrees Conferred (2006)
BS	1973	120	4	No	25	5	25
MBA	1985	52	2	No	5	0	5
PhD	1994	Various	4	Yes	3	0	1

Number of Faculty	Specialized Degree Accreditation	In-State Graduate Tuition	Out-of-State Graduate Tuition	In-State Undergraduate Tuition	Out-of-State Undergraduate Tuition
7	AACSB	$17,110/year	$28,712/year	$12,284/year	$23,152/year

Degree Specializations

BS in finance with a concentration in real estate.
MBA with a concentration in real estate.
PhD in real estate.

Program Description

The program emphasizes the financial analysis of real estate projects through an interdisciplinary approach that includes economics, finance, valuation, law, and social issues.

Core Curriculum

BS in finance with a concentration in real estate: real estate finance, investment, and valuations; institutional real estate investment and portfolio management; real estate securities; international real estate; economics of urban property rights.

MBA with a concentration in real estate: financial analysis of real estate, institutional real estate finance and investment, economics of urban property rights.

PhD in real estate: real estate economics; finance and quantitative analysis.

Financial Aid

Several assistantships and scholarships are available at both the undergraduate and graduate levels.

Lecture Series

Invited speakers—approximately ten per year—include academics in the field of real estate and representatives of various industry groups. Advance Realty Lectures are also held twice each year.

International Programs

Real estate students participate in Penn State's well-known education abroad programs at more than 80 institutions throughout the world.

Program Advisory Group

The Institute for Real Estate Studies maintains an advisory board of donors and supporters.

Internship Placement Assistance

Internships are supported at both the undergraduate and MBA levels.

Job Placement Assistance

Full job placement service is available. The Real Estate Club compiles and distributes annual resume books for the BS and MBA programs. On-campus interviews are scheduled. Support is provided to PhD students for job placement and academic conferences.

Clubs/Alumni Associations

The Real Estate Club is an active student-run organization.

Faculty

Brent W. Ambrose, Jeffery L. and Cindy M. King Faculty Fellow and professor of real estate. PhD, MBA, University of Georgia; BS, Wake Forest University. Real estate markets, corporate finance, real estate finance and investment.

Shaun A. Bond, visiting associate professor of real estate. PhD, MPhil, University of Cambridge; B economics, University of Queensland. Real estate economics, empirical analysis of real estate markets.

Daniel R. Cahoy, associate professor of business law. JD, Franklin Pierce Law Center; BA, University of Iowa. Intellectual property rights, patent law, business law.

David B. Corneal, assistant professor of business law. JD, Stetson University School of Law; BS, Penn State. Real estate law, business law, small-business practice.

Austin J. Jaffe, department chair; Philip H. Sieg Professor of Business Administration; director, Institute for Real Estate Studies. PhD, MS, BS, University of Illinois. Real estate financial analysis, economics of property rights, conceptual basis of property, international real estate markets.

Jeffery M. Sharp, associate professor of business law. JD, MBA, BBA, Uni-versity of Oklahoma. Regulation of land use, aesthetic regulation, regulatory takings, environmental law, financial fraud.

Abdullah Yavas, Elliott Professor of Business Administration; research director, Institute for Real Estate Studies. PhD, University of Iowa; BS, Bogazici University, Istanbul. Financial contracting, agency problems, economics of brokerage, mortgage finance, experimental economics.

University of Pennsylvania

Professor Witold Rybczynski, Director
School of Design
Meyerson Hall, 210 South 34th Street
Philadelphia, PA 19104-2192
215-573-0985; fax 215-573-2192
rybczyns@design.upenn.edu
www.design.upenn.edu/new/real/index.htm

Degree	Year Program Began	Credit Hours	Years to Complete	Full-Time Students (2006–2007)	Degrees Conferred (2007)
CREDD	1998	5 courses	2–3, depending upon degree program	25	14

Degree	Application Deadline	Departmental Requirements
CREDD	December 1	CREDD applicants must be accepted and enrolled in one of the graduate programs in the School of Design (architecture, city and regional planning, landscape architecture, historic design and preservation). The CREDD is not offered as a freestanding program.

Number of Faculty	In-State Graduate Tuition	Out-of-State Graduate Tuition
Standing faculty: 3 Adjunct faculty: 3	$35,640/year	$35,640/year

Degree Specialization
CREDD.

Program Description
The CREDD program is open only to graduate students who are already enrolled in the School of Design. The program is aimed at developing design professionals (architects, city planners, landscape architects, preservationists) who have the requisite skills to understand and participate in real estate development. Students take courses in both the School of Design and the Wharton School. School of Design faculty have secondary appointments in the Wharton Real Estate Department.

Core Curriculum
Real estate finance, real estate law, design and development, real estate development, project management or public/private development or preservation economics or urban markets.

Financial Aid
Students enrolled in School of Design professional programs in architecture, city planning, landscape architecture, and historic preservation are eligible for a variety of need- and merit-based grants and scholarships, as well as teaching assistantships and work-study. Every year, WX awards a $7,500 scholarship to a woman real estate student in the School of Design. Contact Joan Weston at 215-898-6520 or weston@design.upenn.edu.

Lecture Series
The student real estate club organizes regular lectures. Visitors include industry figures, CREDD alumni, and developers.

International Programs
Individual departments regularly schedule international studios and have programs abroad (London, Mexico City) in collaboration with local teaching institutions.

Program Advisory Group
An informal advisory group consisting of professors Rybczynski, Landis, and Sagalyn meets as needed.

Job Placement Assistance
Students participate in Wharton's intern program at the Zell/Lurie Real Estate Center, in a student/mentor program, and in career panels. Students produce a resume book that is available online at http://realestate.wharton.upenn.edu.

Clubs/Alumni Associations
The Real Estate Interest Group is a student club that organizes lectures, roundtables and field trips, and cooperates with the graduate and undergraduate student clubs at the Wharton School, and with the real estate club at the Law School.

Faculty

John D. Landis, Crossways Professor of City and Regional Planning. PhD, University of California at Berkeley; BS, Massachusetts Institute of Technology. Property development.

Witold Rybczynski, professor of real estate; Martin and Margy Meyerson Professor of Urbanism. MArch, BArch, McGill University. Architecture, urban design, housing.

Affiliated Faculty

Charles Arena, lecturer in architecture. MArch, University of Pennsylvania. Project management.

Alicia Glen, lecturer in city planning. JD, Columbia University. Urban markets and residential development.

Donovan Rypkema, lecturer in historic preservation. MS, Columbia University; BA, University of South Dakota. Preservation economics.

University of Pennsylvania

Joseph Gyourko, Director
The Samuel Zell and Robert Lurie Real Estate Center at Wharton
The Wharton School
1412 Steinberg Hall-Dietrich Hall
3620 Locust Walk
Philadelphia, PA 19104-6302
215-898-9687; fax 215-573-2220
lebermaj@wharton.upenn.edu
http://realestate.wharton.upenn.edu

Degree	Year Program Began	Credit Hours	Years to Complete	Full-Time Students (2006–2007)	Degrees Conferred (2007)
BS	1985	37	4	108	45
MBA	1985	19	2	107	48

Degree	Application Deadline	Minimum High School or Undergraduate GPA	Minimum GRE or GMAT Score	Departmental Requirements
BS	January 1	No fixed criteria; no cutoffs for grades or test scores		
MBA	January 1	No minimum	No minimum	Completion of an undergraduate program in an accredited U.S. college or its equivalent in another country; GMAT results

Number of Faculty	Specialized Degree Accreditation	In-State Graduate Tuition	Out-of-State Graduate Tuition	In-State Undergraduate Tuition	Out-of-State Undergraduate Tuition
178	AACSB	$47,236/year	$47,236/year	$37,526/year	$37,526/year

Degree Specializations

BS with a major in real estate.
MBA with a major in real estate.

Program Description

The comprehensive real estate major at Wharton produces sophisticated real estate professionals who have both strong business skills and the ability to sensitively create and maintain working and living environments. Wharton's real estate program has been rated number one by *BusinessWeek, U.S. News & World Report,* and London's *Financial Times.*

Core Curriculum

BS and MBA in real estate: real estate investment, analysis, and finance; real estate law, finance, and development.

BS electives: housing financing and public policy, urban real estate economics, urban fiscal policy, urban public management and private economic development, introduction to planning and design for real estate development.

MBA electives: advanced real estate investment and analysis, real estate entrepreneurship, urban public policy and private economic development, urban real estate economics, housing finance systems and policy, urban fiscal policy, independent study, introduction to planning and design for real estate development.

Financial Aid

Eleven real estate fellowships, ranging from $500 to $5,000, are available. Fellowships are awarded by a faculty committee and based on the student's performance in the first year. Other aid is available through Wharton MBA Admissions and Financial Aid (215-898-3430), and the University of Pennsylvania's Office of Student and Financial Services (215-898-7988).

Lecture Series

Sponsored by the Zell/Lurie Center and funded by center member Max Farash, the Farash Distinguished Lecture Series and the Max M. Farash Real Estate Roundtable bring prominent industry leaders to campus. Recent participants include Robert Rubin, former Secretary of the Treasury; David Gergen, presidential adviser, Harvard professor, and editor-at-large of *U.S. News and World Report*; Peter G. Peterson, chairman and co-founder of the Blackstone Group; and Larry Summer, former Secretary of the Treasury.

International Programs

The International Training Program in Housing Finance educates high-level officials from the public and private sectors in emerging economies and developing countries in the institutional, financial, managerial, and mathematical aspects of housing finance.

Program Advisory Group

Chaired by Michael Fascitelli, of Vornado Realty Trust, the advisory board is made up of more than 250 well-known real estate professionals. The board provides student support and offers guidance on research initiatives, curriculum, and placement.

Job Placement Assistance

Real Estate Center students have access to Wharton's graduate placement office and the university's undergraduate placement office. The center sponsors a summer intern program, a student/mentor program, and a number of career panels. In addition, the Real Estate Club and the Center produce a student resume book, available at http://realestate.wharton.upenn.edu.

Clubs/Alumni Associations

There are four very active real estate clubs on campus: Wharton MBA, Wharton Undergrad, the School of Design, and the Law School of the University of Pennsylvania.

Real Estate Faculty

Fernando V. Ferreira, assistant professor of real estate. Urban economics and real estate, public economics, labor economics.

Joseph Gyourko, Martin Bucksbaum Professor of Real Estate and Finance; chairperson, Real Estate Department; director, Zell/Lurie Real Estate Center. Real estate finance, urban and real estate economics, housing markets.

Peter Linneman, Albert Sussman Professor of Real Estate; professor of finance and business and public policy. Real estate finance and strategy; mergers and acquisitions.

Georgette Phillips, David B. Ford Professor of Real Estate; professor of legal studies and law; vice dean, Wharton Undergraduate Division. Real estate law, urban and regional planning, housing.

Albert Saiz, assistant professor of real estate. Real estate economics, urban economic development, local public finance.

Todd Sinai, associate professor of real estate. Risk and pricing in housing markets, taxation of real estate and capital gains, commercial real estate and real estate investment trusts, air-traffic delays, real estate and public economics.

Susan M. Wachter, professor of real estate, finance, and city and regional planning; Richard B. Worley Professor of Financial Management. Real estate economics, urban economics, housing finance.

Grace Wong, assistant professor of real estate. Applied microeconomics; real estate economics; Asian housing markets; living conditions and health.

Secondary Real Estate Faculty

Robert Inman, professor of finance and economics, business and public policy, and law and economics (Law School); Richard King Mellon Professor of Finance; Real Estate vice dean; director, doctoral programs; Senior Fellow, Leonard Davis Institute of Health Economics. Public finance, political economy, urban fiscal policy.

Michael S. Knoll, professor of real estate; Theodore K. Warner Professor of Law. Corporate finance, international trade, real estate transactions, tax law.

Janice F. Madden, professor of urban studies, regional science, sociology, and real estate; Robert C. Daniels Foundation Term Professor. Urban and regional economics, labor market analysis.

Janet R. Pack, professor of business and public policy and real estate. Fiscal federalism and intergovernmental relations, political economy of economic policy, urban and regional economic development, foreign aid, privatization.

Witold Rybczynski, professor of real estate; Martin and Margy Meyerson Professor of Urbanism. Architecture, urban design, urbanism, housing.

Lynne Sagalyn, professor of real estate development and planning. Urban redevelopment, political economy of preservation, real estate development finance, politics and policy of the built environment, real estate securitization, real estate industry structure.

Emeritus Real Estate Faculty

Anita A. Summers, emeritus professor of public policy and management, real estate, and education. Urban economic development, urban public finance, educational finance.

Adjunct Real Estate Faculty

Marja Hoek-Smit, director, International Housing Finance Program. Housing policy and housing finance for emerging and developing economies.

Asuka Nakahara, adjunct lecturer in real estate; associate director, Zell/Lurie Real Estate Center.

University of Reading

Neil Crosby
Department of Real Estate and Planning
The University of Reading Business School
Reading RG6 6AW
United Kingdom
44 (0) 118 378 8175; fax 44 (0) 118 378 8172
rep@reading.ac.uk
www.reading.ac.uk/rep

Degree	Years in Operation	Credit Hours	Years to Complete	Full-Time Students (2006–2007)	Part-Time Students (2006–2007)	Degrees Conferred (2006)
BSc						
Real estate (formerly land management)	40	360	3	215		67
Investment and finance in property	13	360	3	37		11
BSc in real estate leading to diploma or MSc in urban planning and development	17	360 + 180	4	31		9
MSc (full-time)						
Real estate	20	180	1	57		56
Development planning	4	180	1			
Development planning research		180	1			
MSc (flexible)						
Corporate real estate and facilities management	9	180	2–6		48	4
Real estate appraisal	5	180	2–6		48	4
Real estate investment and finance	5	180	2–6		48	3

Degree	Number of Faculty	In-State Graduate Tuition	Out-of-State Graduate Tuition	In-State Undergraduate Tuition	Out-of-State Undergraduate Tuition
BSc	21			£3,125	£11,300
MSc in real estate (full-time)		£11,300	£11,300		
MSc in development planning (full-time)		£5,200	£10,500		
MSc (flexible)		£1,100/20 credit modules	£1,100/20 credit modules		

Degree Specializations

BSc in real estate (formerly land management).
BSc in investment and finance in property.
BSc in real estate leading to a diploma or master of science in urban planning and development.
MSc in real estate (various specializations).
MSc in corporate real estate and facilities management (flexible block release).
MSc in real estate appraisal (flexible block release).
MSc in real estate investment and finance (flexible block release).

Program Description

The three undergraduate programs offer a broad real estate education with appropriate professional specializations. The MSc in real estate programs are designed to provide a flexible route for students wishing to specialize in commercial real estate studies. The three flexible master's programs offer executive development modules.

The following programs offer exemptions from the RICS professional examinations: the BSc in real estate, the BSc in investment and finance in property, the MSc in real estate, the MSc in corporate real estate and facilities management, the MSc in real estate appraisal, and the MSc in real estate investment and finance. Two programs—the BSc in real estate leading to the MSc in urban planning and development, and the MSc in development planning—offer exemption from the professional examinations of the RICS and the Royal Town Planning Institute.

Core Curriculum

The three undergraduate programs offer a core curriculum consisting of land economics, investment appraisal, planning, law, management, and building. Specializations are available in appraisal, investment, and development.

Students in the full-time MSc programs select a specialization with core and optional units in economics, finance, appraisal, and law.

Students in the flexible MSc programs choose from a suite of executive development modules.

Financial Aid

Occasional scholarships are available. Contact the head of department at 44 (0) 118 378 8175.

Lecture Series

More than 20 visiting speakers participate in speakers' programs at the undergraduate level. The Reading Real Estate Foundation also offers an evening lecture series.

International Programs

European Erasmus and Socrates programs offer students the chance to study abroad.

Job Placement Assistance

All undergraduates are advised by the Careers Advisory Service and are given assistance with arranging interviews with visiting employers. All postgraduates are advised by Careers Advisory Service and course directors. Contact the head of department at 44 (0) 118 378 6340.

Faculty

Real Estate and Planning

Philip Allmendinger, professor. PhD, Oxford University; BSc, University of Edinburgh. MRICS, MRPTI. Planning and development.

Michael Ball, professor. MSc, BSc, University of London. Housing studies and urban economics.

Andrew E. Baum, professor. PhD, MPhil, BSc, University of Reading. FRICS, AIIMR. Valuation, appraisal, investment.

Peter J. Byrne, professor. BA, University of Manchester. Management information systems.

Alina Congreve, PhD, MSc, BSc, University of London. Eco-buildings and environmental issues.

F. Neil Crosby, professor. PhD, University of Reading. ARICS. Valuation, appraisal, investment.

Eamonn D'Arcy, senior lecturer. MA, BA, Dublin. Economics of planning and property, European real estate.

Andrew J. Doak. MPhil, BA, University of London. MRTPI. Town and country planning.

Henry L. Foster. ARICS, IRRV. Management and housing.

Franz Fuerst. PhD, Berlin; MSc, BSc, University of Dortmund. Real estate economics and finance.

Roger Gibbard. BSc, University of Reading. Property taxation, rural land management.

Virginia A. Gibson, professor. MSc, University of Reading; BA, University of Western Ontario. Marketing and corporate real estate.

Catherine Hughes. BSc, University of Manchester. Valuation and management.

Colin M. Lizieri, professor. PhD, LSE, BA, Oxford University. Urban economics and real estate investment.

Gianluca Marcato. PhD, MSc, University of London; BSc, Bocconi University. FSA.

Patrick McAllister. MPhil, University of Cambridge; BA, University of Kent. Valuation and real estate investment.

Gavin Parker. PhD, University of Bristol; MPhil, University of London; BSc, University of East London. MRTPI, FRGS. Land use, citizenship, politics and planning.

Alan R. Rowley. MA, DipTP, University of Manchester. FRICS, MRTPI. Urban design.

Charles W.R. Ward, professor. PhD, University of Reading; MA, University of Cambridge; MA, University of Exeter. AIIMR. Property/real estate investment.

Law

Sandra E. Murdoch, senior lecturer. LLM, University of Birmingham. Law of landlord and tenant.

Peter Smith, reader. MA, BCL, Oxford University. Property law, law of landlord and tenant.

Roosevelt University

Jon DeVries, Director
Marshall Bennett Institute of Real Estate
Walter E. Heller College of Business Administration
Chicago School of Real Estate
430 S. Michigan Ave, Gage Building 830
Chicago, IL 60605
312-281-3358; fax 312-281-3123
jdevries@roosevelt.edu
www.roosevelt.edu/realestate/

Degree	Year Program Began	Credit Hours	Years to Complete	Full-Time Students (2006–2007)	Part-Time Students (2006–2007)	Degrees Conferred (2006)
MSRE	2005	31	2	8	40	9
MBA REES	2002	27	2	10	46	15

Degree	Application Deadline	Minimum Undergraduate GPA	Minimum GMAT Score	Departmental Requirements
MSRE	Rolling admissions	3.25 preferred	450	If your GPA is 3.25 or better, no further materials are required. If your GPA is between a 2.8 and 3.24, submit a goal statement and resume. If your GPA is 2.79 or below, submit a goal statement, resume, and GMAT scores.

Number of Faculty/FTE	Specialized Degree Accreditation	In-State Graduate Tuition	Out-of-State Graduate Tuition
3/3	MSRE: ACBSP MBA: ACBSP	$709/credit	$709/credit

Degree Specializations

The Chicago School of Real Estate offers three academic programs: a master of science in real estate, a master of business administration with a concentration in real estate; and a certificate in commercial real estate development. The MS in real estate offers specialized classes and an interdisciplinary approach that combines urban economics with hands-on real estate experience. The certificate program is designed for students who already have a master's degree in a related field.

Program Description

The mission of the Chicago School of Real Estate is to raise the quality bar within the real estate profession. Our aim is to create career opportunities and enhance the resource base for the industry through a diversified program that attracts the best and the brightest individuals to the school.

The MBA program in real estate is the most innovative MBA in the Chicago area. Roosevelt's MBA represents a complete rethinking of what we teach and how we teach. The focus of the learning process is the shared responsibility of the student and instructor. Our classes are small, and the contact is personal. We stress teamwork and group projects. Because we believe that adult learners have considerable expertise to share with classmates, we expect each student to contribute to the education of his or her colleagues.

The MSRE program is designed to serve students seeking either to enter the real estate profession or to enhance their careers within it. The courses are designed to develop real estate professionals who will not only be able to manage and broker real estate, but to provide guidance for future planning and development in their communities. Graduates will have the necessary knowledge to enter the real estate profession as developers, managers, or researchers.

The courses that lead to the certificate in commercial real estate development build on students' graduate education in business and provide the academic and practical knowledge necessary to succeed in commercial development.

Core Curriculum

See www.roosevelt.edu/realestate.

Financial Aid

The Marshall Bennett Institute provides three Future Leader programs—the Goldie B. Wolfe Miller: Women Leaders in Real Estate Initiative; the Teresa and Hipolito Roldan Scholarship Program for Tomorrow's Hispanic Leaders in Community Development and Real Estate; and the Joseph and Joyce Freed Tomorrow's Leaders in Real Estate Initiative. Each program provides scholarship assistance, counseling, mentoring, job placement, and professional development courses to support students from their initial registration through graduation, and as they move into leadership-track positions in the real estate industry.

Additional partial scholarships are available through the graduate business office; award amounts vary depending on the scholarship. Only students who have been accepted to a real estate program as degree-seeking candidates may apply for scholarships. To be eligible for scholarship consideration on admission, students must have an undergraduate GPA of at least a 3.0, and must be enrolled in at least six semester hours per term. Real estate scholarships may be used only as tuition credits. For a list of available scholarships and applications, see www.roosevelt.edu/realestate.

Other standard forms of financial aid are available through the graduate school. See www.roosevelt.edu/financialaid/graduate for more information.

Lecture Series

The institute hosts two distinguished-speaker series: the Gerald Fogelson Forum on Real Estate and the Goldie B. Wolfe Miller: Women Leaders in Real Estate Lecture Series. Both events focus on best practices in development, finance, appraisal, brokerage, property management, design, environment, sustainability, land planning, market research, construction, regulatory approvals, management, and other leading issues of the development industry. For information on all Chicago School of Real Estate events, see www.roosevelt.edu/realestate.

Program Advisory Group

The Marshall Bennett Institute of Real Estate owes its reputation to the quality and commitment of its industry support. Since 2000, the institute's prestigious 80-member advisory board has been guiding the activities of the Chicago School of Real Estate. Members are prominent local and national industry leaders. They serve on the board under the direction of co-founders Marshall Bennett and Gerald Fogelson, and co-chairmen John Newman and Anthony Pasquinelli. Board members review curricula, suggest new programs, organize and participate in conferences, raise funds, and support the institute's other activities. A number of committees support specialized segments of the institute's programs.

Job Placement Assistance

The Marshall Bennett Institute of Real Estate assists all students in exploring employment opportunities within the real estate and construction industries. In addition, all students have access to the Urban Retail Professional Development and Research Center for career evaluation, planning, and counseling. The center provides real estate faculty and career professionals to assist students in developing their resumes, and in obtaining and preparing for job interviews. For participants in the Future Leader programs (see "Financial Aid"), the center also provides a staff professional who meets with students to evaluate their class mix, to help them determine which industry events will best prepare them for placement in their chosen field, and to review and explore career options.

Clubs/Alumni Associations

The Student Real Estate Club is a group for Roosevelt University students with an interest in real estate and urban development.

The club's primary objective is to strengthen the relationship between faculty, students, and practitioners interested in development issues: the club offers a forum for ongoing discussions with leading professionals in the field. Among other activities, the club sponsors speakers from the real estate community.

Other

The Chicago School of Real Estate benefits from the Marshall Bennett Institute of Real Estate , which is housed in the Walter E. Heller College of Business. The institute recruits speakers and sponsors real estate research, industry roundtables, and the annual Real Estate Gala. The institute also provides mentoring and internship and job placement services to students, and field experiences and guest speakers for classes. Institute staff—director Jon B. DeVries, assistant director Kristin Nance, and administrative assistant Ivrea Vinson—are available to assist students and faculty to access the best resources in the industry.

The Urban Retail Professional Development and Research Center is located in the Marshall Bennett Institute of Real Estate. The purpose of the center is to provide on-site resources for faculty, students, and professionals associated with the program to undertake research, use online data resources, and discuss real estate topics. The center also provides professional development services to students and recruitment services to the industry. Finally, there is a fully equipped media center for the creation and viewing of presentations for classes, for executive education, and for student training in presentation skills.

Faculty

Stephen L. Cleary, lecturer, real estate law, property management, and real estate process. JD, Northern Illinois University; MBA, DePaul University; BA, University of Illinois. President, Cleary and Associates, LTD.

Sofia Dermisi, associate professor of real estate, Walter E Heller College of Business. PhD, design studies; MDesS, Harvard University; diploma in planning and regional development engineering, University of Thessaly. Office real estate, security and terrorism prevention, Internet technology, residential real estate, redevelopment patterns.

Jon B. DeVries, lecturer in real estate development; director, Marshall Bennett Institute of Real Estate. MUPP, University of Illinois at Chicago; Masters of Divinity, Union Theological Seminary; BA, St. Olaf College. CRE, AICP.

Robert L. Finke, lecturer, construction project management. MBA, University of Illinois; BS, University of Illinois. President, Phynyx Realty Services Inc.

David Nickerson, professor and Marshall Bennett Chair, Walter E Heller College of Business. PhD, economics, Northwestern University; BA, University of Missouri. Real estate finance, financial intermediation, market microstructure.

Royal Institute of Technology

Professor Stellan Lundstrom
Real Estate and Construction Management
Architecture and Built Environment
Brinellvagen 1
Stockholm SE 10044, Sweden
+468790 6963; fax +468411 7436
Contact: Samuel Azasu, azasu@infra.kth.se
coordinator_rem@infra.kth.se
www.kth.se/studies/master/programmes/abe/2.1728?l=en

Degree	Year Program Began	Credit Hours	Years to Complete	Thesis or Final Product	Full-Time Students (2006–2007)	Degrees Conferred (2006)
MSc	1984	120	2	Yes	30	18

Degree	Application Deadline	Departmental Requirements
MA/BSc (minimum)	February 1	Academic transcripts, resume, personal statement, 2 letters of reference

Degree Specialization

MSc in real estate management.

Program Description

The Royal Institute of Technology is the oldest institution providing real estate education in Sweden. The Division of Building and Real Estate Economics draws on many years of experience in designing our education programs. Because of our hands-on approach to teaching and learning, students gain practical, job-related skills. Our close links with industry and local professional bodies and our strong alumni network allow us to stay abreast of current industry developments and integrate them into our programs. Our informal atmosphere encourages interaction with teachers and fellow students.

Core Curriculum

The courses given from periods one to three are foundation courses and are therefore compulsory. Period four courses, which are essentially applied courses, are electives. During period four, students will also be free to select electives courses from other programs within the school, subject to the coordinator's approval. The first two terms emphasize finance and management within the real estate discipline, and cover principles, theories, methods, and applications. The first half of the second year is devoted to research training and an introduction to leadership and organizational principles.

Financial Aid

All graduate programs are tuition-free. There are no additional scholarships offered by the school beyond this. Students can, however, apply for scholarships from the Swedish Institute.

Lecture Series

Guest speakers from the real estate industry provide additional perspectives on the real estate body of knowledge.

International Programs

There is a bilateral exchange program with the University of Aberdeen Business School.

Online Courses

One course is delivered almost exclusively online. There is also a Web platform that supports the rest of the courses.

Program Advisory Group

All faculty and administrators review the program curriculum and student support processes annually.

Internship Placement Assistance

The program has close links with industry, which students are encouraged to use to find their own internships.

Job Placement Assistance

There is no job placement assistance, but there are multiple job fairs on campus and students are encouraged to participate in them.

Other

Because of its location, our program offers students a gateway to the East European and Russian real estate job market. With a rapidly expanding real estate sector, the demand for our graduates is as strong as ever.

Faculty

Roland Andersson, professor emeritus. Regional and urban economics.

Samuel Azasu, MPhil, MSc, BA (Hons.). Economics, real estate investments, real estate valuation.

Mats Bohman, associate professor, economics.

Fredrik Brunes, MPhil, MSc. Economics, real estate investments, real estate valuation, regional and urban economics.

Kent Eriksson, professor. Management and leadership.

Åke Gunnelin, PhD, associate professor.

Sigrid Katzler, MPhil, MSc. Real estate management, financial economics.

Kerstin Klingborg, MPhil, MSc.

Hans Lind, PhD, professor. Business cycles in real estate markets.

Berndt Lundgren, MPhil, MSc. Real estate market analysis.

Stellan Lundström, PhD, professor. Real estate management, advanced issues in real estate economics.

Svante Mandell, PhD. Contract theory, real estate valuation.

Bo Nordlund, MPhil, MSc.

Erik Persson, PhD, associate professor. Real estate valuation.

Kurt Psilander, PhD, associate professor. Real estate market analysis and development.

Han-Suck Song, MPhil, MSc. Financial economics, portfolio management, real estate finance.

Abukar Warsame, MPhil, MSc. Regional and urban economics.

Mats Wilhelmsson, PhD, associate professor. Econometrics, regional and urban economics, research methods.

University of San Diego

Dr. Norm Miller
Burnham-Moores Center for Real Estate
School of Business Administration
5998 Alcala Park
San Diego, CA 92110
619-260-4150; fax 619 260-2760
Contact: Lisa Chambers
realestate@sandiego.edu
www.usdrealestate.com

Degree	Year Program Began	Credit Hours	Years to Complete	Full-Time Students (2006–2007)	Part-Time Students (2006–2007)	Degrees Conferred (2006)
BBA, emphasis in real estate	2001	124	4	100		40
MSRE	2004	32	1	24		24
MBA, emphasis in real estate	1999	48	2	15	5	10
Joint MBA/MSRE	2004	68	2.5	5		5

Degree	Application Deadline	Minimum High School or Undergraduate GPA	Minimum SAT, GRE, or GMAT Score	Departmental Requirements
BBA, emphasis in real estate	Fall: January 5 Spring: October 1	No requirement; entering freshmen average 3.8	No requirement; entering freshment have average SAT of 1200	Official transcripts, SAT or ACT scores, essay on topic provided, academic recommendation (other recommendations optional); optional essay on extracurricular activities, resume
MSRE	March 14 (first priority)	3.0	550	Application, official college or university transcripts, 3 recommendations, statement of interest in a real estate career, resume, TOEFL score (for international students)
MBA, emphasis in real estate	May 1 (first priority)			Application, resume, letters of recommendation, GMAT score, transcripts, statement of purpose
Joint MBA/MSRE	March 14 (first priority)	3.0	550	Application for joint degree, official college or university transcripts, 3 recommendations, statement of interest in a real estate career, resume, TOEFL score (for international students)

Number of Faculty/FTE	Specialized Degree Accreditation	In-State Graduate Tuition	Out-of-State Graduate Tuition	In-State Undergraduate Tuition	Out-of-State Undergraduate Tuition
MSRE: 11/5.5	MSRE: AACSB	$1,130/unit	$1,130/unit	$17,000/semester	$17,000/semester

Degree Specializations

BBA with a minor in real estate.
MSRE.
MBA with an emphasis in real estate.
Joint MBA/MSRE.

Program Description

The MSRE program is designed to develop the specialized skills needed by real estate professionals. Through an interactive approach, students gain the leadership, communication, and interpersonal skills necessary to compete for middle- to upper-management positions in real estate or to become real estate entrepreneurs. Through personalized teaching methods, including numerous "live," project-based courses, students gain a full understanding and appreciation of the many different facets of the real estate profession. Specifically, the MSRE program produces graduates who have decision-making skills; skills in financial and quantitative analysis; negotiating skills; an understanding of ethical issues in the real estate profession; business writing, critical thinking, and problem-solving skills; oral communication and interpersonal skills; and technology-related skills, including knowledge of ARGUS and other real estate databases.

Core Curriculum

BBA: Principles of Real Estate, Financing Real Estate, Legal Aspects of Real Estate, Commercial Real Estate Valuations, Real Estate Economics.

MSRE: The Real Estate Process, Real Estate Law, Legal Transactions and Land Use, Commercial Real Estate Finance and Investments, Urban Land Economics, Construction Management, Urban and Suburban Development, Commercial Real Estate Valuation, Commercial Real Estate Capital Markets.

MBA, real estate emphasis: Organizational Concepts and Techniques, Information and Analysis, Financial Reporting and Control, Customers and Markets, Financial Management and Analysis, Operational Processes, Global Business Environment, Law and Ethics in the Business Environment, Managerial Decision Making, Strategic Management, Real Estate Law, Residential Real Estate Markets, Financing and Institutions, and Commercial Real Estate Finance.

Joint MBA/MSRE: All MSRE courses and MBA core courses listed above.

Financial Aid

At the University of San Diego (USD), more than 100 assistantships and limited university grants that are credited toward tuition are available for both part-time and full-time graduate students. Other scholarships are offered by the Burnham-Moores Center for Real Estate through various trade associations. For more information, visit the scholarship section at www.usdrealestate.com; visit the Financial Aid Office Web site at www.sandiego.edu; call 619-260-4514; or e-mail usdofas@sandiego.edu.

Lecture Series

The MBA Speaker Series sponsors speakers in a variety of fields, offering graduate students the opportunity for conversation in intimate professional settings. Professors also invite local business leaders into their classes for discussion. In some courses, students are encouraged or required to invite leaders of their own organizations to speak in class. USD also sponsors the Executive in Residence program, through which out-of-town business leaders reside on campus for a week, hold counseling sessions during scheduled office hours, participate in classes, and attend social functions.

International Programs

The International Business Practicum provides opportunities for graduate students to engage in international consulting projects with overseas firms. Students begin the work at USD and spend the final week at the company, in its home country. Sponsored by the Ahlers Center for International Business, the program has been offered in Rio de Janeiro, Lima, Cape Town, and other cities around the globe.

USD also sponsors the International Collegiate Business Strategy Competition, a sophisticated computer simulation in which graduate students act as senior management teams, competing with other graduate students from universities worldwide. At the final stage of the competition, which is hosted in San Diego, business leaders participate as "boards of directors" to judge the competency of the senior management teams.

Program Advisory Group

The Executive Committee of the Burnham-Moores Center for Real Estate is made up of 30 senior executives in business and real estate who provide policy guidance and financial support to the center's real estate program. The Commercial Real Estate Committee oversees the commercial real estate program, the Residential Real Estate Committee oversees the residential real estate program, and the Curriculum and Research Committee provides guidance on curriculum and research topics.

Internship Placement Assistance

For information on internships, contact Career Services at 619-260-4654 or careers@sandiego.edu. Graduate students may contact Lauren Lukens, student and alumni services manager, at 619-260-7619 or llukens@sandiego.edu. Undergraduates may contact John Ferber, associate director of commercial real estate, Burnham-Moores Center for Real Estate, at 619-260-7513 or jferber@sandiego.edu.

Job Placement Assistance

For information on job placement, contact Career Services at 619-260-4654 or careers@sandiego.edu. Graduate students may contact Lauren Lukens, student and alumni services manager, at 619-260-7619 or llukens@sandiego.edu. Undergraduates may contact John Ferber, associate director of Commercial Real Estate, Burnham-Moores Center for Real Estate, at 619-260-7513 or jferber@sandiego.edu.

Clubs/Alumni Associations

The Real Estate Society is a student organization for both undergraduate and graduate students. Through guest speakers, panel discussions at monthly meetings, and off-campus tours of project sites, the society helps students gain direct exposure to industry projects and personnel.

The Real Estate Chapter of the USD Alumni Association provides a forum in which USD graduates who are working in real estate can network, and promote USD's and the Burnham-Moores Center's commitment to socially responsible leadership within the academic and business communities.

Other

The MSRE is dedicated to the values-based education philosophy of the University of San Diego. We stress the critical role real estate professionals play in building our communities, regardless of the career path they choose. We are committed to providing our students with the knowledge and skills necessary to become socially responsible leaders in the multidisciplinary world of real estate.

We are dedicated to providing a high-quality learning experience for students. The program's strong affiliation with industry, through USD's Burnham-Moores Center for Real Estate, allows students to gain technical expertise and hands-on experience through interaction with real estate executives and practicing professionals during their graduate program.

Faculty

John Demas, instructor. JD, University of Denver; MBA, New Mexico State University.

Louis Galuppo, adjunct professor. JD, California Western School of Law; BS, business administration, San Diego State University.

Norm Miller, professor and director of academic programs. PhD, MBA/MS, BBA, finance, Ohio State University.

Mark Riedy, professor and director. PhD, business economics, University of Michigan.

Charles Tu, associate professor. PhD, business administration, MBA; finance and investments, George Washington University; BS, mechanical engineering, National Chiao-Tung University, Taiwan.

Affiliated Faculty

Craig Barkacs, professor of law. JD, MBA, University of San Diego; BA, philosophy, Kenyon College.

Alan Gin, associate professor of economics. PhD, MA, economics, University of California, Santa Barbara; BS, economics, California Polytechnic State University.

Andrew Narwold, professor of economics. PhD, economics, University of California, Santa Barbara; MBA, Virginia Commonwealth University; BA, economics, University of Virginia.

Daniel Rivetti, associate professor of finance. DBA, Kent State University; BA, finance, Penn State University.

University of Southern California

Raphael Bostic, Director
School of Policy, Planning and Development
Lusk Center for Real Estate
650 Childs Way
Los Angeles, CA 90089
213-740-6842; fax 213-740-7573
Contact: Sonia Savoulian, Associate Director
sonias@usc.edu
sppd@usc.edu
www.usc.edu/sppd/mred

Degree	Years in Operation	Credit Hours	Years to Complete	Thesis or Final Product	Full-Time Students (2006–2007)	Part-time Students (2006–2007)	Degrees Conferred (2007)
MRED	21	44	Full-time: 11 months Part-time: 2 years	Comprehensive exam	43	25	52

Degree	Application Deadline	Minimum Undergraduate GPA	Minimum GRE or GMAT Score	Departmental Requirements
MRE	February 1	3.0	GMAT: 300 GRE: 1100 (verbal + quantitative)	Resume (minimum 2 years related work experience), written statement, 3 letters of recommendation, completion of prerequisites (listed on MRED Web site)

Number of Faculty/FTE	In-State Graduate Tuition	Out-of-State Graduate Tuition
33/7.31	$49,600/year	$49,600/year

Degree Specializations

MRED.
MRED/MBA.
MRED/JD.
MRED/Master of Planning.

Program Description

The University of Southern California (USC) MRED program brings together the three main elements of real estate development: design, finance, and policy; the goal is to prepare students for key positions in real estate development. Students are exposed not only to the full range of development functions—market analysis, finance, site planning, and project management and operations—but also to all product types, including residential, retail, office, hospitality, and industrial. Whether in the context of urban redevelopment, historic preservation, or suburban growth, MRED students learn, from the developer's perspective, the importance of relevant issues in real estate law, economics, finance, market analysis, negotiation, architecture, urban history, planning, and project management. Among other distinctive features, the MRED program is taught by full-time USC faculty as well as by developers, lawyers, architects, planners, and other prominent professionals who link learning with practice.

The USC MRED is one of the few graduate degrees focused on real estate development. The USC Lusk Center for Real Estate provides MRED students with a forum for professional development and offers opportunities to connect with southern California's real estate development community. In addition, the Los Angeles metropolitan area and its surrounding counties provide a rich urban environment within which MRED students can study a wide range of projects.

Core Curriculum

Real Estate Development and the Economy, Market Analysis for Real Estate, Finance of Real Estate Development, Real Estate Capital Markets, Applications of Real Estate Finance to Problems of Development, Project Management and Construction, the Approval Process, Legal Issues in Real Estate Development, Design History and Criticism, Building Typologies, Community Design and Site Planning, Real Estate Product Type Development.

Financial Aid

Seven to eight graduate assistantships are awarded each year to full-time students. The award provides 16 units of tuition credit and a nine-month stipend of $9,000. Students work with a member of the real estate faculty for ten hours per week. MRED students also are eligible for federally subsidized student loans administered through the USC Financial Aid Office.

Lecture Series

The Lusk Real Estate Speaker Series features prominent developers, consultants, and industry leaders at weekly noontime discussions. Topics include current development projects, industry trends, and company profiles.

International Programs

The School of Policy, Planning and Development has a strong international focus and a large number of international students. The Summer International Workshop provides students with project experience abroad. Recent groups have traveled to Australia, Hong Kong, China, England, Croatia, and Germany. There are also ten-day professional-level overseas visits (e.g., Sydney, Hong Kong, and Dortmund/Berlin), during which students meet with leading developers, government officials, prominent businesspeople, and consultants actively involved in the development community of the international site.

Program Advisory Group

The Lusk Center Executive Board provides professional support for the MRED program, serving as the liaison between the academic program and the professional community. The MRED faculty meet on a regular basis to oversee program administration and curriculum.

Job Placement Assistance

The Lusk Center supports the professional development of MRED students. Through the Lusk Center Mentor program, students establish one-on-one relationships with senior-level industry leaders. The Lusk Center publishes an annual real estate resume book and holds two annual career networking events. In the spring, Industry Night provides an opportunity to network with more than 60 real estate firms. The Lusk Center's Real Estate Employment Report summarizes the placement of USC real estate graduates.

Clubs/Alumni Associations

More than 90 percent of USC MRED alumni are employed in the real estate industry. USC alumni are members of a proud tradition known as the Trojan Family. MRED alumni are loyal representatives of the program and USC, and play an active role in supporting current students. LuskREAF, the Lusk Real Estate Alumni and Friends organization, serves as a focal point for professional and social interaction among alumni and friends of USC's various real estate programs. The group acts as a resource for the USC real estate programs and facilitates interaction between industry professionals and current students in the MRED, MBA, MCM, MPL, and undergraduate real estate programs. LuskREAF offers recent alumni an opportunity to work on events and programs for alumni and students, maintain contact with the university, and interact with Lusk Center members.

Faculty

Raphael Bostic, professor, School of Policy, Planning and Development; director, MRED. PhD, economics, Stanford University. Financial markets and institutions; the role and effects of regulation in banking, housing, and homeownership; urban economic growth; wage and earnings profiles; policy analysis.

Delores Conway, associate professor, Marshall School of Business. PhD, Stanford University. Economic analysis, employment discrimination, forecasting.

Yongheng Deng, associate professor, School of Policy, Planning and Development. PhD, economics, University of California at Berkeley. Real estate economics and finance, modeling and quantitatively analyzing housing and mortgage markets, policy.

Peter Gordon, professor, School of Policy, Planning and Development and Department of Economics. PhD, regional science, University of Pennsylvania. Urban and regional economics, real estate economics, regional policy analysis.

Christian Redfearn, assistant professor, School of Policy, Planning and Development. PhD, economics, University of California at Berkeley. Public finance, urban and regional economics, macroeconomics, real estate finance, economic geography.

Adjunct Faculty

Bruce Baltin, senior vice president, PKF Consulting.

David Brown, co-president, Grand Pacific Resorts.

Nancy G. Burke, land use manager, Kaiser Permanente.

Robert Champion, president, Champion Development Corporation.

Terri Dickerhoff, director of development, Josephson Properties.

Elizabeth Falletta, clinical assistant professor, USC School of Policy, Planning and Development.

Marcia Z. Gordon, administrative chair, Real Estate Group, Buchalter, Nemer, Fields & Younger.

Stanley L. Iezman, president and chief executive officer, American Realty Advisors.

Bryan C. Jackson, partner, Allen Matkins Leck Gamble & Mallory, LLP.

James Kasim, executive vice president and chief financial officer, Bentley/Forbes.

Steve Kellenberg, principal, EDAW, Inc.

Michael Keston, chairman and chief executive officer, Larwin Company.

Allan D. Kotin, principal, Allan D. Kotin & Associates.

Alon I. Kraft, vice president, Lowe Enterprises, Inc.

Carl F. Meyer, partner, Rosetti.

Dusan Miletich, president, Arenda Capital, Inc.

Ehud G. Mouchly, vice president and general manager, UniDev, LLC.

Tom Muller, partner, O'Melveny & Myers.

Ira C. Norris, chief executive officer, Horizon Communities, LLC.

Paul Novak, planning deputy, Los Angeles County Supervisor's Office.

Mark E. Oliver, appraiser, Cushman & Wakefield, Inc.

Richard Ortwein, partner, Focus Real Estate.

Kirk Roloff, senior vice president, Shea Properties.

Tracey Seslen, assistant professor of clinical finance, Marshall School of Business.

Renata Smith Simril, senior vice president, Forest City Residential West, Inc.

Johannes Van Tilburg, principal, Van Tilburg, Banvard & Soderbergh, AIA.

Chris Wilson, president, Wilson Commercial Real Estate.

Southern Polytechnic State University

Khalid M. Siddiqi, Chair, Construction Program
Department of Construction Management
Architecture, Engineering Technology and Construction
1100 South Marietta Parkway
Marietta, GA 30060
678-915-7221; fax 678-915-4966
ksiddiqi@spsu
http://cnst.spsu.edu

Degree	Year Program Began	Credit Hours	Years to Complete	Thesis or Final Product	Full-Time Students (2006–2007)	Degrees Conferred (2006)
BSCM, land development concentration	1999	128	4	Capstone project	40	24
Certificate in land development	2002	21	1		2	2

Degree	Application Deadline	Minimum High School or Undergraduate GPA	Minimum SAT, GRE, or GMAT Score	Departmental Requirements
BSCM	Fall: August 1 Spring: December 1 Summer: May 1	2.5	1000	Application package
Certificate in land development	Fall: August 1 Spring: December 1 Summer: May 1	2.5	1000	Application package

Number of Faculty	Specialized Degree Accreditation	In-State Undergraduate Tuition	Out-of-State Undergraduate Tuition
10	ACCE	$1,762/semester	$5,969/semester

Degree Specializations

BSCM with a concentration in land development.
Certificate in land development.

Program Description

The construction management degree with a concentration in land development follows the "School of the Built Environment" educational model. Students are provided with a holistic educational program that includes construction management, investment real estate finance and feasibility, land planning, construction law, land development law, project management and marketing, leasing, property management, and brokerage. Electives are available in a wide range of disciplines, from architecture and engineering to management, technical communications, and computer technology.

Core Curriculum

Core courses, BSCM: Introduction to Land Development; Site Planning; Development Finance and Feasibility; Development Marketing and Management; Development Law; Construction Graphics; Surveying; Structures; Residential Construction Materials and Methods; Commercial Construction Materials and Methods; Mechanical, Electrical, and Plumbing Materials and Methods; Construction Scheduling; Construction Project Management; Construction Estimating; Computer Applications to Construction; Building Codes; Management; and Accounting.

Core courses, certificate in land development: Commercial Construction Materials and Methods, Introduction to Land Development, Site Planning, Development Finance and Feasibility, plus seven semester hours of electives in construction and development.

Financial Aid

In-state students with a B average may apply for a HOPE Scholarship; scholarships are also available from private foundations and professional organizations. For more information, contact the Financial Aid Office at 678-915-7468 or finaid@spsu.edu.

Lecture Series

A seminar in land development and construction topics is offered annually. Fifteen to 20 industry professionals speak at each seminar.

Program Advisory Group

The Industry Advisory Board consists of 25 professionals from the development and construction industry; it meets quarterly to review the curriculum in relation to industry trends and needs. For more information, see http://cnst.spsu.edu/CNSTWEB/General%20Information/Industry_Committee.htm.

Internship Placement Assistance

The Career and Counseling Center handles internship placement on a university-wide basis. The Construction Management Department maintains a job bank, with postings updated daily, for the Construction Department's network of employers. Thirty to 40 companies visit the Construction Department each semester for recruitment. Internships are available but not required. Contact Phyllis Weatherly at 678-915-7391 or pweatherly@spsu.edu.

Job Placement Assistance

The Career and Counseling Center handles job placement on a university-wide basis. The Construction Management Department maintains a job bank, with postings updated daily, for the Construction Department's network of employers. Thirty to 40 companies visit the Construction Department each semester for recruitment. Contact Khalid Siddiqi, chairman, Construction Management Department, at 678-915-7221 or ksiddiqi@spsu.edu.

Clubs/Alumni Associations

Sigma Lambda Chi.

Other

The concentration in land development is part of Georgia's largest accredited program in construction management and covers a broad range of topics. There are currently 500 students in various construction management programs. The department offers late afternoon and evening classes and uses a flexible teaching format to facilitate student achievement. Hands-on learning and a solid reputation make program graduates market-ready for employment. Students develop business skills to plan and complete projects on time and within budget. The program is accredited by the American Council for Construction Education. Students and faculty belong to numerous professional organizations. The networking opportunities and connections that are made through the program afford students a definite advantage. The department's growing reputation outside the United States attracts a high proportion of international students, which provides a diverse environment that reflects the diversity of the workplace. The program exists within a teaching university, where teaching is the number-one criterion for promotion and tenure. Small classes and individual attention to the students' needs are central to the program.

Faculty

Hussain Abaza, assistant professor. PhD, MASc, BA, Virginia Polytechnic State University.

Gouranga C. Banik, professor. PhD, Iowa State University; MS, University of Manchester; MS, BS, Bangladesh University of Engineering and Technology. PE. Construction safety, applied structures, value engineering.

Wilson C. Barnes, dean, School of Architecture, Engineering Technology and Construction. PhD, University of Central England; MArch, Harvard University; MS, University of Pennsylvania; BS, United States Military Academy. Registered architect. AIA, MCARB, AIC, MCIOB. Construction graphics.

Zuhair El Itr, associate professor. PhD, MSCE, Georgia Institute of Technology; BSEE, American University of Beirut. PE. Construction estimating, strategic bidding.

Shariar Makarechi, assistant professor. PhD, Georgia Institute of Technology; MS, George Washington University; BS, Aryamehr University of Technology, Tehran. PE, California; Washington, D.C.; Georgia; Maryland; Virginia; West Virginia.

Pavan Meadati, assistant professor. PhD, University of Nebraska–Lincoln; MS, Indian Institute of Technology, Madras; BS, Osmania University, Hyderabad, India.

John Mench, lecturer. PhD, California Coast University; MBA, Ohio University; BSEE, University of South Carolina. Mechanical, electrical, and plumbing materials and methods; construction estimating; construction finance and feasibility; construction process simulation; capstone project.

David R. Pierce, professor. MBA, University of West Florida; BS, Virginia Polytechnic State University. Commercial construction materials and methods, project management, construction scheduling and cost control.

Khalid M. Siddiqi, professor and chairman, Construction Management Department. PhD, Georgia Institute of Technology; MS, Asian Institute of Technology, Thailand; BS, University of Engineering and Technology, Lahore, Pakistan. PE. Building failures and defective work, research methodology.

Temple University

Forrest E. Huffman, Program Director
Finance and Real Estate
Fox School of Business
1810 N. 13th Street
Philadelphia, PA 19122
215-204-6675; fax 215-204-1697
fhuffman@etemple.edu
www.sbm.temple.edu/dept/finance/undergraduate/undergrad-real.html

Degree	Year Program Began	Credit Hours	Years to Complete	Full-Time Students (2006–2007)	Part-Time Students (2006–2007)	Degrees Conferred (2007)
BBA, major in real estate	1975	123	4	249	47	20

Degree	Application Deadline	Minimum High School GPA	Specialized Degree Accreditation	In-State Undergraduate Tuition	Out-of-State Undergraduate Tuition
BBA, major in real estate	May 1	2.0	Middle States AACSB	$10,996/year	$19,120/year

Degree Specialization

BBA with a major in real estate.

Program Description

The real estate major at Temple University consists of five courses in the real estate area combined with the necessary requirements for the completion of a BBA. The real estate curriculum focuses on real estate brokerage and real estate investment and finance. All real estate majors must take a major capstone course that is writing intensive, team oriented, case-study oriented, and includes a project analysis component.

Core Curriculum

The Temple University core curriculum requirements are currently under revision. For details, see www.temple.edu.

Financial Aid

E. Fred Kemner Award for Real Estate Students, $500 to $1000 annually.

Lecture Series

Rho Epsilon, a student club, offers a speakers' series each semester. The real estate program frequently hosts speakers and guests from the local real estate community.

International Programs

Temple University has exchange programs and international campuses in Rome and Tokyo. Real estate students can also take summer courses in Rome.

Internship Placement Assistance

The real estate program works in concert with the Fox School of Business Center for Student Professional Development to place students in part-time and full-time positions. Information on careers in real estate is available from the real estate program. See Professor Huffman, program director, for information and guidance.

Job Placement Assistance

The real estate program works in concert with the Fox School of Business Center for Student Professional Development to develop full- and part-time job opportunities in the Philadelphia region for students and alumni.

Clubs/Alumni Associations

Temple has an active chapter of Rho Epsilon, the student professional organization for real estate students. Temple University also hosts a chapter of the Alpha Sigma Gamma Society, the International Real Estate Honorary Society for students.

Other

Temple University, located just north of Center City Philadelphia, is one of the largest universities in the United States. The real estate faculty is known for high-quality academic research and for its involvement in the real estate and legal community.

In addition to the Main Campus, on North Broad Street, Temple University has the Center City campus, and the suburban Ambler Campus, in Montgomery County. The real estate program at Temple reflects the diversity of the Temple University student body, the educational opportunities available at a large university, and the excitement available in a dynamic urban environment.

Faculty

Paul K. Asabere, professor, Department of Finance and Real Estate. PhD, University of Illinois. Real estate investment and finance.

Joseph Beller, adjunct professor, Department of Legal Studies. LLB, University of Pennsylvania Law School. Real estate fundamentals.

Robert Franklin, adjunct professor, Department of Legal Studies. JD, Temple University School of Law. Real estate fundamentals.

Forrest E. Huffman, program director and professor, Department of Finance and Real Estate. PhD, University of South Carolina. Real estate investment and finance.

James Lammendola, adjunct professor, Department of Legal Studies. JD, University of Tulsa College of Law. Real estate fundamentals, real estate practice.

Vanessa Lawrence, assistant professor, Department of Legal Studies. JD, University of Pennsylvania Law School. Real estate fundamentals.

Joseph London, adjunct professor, Department of Legal Studies. JD, Temple University School of Law. Real estate practice.

E. Stoney Read, adjunct professor, Department of Legal Studies. LLM, University of London, School of Economics. Real estate fundamentals, real estate practice.

Barbara Schneller, adjunct professor, Department of Legal Studies. JD, Villanova University School of Law. Real estate fundamentals.

Michael A. Valenza, associate professor, Department of Legal Studies. JD, Temple University School of Law. Real estate fundamentals, real estate practice.

Texas A&M University

Cydney Donnell, Director
Finance Department
Mays Business School
4218 TAMU
College Station, TX 77843-4218
979-845-4858; fax 979-845-3884
adegelman@mays.tamu.edu
http://mays.tamu.edu/grad/masters.realestate/index.htm

Degree	Year Program Began	Credit Hours	Years to Complete	Thesis or Final Product	Full-Time Students (2006–2007)	Degrees Conferred (2006)
MSRE	1976	37	1.5	Oral examination	72	44

Degree	Application Deadline	Minimum Undergraduate GPA	Minimum GRE or GMAT Score	Departmental Requirements
MSRE	March 1; October 1	3.25	Competitive	Essays, 3 letters of reference, resume, application, interview

Number of Faculty/FTE	Specialized Degree Accreditation	In-State Graduate Tuition	Out-of-State Graduate Tuition	In-State Undergraduate Tuition	Out-of-State Undergraduate Tuition
23/5	AACSB	$170.50/credit	$428.50/credit	$122.50/credit	$380.50/credit

Degree Specializations

MSRE.
Other options at Texas A&M University:
MBA with a concentration in real estate (Mays Business School)
Master of Land Development (College of Architecture)
Undergraduate finance degree with real estate emphasis (Mays Business School).

Program Description

The MSRE program is a professional rather than a research-focused program, and is designed to meet the demand for real estate specialists. Our program integrates the studies of real estate and business through a broad curriculum, including accounting, finance, development, law, and a professional internship. The program was started over 30 years ago, and originally had a strong emphasis on valuation. In keeping with the evolutionary nature of the industry, the curriculum today is more focused on finance and capital markets. Unlike most MBA programs, the MSRE program does not require work experience.

The Mays Business School also offers an MBA with a concentration in real estate. Information on our MBA degree is available at mba.tamu.edu. For some degree candidates, this course of study may be recommended.

Core Curriculum

Students who have completed the prerequisite courses (or their equivalent) will normally complete the following core courses: AGEC 603, Land Economics; FINC 670, Real Property Analysis; FINC 672, Real Property Finance; FINC 673, Real Property Valuation I; FINC 674, Real Property Valuation II; FINC 675, Financing Real Estate Investments; FINC 676, Commercial Real Estate Law; FINC 677, Real Estate Development Analysis; FINC 684, Professional Internship; FINC 685, Directed Studies; GEOG 662, Real Property Geographic Information Systems Applications. In addition to core courses, students will normally complete two elective courses in land development, finance, or construction science.

Financial Aid

Generally, one teaching assistantship and four merit-based endowed scholarships are available. There are also opportunities for industry and collegewide scholarships. See https://financialaid.tamu.edu.

Lecture Series

The Real Estate Program office organizes a weekly lecture series. Common topics include current issues affecting mortgage lending, the investment climate for real estate, and career issues. Represented companies include Integra, Exxon Mobile, Alvarez & Marsal, Marcus & Millchap, Capmark, Principal, Ernst & Young, Grant Thornton, ProLogis, USAA, Trammell Crow, and CB Richard Ellis.

Program Advisory Group

Mission: Mentoring students, outreach.
Requirements: Financial, time.
Major activities: Real Estate Career Day, sponsoring luncheon, counseling director.

Internship Placement Assistance

Internships are required as coursework. Students obtain internships through the alumni network and their own initiative. Graduate Business Career Services assists with interviews and resumes, and provides job postings and employer recruitment services. See http://gbcs.tamu.edu/DotNetNuke/.

Job Placement Assistance

See "Internship Placement Assistance." Contact Cindy Billington at 979-458-3048 or c-billington@tamu.edu.

Clubs/Alumni Associations

Alumni club: STAMREP (Society of Texas A&M Real Estate Professionals); aggierealestatenetwork.com, stramrep@gmail.com. Student clubs: REA (Real Estate Association); GREW (Graduate Real Estate Women).

Faculty

Cydney Donnell, executive professor and director of the Real Estate Program. MBA, Southern Methodist University; BBA, Texas A&M University. Real estate in capital markets.

O.E. Elmore, senior lecturer. JD, BA, University of Texas at Austin. Commercial real estate law.

Anthony Filippi, assistant professor. PhD, University of South Carolina. Real property geographic information systems applications.

Charles E. Gilliland, research economist, Real Estate Center. PhD, Texas A&M University; MS, resource economics; BS, Regis College. Real property analysis.

Richard L. Haney, Jr., professor in real estate and finance. DBA, MBA, Indiana University; BS, University of Colorado. Real property finance, real estate development analysis.

Thomas O. Jackson, clinical associate professor, Department of Finance. PhD, Texas A&M University; MRP, University of North Carolina at Chapel Hill; MA, Ohio State University; BA, University of South Florida. Real estate valuation.

David Newburn, assistant professor, Department of Agricultural Economics. PhD, University of California at Berkeley; BS, University of Maryland. Land economics.

Affiliated Faculty

Amanda Adkisson, clinical associate professor. PhD, finance; MS, finance; MAgri, animal science; BS, entomology, Texas A&M University. Investment management.

Leonard Bierman, professor. MA, University of California; JD, University of Pennsylvania; BS, Cornell University. Business negotiations.

Jose Fernandez-Solis, assistant professor. PhD, BArch, Georgia Institute of Technology; M, theology, St. Vincent de Paul Seminary. Construction science.

Donald R. Fraser, Hugh Roy Cullen Chairholder in Business. PhD, BA, University of Arizona; MS, University of Rhode Island. Analysis of money and capital markets.

John C. Groth, professor, Department of Finance. PhD, MSLA, BS, Purdue University. Financial management.

Scott Lee, associate professor, Department of Finance. PhD, University of Oregon; BS, University of Utah. Financial management.

Jesse Saginor, assistant professor, College of Architecture. PhD, Cleveland State University; MPA, Ohio State University; BA, Michigan State University. Market analysis for development.

Robert Segner, professor, College of Architecture. MA, BS, Texas A&M University. Construction science.

M. Atef Sharkawy, professor; coordinator, Master of Science of Land Development. PhD, University of Wisconsin; MS, University of Oregon; BS, Cairo University. Design and development economy.

Elizabeth Umphress, assistant professor of management and Mays Research Fellow. PhD, Tulane University; BA, University of Texas at Austin. Business negotiations.

Texas A&M University

Dr. Atef Sharkawy, Professor and Program Director
Landscape Architecture and Urban Planning
College of Architecture
Langford Architecture Center
3137 TAMU
College Station, TX 77843-3137
979-458-4306; fax 979-862-1784
Contact: Thena Morris
t-morris@tamu.edu
http://archone.tamu.edu/laup/Programs/msld_index.html

Degree	Year Program Began	Credit Hours	Years to Complete	Full-Time Students (2006–2007)	Part-Time Students (2006–2007)	Degrees Conferred (2007)
MSLD	1983	45	1.5	30	1	13
MSLD Plus	1995	36	1	7		4

Degree	Application Deadline	Minimum Undergraduate GPA	Minimum GRE or GMAT Score	Departmental Requirements
MSLD	March 1	About 3.0	About 1100 (verbal and quantitative)	Resume, personal statement, 3 letters of reference
MSLD Plus	March 1	About 3.0	1100 (verbal and quantitative)	Resume, personal statement, 3 letters of reference

Number of Faculty/FTE	In-State Graduate Tuition	Out-of-State Graduate Tuition
29/4 (plus 5 adjunct)	$206.00/credit	$470.00/credit

Degree Specialization

Centered exclusively on land and real estate development, the MSLD is an entrepreneurship-oriented program of study that combines MBA-type courses with physical planning, design, and construction in an international context. It deals with both the development of physical form and the structure of financial ventures in a manner that aligns site ecology and market economy with entrepreneurial interests and regulatory guidelines.

MSLD Plus plans provide two-degree options that cross disciplinary lines and/or national borders. An interdisciplinary, two-degree option enables a graduate student to pursue two complementary degrees, or a master's degree and a certificate. Fewer credit hours are required than for two degrees taken separately, and the content is more integrated.

Program Description

The MSLD is a 45-credit program of individually tailored curricula including 12 credits of "leveling" and "emphasis" courses, 24 credits of "core" courses, and 9 credits of "cap" courses. A wide variety of leveling and emphasis courses are available at Texas A&M in finance, construction management, planning, and other topics, depending on each student's education, experience, interests, and future plans. Cap courses link together skill sets in the MSLD curriculum through developer-sponsored projects. Such courses also focus on the development of teamworking skills, and are anchored by lectures and field trips with program alumni and industry leaders.

Core Curriculum

Core and cap courses include development process, residential development, income-property development, site analysis and construction for development, development law, sustainable development, financial analysis, due diligence for development, and development design and feasibility. All courses are offered by the program except financial analysis, which is offered by the Department of Finance.

Financial Aid

The university's financial aid office arranges student loans. Candidates for the MSLD and MSLD Plus are eligible for several competitive graduate assistantships and fellowships, with annual awards of up to $12,000, plus tuition. Competitive $1,000 scholarships are also available. Assistantships and scholarships enable students to pay in-state tuition rates. A tuition waiver is worth over $9,000 in tuition savings. Texas A&M also offers substantial scholarships to students with exceptional academic scores. Contact the financial aid office at 979-845-3236.

Lecture Series

The College of Architecture sponsors the Built Environment lecture series. The Department of Landscape Architecture and Urban Planning has a lecture series, and the MSLD program regularly includes alumni and development-industry professionals in development classes.

International Programs

The College of Architecture offers study abroad programs in China, Germany, Italy, and the UK. The MSLD program offers a transnational, two-degree program in project administration and land and real estate development with Universidad Francisco Maroquin, in Guatemala, Central America's leading business school.

Program Advisory Group

The Development Industry Advisory Council (DIAC) meets twice a year to coordinate the work of the council's geographically based committees and members. The Executive Committee meets quarterly to provide guidance on curriculum, to support mentoring and networking opportunities for students, and to fund scholarships.

Internship Placement Assistance

Internships are not required, but are facilitated by the program director and through the DIAC. Contact Dr. Atef Sharkawy at 979-575-5834 or sharkawy@tamu.edu.

Job Placement Assistance

The university has a career center. At least three job markets are held annually for the "Built Environment" industries within the College of Architecture. Job placement assistance is also offered by the program director and the DIAC.

Clubs/Alumni Associations

The program's student association, REDA, focuses on the development of leadership, communication, and interpersonal skills, and on assisting students to build industry networks. Student leaders become industry leaders and join the DIAC. DIAC members participate in program management, fund scholarships, and provide guidance to students through DIAC committees, such as the MSLD Mentors and the Collaborative Teaching committees.

Faculty

S. Kent Anderson. PhD, Texas A&M University; MA, BA, Sam Houston State University. Residential development, due diligence for development.

Samuel D. Brody. PhD, University of North Carolina; MS, University of Michigan; BA, Bowdoin College. Environmental planning and policy, resource policy and behavior, environmental studies, sustainable development.

Cecilia Giusti. PhD, University of Texas; MA, Institute of Social Studies, The Hague; BA, Catholic University of Peru. International development, economic development, development trends.

Jesse Saginor. PhD, Cleveland State University; MPA, School of Public Policy and Management, Ohio State University; BA, Michigan State University. Economic development, market analysis, public/private finance.

M. Atef Sharkawy, professor of land and real estate development. PhD, University of Wisconsin; MArch, University of Oregon; BSArch, Cairo University. Development design and feasibility, executive real estate development training.

Affiliated Faculty

O.E. Elmore, lecturer in finance. JD, BA, University of Texas at Austin. Commercial real estate law.

Charles E. Gilliland, research economist, Real Estate Center. PhD, MAgr, Texas A&M University; BS, Regis College. Land economics, rural appraisal, property taxation.

Richard L. Haney, Jr., professor, real estate and finance. DBA, MBA, Indiana University; BS, University of Colorado. Real estate development, real estate finance, real estate valuation, real estate market analysis.

Adjunct Faculty

Peter Barnhart. MSLD, Texas A&M University. Vice president for development, Caldwell Watson, Houston, Texas.

Jonathan Brinsden. MSLD, Texas A&M University. Executive vice president, Midway Companies, Houston, Texas.

Tim Crawford. MSLD, Texas A&M University. President, Cityline Development, Charlotte, North Carolina.

Tim Early. MSLD, Texas A&M University. Vice president for acquisitions, Hovanian Homes, Houston, Texas.

Joe Rodriguez. MSLD, Texas A&M University. President, Brass Real Estate Fund, San Antonio, Texas.

University of Texas at Austin

Jay Hartzell, Associate Professor
Director, Real Estate Finance and Investment
Red McCombs School of Business
Department of Finance, CBA 6.222
1 University Station B6600
Austin, TX 78712
512-471-6779; fax 512-471-5073
jay.hartzell@mccombs.utexas.edu
http://cref.bus.mccombs.utexas.edu

Degree	Years in Operation	Credit Hours	Years to Complete	Full-Time Students (2006–2007)	Degrees Conferred (2007)
BBA	27	120	4	4,317	1,103
MBA	27	60	2	520	258
PhD	27		4–5	23	4

Number of Faculty/FTE	Specialized Degree Accreditation	In-State Graduate Tuition	Out-of-State Graduate Tuition	In-State Undergraduate Tuition	Out-of-State Undergraduate Tuition
10/7	AACSB	$7,441/semester	$15,843/semester	$4,454/semester	$7,584/semester

Degree Specializations

BBA with a major in finance/real estate.
MBA with a concentration in finance/real estate.
PhD with a concentration in finance/real estate.

Program Description

The goal of the real estate program is to prepare undergraduate and MBA students for advanced careers in real estate and related fields. The Real Estate Finance and Investment Center benefits from exceptional faculty with diverse backgrounds in real estate and finance. Students receive training in urban land markets, real estate investment and finance, real estate equity and debt markets, and urban development. The PhD program prepares students of high intellectual capacity for university teaching and research positions in the real estate disciplines. The doctoral program is oriented toward research and requires students to demonstrate general proficiency and distinctive achievement in the fields of real estate, finance, and economics, as well as an ability to conduct independent investigation.

Today's real estate companies have a growing need for well-trained managers in areas such as financial analysis, project evaluation, equity, and debt securitization. The center's goal is to meet that need at both the graduate and undergraduate levels.

Core Curriculum

BBA: real estate and urban development, finance, investment.

MBA: real estate and investment decisions, finance, equity and debt markets, regional and urban analysis.

PhD: microeconomics, macroeconomics, statistics, urban economics, real estate research, asset pricing, corporate finance.

Financial Aid

A wide variety of undergraduate scholarships are available. At the graduate level, a fellowship program and teaching/research assistantships are available. Contact Laura Starks, chairman, Department of Finance.

Lecture Series

The graduate and undergraduate real estate societies invite a large number of real estate professionals to the campus each semester. The Department of Finance also sponsors an active research seminar series.

Job Placement Assistance

The Ford Career Center is one of the largest placement centers in the nation. Real estate professionals who serve on the program's council also assist in career placement.

Faculty

Andres Almazan, associate professor. PhD, finance, Massachusetts Institute of Technology. Real estate economics and finance.

George W. Gau, dean; second professorship; Watson Centennial professor. PhD, finance, University of Illinois at Urbana-Champaign. Real estate finance and investment.

Greg Hallman, lecturer. PhD, finance, University of Texas at Austin. Real estate debt and equity markets.

Jay Hartzell, associate professor. PhD, finance, University of Texas at Austin. Real estate finance and investment.

Steve LeBlanc, lecturer. BBA, finance, University of Texas at Austin. Real estate and finance.

Paula C. Murray, professor. JD, University of Texas at Austin. Real estate law.

Jeremy Smitheal, lecturer. MBA, finance, University of Texas at Austin. Real estate finance.

Lenore M. Sullivan, lecturer. MBA, Harvard University. Real estate investments, development, equity markets.

Sheridan Titman, McAllister Centennial Chair. PhD, economics, Carnegie Mellon University. Real estate economics and finance.

Stathis Tompaidis, associate professor. PhD, finance, University of Texas at Austin. Real estate debt markets.

University of Texas at San Antonio

Thomas A. Thomson, Professor of Finance and Real Estate
Director, Real Estate Finance and Development Program
University of Texas at San Antonio
One UTSA Circle
San Antonio, TX 78249-0637
210-458-5306; fax 210-458-6320
thomas.thomson@utsa.edu
http://refd.utsa.edu

Degree	Years in Operation	Credit Hours	Years to Complete	Full-Time Students (2007–2008)	Degrees Conferred (2007)
BBA in real estate finance and development	25	120	4	165	25
MBA with a concentration in real estate finance	0	36	1–2	1	0
MS in finance with a concentration in real estate finance	0	33	1–2	2	0

Degree	Number of Faculty	Specialized Degree Accreditation	In-State Graduate Tuition	Out-of-State Graduate Tuition	In-State Undergraduate Tuition	Out-of-State Undergraduate Tuition
BBA	6	AACSB			$223/credit	$501/credit
MBA	2	AACSB	$273/credit	$829/credit		
MS	2	AACSB	$273/credit	$829/credit		

Note: Tuition per semester credit hour, which includes student fees, is based on full-time enrollment for spring 2008.

Degree Specializations

BBA in real estate finance and development; may be pursued with minors, including a minor in building and development (construction).

MBA with a concentration in real estate finance.

MS in finance with a concentration in real estate finance.

Program Description

The Real Estate Finance and Development Program meets the needs of those interested in managing businesses associated with real estate; it covers planning, investing, financing, development, and construction of buildings. By synthesizing training in the areas of business management and architectural design, planning, and construction, the program provides students with an educational background that spans initiation to final management of the completed project. Students gain the full range of knowledge and skills for real estate–related careers, including the ability to determine project costs; develop design and production schedules; and manage various aspects of construction.

Core Curriculum

In addition to the core curriculum requirements of the university and the College of Business, candidates for the BBA in real estate finance and development must complete 18 credit hours of Real Estate Principles, Mortgage Banking and Real Estate Finance, Real Estate Investment, Real Estate Development, and Real Estate Law. For a minor in building and development, students must also complete five courses in architecture (Building Materials, Construction Estimating I and II, Construction Management I and II), plus an internship. Students may also take other real estate courses or related courses, or may undertake a minor—such as finance or marketing—in the College of Business.

Financial Aid

The University of Texas at San Antonio (UTSA) has work-study programs available for students who meet the criteria. In addition, several scholarships are available specifically for students in real estate programs, and others are available through the College of Business. See http://refd.utsa.edu/scholarships.htm.

Lecture Series

UTSA and the College of Business offer students the Frost Bank Distinguished Lecture Series four times a year. Prominent local business and community leaders give presentations on career advancement, leadership skills, and entrepreneurship opportunities.

International Programs

UTSA has exchange programs with universities in Canada, Mexico, Italy, and Japan.

Program Advisory Group

Four faculty members constitute the formal advisory group for the Real Estate Finance and Development Program. There is also an advisory board, made up of 25 prominent business leaders, which provides advice on program and curriculum issues and supports the program in the community. See http://refd.utsa.edu/advisoryboard2007.htm).

Internship Placement Assistance

An internship is required for the building and development minor and is optional for all other students. Our office maintains a list of companies that are interested in having an intern or that have had interns in the past. The Center for Student Professional Development also assists with internships; see http://business.utsa.edu/cspd/.

Job Placement Assistance

The Center for Student Professional Development and UTSA Career Services have Web sites; all UTSA students and alumni are permitted to view all jobs listed there. The center offers an employer module, through which prospective employers can register with UTSA to list job opportunities and to scan resumes. UTSA conducts fall and spring on-campus interviews with companies seeking job applicants. Finally, the program offers an annual Career Expo, where students can meet potential employers and learn about job opportunities. See http://business.utsa.edu/cspd/ and http://refd.utsa.edu/expo2008.htm.

Clubs/Alumni Associations

The student organization Future Leaders in Real Estate, Development, and Construction is associated with the Real Estate Finance and Development Program. Officers are elected each semester, and the group's activities include field trips and guest speakers from the local real estate and construction community.

Faculty

Marc Giaccardo, associate professor of architecture. AIA. Construction science.

Ronald C. Rutherford, professor of finance and real estate; Elmo J. Burke, Jr., Chair in Building Development. PhD, MBA, University of Georgia; MS, BA, Valdosta State College. Real estate and finance.

Richard R. Tangum, professor of architecture. DED, Texas A&M; MArch, Virginia Polytechnic Institute; BArch, Texas Tech University. Project development, housing design and development.

Raymond H.C. Teske, lecturer I. JD, South Texas College of Law; BA, Baylor University. Real estate, real estate law.

Thomas A. Thomson, professor of finance and real estate; director of the Real Estate Finance and Development Program. PhD, University of Michigan; PhD, University of California at Berkeley; MS, Virginia Polytechnic Institute and State University; BSF, University of British Columbia. Real estate finance.

Affiliated Faculty

Larry Bruner, lecturer II. JD, St. Mary's University School of Law; BBA, University of Texas at San Antonio. Real estate law.

Andrew Perez III, associate professor of architecture. BArch, University of Texas at Austin. Construction estimating.

Bob Reynolds, lecturer I. MBA, Golden Gate University; BA, Louisiana State University. Real estate marketing.

Virginia Commonwealth University

Robert W. Taylor, Director
The Virginia Real Estate Center
Real Estate Program
Department of Finance, Insurance, and Real Estate
Snead Hall
301 W. Main Street
P.O. Box 844000
Richmond, VA 23284-4000
804-828-3169
rwtaylor@vcu.edu
www.realestate.bus.vcu.edu

Degree	Year Program Began	Credit Hours	Years to Complete	Thesis or Final Product	Full-Time Students (2006–2007)	Part-Time Students (2006–2007)	Degrees Conferred (2007)
BS in real estate	1973	120	4		91	10	41
MBA, real estate concentration	1973	60	2		70	164	2
MSB, real estate valuation concentration	1973	54	2	Yes	2	4	1
Graduate certificate	2000	18	1		0	7	3

Degree	Application Deadline	Minimum Undergraduate GPA	Minimum GRE or GMAT Score	Departmental Requirements
BS in real estate	Fall: February 1 Spring: December			Candidates are reviewed based on academic performance in an accredited high school and either SAT I or ACT scores; college preparatory curriculum is highly preferred, and a minimum of 20 units are required for admission to all programs on the academic campus; see www.vcu.edu/ugrad/.
MBA, real estate concentration	Fall: April 1 Spring: November 1 Summer: March 1	2.7	550	A written personal statement of intent, 3 letters of reference; see www.vcu.edu/vcu/pro/info_grad.html.
MSB, real estate valuation	Fall: April 1 Spring: November 1 Summer: March 1	2.7	550	A written personal statement of intent, 3 letters reference; see www.vcu.edu/vcu/pro/info_grad.html.
Graduate certificate	Fall: July 15 Spring: November 15 Summer: March 15	2.7		A wirtten personal statement of intent to obtain the certificate; 3 letters of reference; minimum of 5 years experience preferred; see www.vcu.edu/vcu/pro/info_grad.html.

Number of Faculty	Specialized Degree Accreditation	In-State Graduate Tuition	Out-of-State Graduate Tuition	In-State Undergraduate Tuition	Out-of-State Undergraduate Tuition
Real estate program: 3 Finance, Insurance, and Real Estate Department: 13 School of Business: 95	AACSB	$8,341/year	$17,582/year	$5,819/year	$17,616/year

Degree Specializations

BS with a major in real estate.
MBA with a concentration in real estate.
MSB with a concentration in real estate valuation.
Graduate certificate in real estate.

Program Description

The major focus of the MBA with a real estate concentration is on finance, development, and research. Internships are encouraged, and several scholarships are available. Students who have taken business policy earlier may participate in a research project with a faculty member. The program has an endowed chair of real estate, as well as the Virginia Real Estate Center, which offers research training for graduate students.

The graduate valuation program emphasizes real estate valuation while providing a comprehensive education in related disciplines to enhance graduates' analytical skills and ability to communicate with other professionals. The valuation concentration is approved by the Appraisal Institute; graduates satisfy most of the educational requirements for the MAI designation.

Core Curriculum

MBA: managerial accounting, cases in financial management, organizational behavior, operations research, management information systems, marketing management, managerial economics. Specialized courses for a concentration in real estate include real estate development, real estate investment analysis, real property investment law, commercial mortgage lending, and geographic information systems (GIS).

MSB: financial markets, statistical analysis, financial management, and market research. Specialized courses include real estate development, real estate investment analysis, real property investment law, commercial mortgage lending, and GIS.

Financial Aid

Numerous annual and endowed scholarships are available, plus two graduate research assistantships and an undergraduate assistantship. Contact Robert W. Taylor at 804-828-3169 or rwtaylor@vcu.edu.

International Programs

Each year, faculty members lead short-term summer study with intensive instruction in an international context.

Program Advisory Group

The Real Estate Circle of Excellence, an advisory board, is made up of executives of leading development, mortgage lending, and brokerage firms and real estate investment trusts. The board strengthens the quality and relevance of educational efforts and brings practical, real-world experience to the Real Estate Program.

Internship Placement Assistance

Partnerships with local and regional employers provide internships at leading brokerage firms, development companies, financial institutions, governmental agencies, etc. Contact Robert W. Taylor at 804-828-3169 or rwtaylor@vcu.edu.

Job Placement Assistance

Two lists are maintained: (1) available full-time and part-time positions and internships and (2) students seeking jobs. For several years after graduation, graduates receive assistance in locating positions. Contact Robert W. Taylor at 804-828-3169 or rwtaylor@vcu.edu; or Darlene Ward at 804- 827-0410 or dward@vcu.edu.

Clubs/Alumni Associations

A chapter of Rho Epsilon, the national professional real estate fraternity, is an integral part of the Real Estate Program. Membership is available to students with a major interest in real estate. Members have an opportunity to participate in fraternity-sponsored lectures, career programs, and field trips. The fraternity presents annual awards for outstanding residential and commercial developments in the Richmond area. Rho Epsilon has been selected twice as the nation's most outstanding chapter.

Each year, faculty nominate students who have achieved distinguished academic performance for membership in Alpha Sigma Gamma, the international real estate honor society.

The Association of Real Estate Alumni advances real estate education, stimulates continuing interest and professional relationships between the Real Estate Program and its alumni, and supports and promotes the program by recruiting students; providing mentors, internships, and scholarships; and assisting in job placement.

Faculty

James H. Boykin, professor emeritus. PhD, American University; MCom, University of Richmond; BS, Virginia Polytechnic Institute. MAI.

David H. Downs, professor; Alfred L. Blake Chair; director, Kornblau Institute. PhD, University of North Carolina at Chapel Hill; MBA, George Washington University; BS, James Madison University.

Richard A. Phillips, associate professor. PhD, University of North Carolina at Chapel Hill; BA, Old Dominion University.

Brent C. Smith, assistant professor. PhD, Indiana University; MBA, University of Notre Dame; BA, Indiana University–Purdue University at Indianapolis.

Robert W. Taylor, director, Virginia Real Estate Center. MBA, BA, Virginia Commonwealth University. MAI, SRA.

Adjunct Faculty

Steven B. Brincefield. MS, Virginia Commonwealth University; BS, Virginia Polytechnic Institute. Senior vice president, Thalhimer Commercial Real Estate. CPM.

Andrew M. Condlin. JD, School of Law, College of William and Mary; BA, Potsdam College. Partner, Williams Mullen.

Holly Law Eve, real property manager, Virginia Department of Game and Inland Fisheries. MS, Virginia Commonwealth University; BS, Virginia Polytechnic Institute. CCIM.

Donna Procise. BS, Virginia Commonwealth University. Director of sales and training, Long and Foster Realtors. ABR, ABRM, GRI.

University of Washington

James R. DeLisle, Runstad Professor of Real Estate
Director, Graduate Real Estate Studies
Department of Urban Design and Planning
College of Architecture and Urban Planning
440 3949 15th Avenue, N.E.
Seattle, WA 98195
206-616-2090; fax 206-770-7256
jdelisle@u.washington.edu
www.reuw.washington.edu

Degree	Year Program Began	Credit Hours	Years to Complete	Thesis or Final Product	Full-Time Students (2006–2007)	Part-Time Students (2006–2007)	Degrees Conferred (2007)
MSRE	2009	72	2	No	20 new in 2009		
Master's degree with real estate concentration	2002	28	1+	Required if master of urban planning	20	2	8
MBA, real estate track	2003	15	1	Optional	10	2	In own master's
Non-MBA (MArch MPA), real estate track	2003	16	1	Optional	8	2	In own master's

Degree	Application Deadline	Minimum Undergraduate GPA	Minimum GRE or GMAT Score	Departmental Requirements
MSRE	February	Competitive	Competitive	Interest in real estate career, interdisciplinary background; experience a plus
Master's degree with real estate concentration	February	Competitive	Competitive	Depends on department from which degree is obtained
MBA, real estate track	See college	Competitive	Competitive	Depends on department from which degree is obtained
Non-MBA, real estate track	See college	Depends on the choice of master's degree	Depends on the choice of master's degree	Depends on department from which degree is obtained

Number of Faculty	In-State Graduate Tuition	Out-of-State Graduate Tuition	In-State Undergraduate Tuition	Out-of-State Undergraduate Tuition
3.5	$289/credit	$615/credit	$142/credit	$492/credit

Degree Specializations

Master of science in real estate (MSRE).

Master of urban planning (MUP) with a real estate concentration or real estate track.

Master of Business Administration (MBA) with a real estate concentration or real estate track.

Master of Architecture (MArch) with a real estate concentration or real estate track.

Master of Public Administration (MPA) with a real estate concentration or real estate track.

Any other master's or undergraduate degree with a real estate concentration or real estate track.

Program Description

A series of interdisciplinary degree programs offered by the Department of Urban Planning and Design in the College of Architecture and Urban Planning.

Core Curriculum

The curriculum depends on the degree chosen.

Master of Science in Real Estate

The MSRE is a two-year interdisciplinary program. Students complete six core real estate courses, six elective real estate courses, and six non-real-estate electives from a list of approved courses from across campus. Students are encouraged to pursue internships.

Concentration

Four core courses, including real estate process, real estate finance, and real estate appraisal and feasibility analysis, plus two of the following: fundamentals of real estate, real estate investments, market analysis, real estate development, and a real estate studio. One additional outside elective is also required.

MBA, Real Estate Track

Fundamentals of real estate bridge elective and three of the following: real estate finance, real estate investments, market analysis, real estate development, real estate studio, and real estate appraisal and feasibility analysis.

Non-MBA, Real Estate Track

Real estate process and real estate finance plus two of the following: real estate investments, market analysis, real estate development, real estate studio, and real estate appraisal and feasibility analysis.

Financial Aid

Endowed scholarships for graduate students are available through the real estate program. For resident graduate students, the following would be available: Graduate Tuition Exemption, Graduate University Grant, Academic Scholarship, federal Perkins Loan, Primary Care/Health Professionals/Nursing Loan, federal Direct Stafford/Ford Loan, and federal and state work-study. For nonresident graduate students, the following would be available: federal Perkins loan, Primary Care/Health Professionals/Nursing Loan, federal Direct Stafford/Ford Loan, federal and state work-study.

For resident undergraduates, the following would be available: federal Pell Grant, Federal Supplemental Grant, State Need Grant, Undergraduate Tuition Exemption, Undergraduate University Grant, University Opportunity Grant, Academic Scholarship, federal Perkins Student Loan, Health Professionals/Nursing Loan, federal Direct Stafford/Ford Loan, federal Direct PLUS Loan, federal and state work-study. For nonresident undergraduates, the following are available: federal Pell Grant, federal Supplemental Grant, federal Perkins Student Loan, Health Professionals/Nursing Loan, federal Direct Stafford/Ford Loan, federal Direct PLUS Loan, federal and state work-study.

A limited number of teaching assistantships and research assistantships will be offered. Students may also work in the Runstad Center for Real Estate Studies. Contact the Office of Financial Aid at www.washington.edu/students/osfa/.

Lecture Series

The Real Estate Forum is a speakers' series, offered in the fall quarter, that features industry leaders. The Real Estate Club also hosts events and discussions with industry professionals such as developers, presidents of development companies, and their key staff; typically, one event is held each quarter. Lectures often include a tour and a discussion of past or upcoming real estate development projects.

Internship Placement Assistance

Program assistance (listings on Web site); graduate school assistance. Generally, however, an internship is not required for gradu-

ation unless the selected master's degree specifically requires it. Internships are also available in the Runstad Center for Real Estate Studies. For more information, contact James DeLisle at jdelisle@u.washington.edu.

Job Placement Assistance

Program assistance (listings on Web site); graduate school assistance; Web site listings; professional networking. See www.reuw.washington.edu.

Clubs/Alumni Associations

For information on the Real Estate Club, see www.reuw.washington.edu.

Other

As of summer 2008, the program is actively recruiting two additional tenure-track faculty. The program is also supported by affiliate and adjunct faculty as warranted.

Faculty

James R. DeLisle, associate professor of urban design and planning; director, Runstad Center for Real Estate Studies. PhD, real estate and urban land economics; MS, market research; BBA, real estate, University of Wisconsin–Madison. Interdisciplinary and behavioral real estate.

George Rolfe, associate professor of urban design and planning, construction management. MArch, MCP, University of Pennsylvania; BArch, Iowa State University. Real estate finance and development.

University of Western Ontario

Jason Gilliland, Director
Urban Development Program
Department of Geography
1151 Richmond Street
London, Ontario N6A 5C2
Canada
519-61-3423; fax 519-61-3750
jgillila@uwo.ca
www.geography.uwo.ca/urban/index

Degree	Year Program Began	Credit Hours	Years to Complete	Full-Time Students (2006–2007)	Degrees Conferred (2006)
BAhon (urban development)	1980	40	4	11	2

Degree	Application Deadline	Minimum GPA
BAhon (urban development)	May 15	80%

Number of Faculty/FTE	In-State Undergraduate Tuition	Out-of-State Undergraduate Tuition
8/5	Can$5,039/year	Can$13,931/year

Degree Specialization

BA honors in urban development.

Program Description

The Urban Development Program started in 1980 and produced its first graduating class in 1983. At the time of its inception, the program was unique in Canada. Its focus is on understanding urban process and factors affecting land and property value and the measurement of development feasibility. The objective of the program is to develop students' understanding of the processes of urban growth and change. Its emphasis is on analytic rigor and, reflecting the relative importance of the enterprises influencing the urban landscape, its orientation is toward the behavior of businesses and individuals rather than that of local government agencies.

The program provides an excellent background for graduates who intend to work in real estate research firms, appraisal firms, financial institutions, or retail organizations; as planning consultants, land developers, or industrial location consultants; or in federal or provincial ministries concerned with property taxation, housing, and urban and regional development. Program graduates are now pursuing careers in all of these areas in Canada, the United States, and Asia, and many are now in the middle and upper echelons of both corporations and governments.

Core Curriculum

- Geography: A Systems Introduction to Spatial Analysis; Urban Development; Quantitative Analysis; Spatial Statistics; Economic Geography; Land Use Planning; Land Use and Development Issues; Advanced Urban Development; Introduction to Geographic Information Systems (GIS); Geographical Research Methods; Field Methods and Practices; Housing.
- Economics: Introduction to Economics, Microeconomics, Urban Economics.
- Business Administration: Accounting and Business Analysis.
- Management and Organizational Studies: Management Accounting, Business Law.
- Political Science: Local Government, Urban Political Analysis, Issues in Urban Governance.
- Sociology: The Evolution of Cities, Life in the Contemporary City, Population and Society.
- History: History of Urbanization, the Canadian Elite and Its Urban Base.
- Anthropology: The Anthropology of Towns and Cities.

Financial Aid

Numerous scholarships are available. Contact Student Financial Services at 519-661-2100 or bursary@uwo.ca.

Lecture Series

The faculty members who teach key courses for the program invite guest speakers for their classes. All the students in the program are invited. These events occur randomly and are not organized as a lecture series.

International Programs

Half-year student exchange with Sheffield Hallum University, Sheffield, England.

Program Advisory Group

There is no an advisory group for the program; however, there is a program adviser who serves all undergraduate geography students, including those in the Urban Development Program. The director of the program advises students on matters of curriculum and career planning.

Job Placement Assistance

The program does not offer job placement assistance on a regular basis; however, the director of the program is available for students who need help. There is a Career Office that serves all social science students.

Clubs/Alumni Associations

The Geography Students' Association is open to all undergraduates. For information, e-mail western-gsa@uwo.ca.

Faculty

Godwin Arku, assistant professor. PhD, McMaster University. Urban development, housing.

William R. Code, professor emeritus. PhD, University of California at Berkeley; BA (Hons.), Queens University. Urban development.

Jason Gilliland, associate professor and director, Urban Development Program. PhD, MArch, MA, McGill University; BA (Hons.), McMaster University. Urban development, urban planning, urban morphogenesis, GIS.

Milford B. Green, professor. PhD, MA, Ohio State University. Economic geography, quantitative analysis.

Jeffrey S.P. Hopkins, associate professor. PhD, McGill University. Cultural geography, urban social geography.

Jacek Malczewski, PhD, professor. Quantitative analysis, GIS.

Diana Mok, assistant professor, BMath, BES, University of Waterloo; MPI, Queen's University; PhD, University of Toronto. Development feasibility modeling, urban development.

James Voogt, associate professor. PhD, MA, University of British Columbia; BA, Queen's University. Urban climatology.

Wichita State University

Stanley D. Longhofer
Director and Clark Chair of Real Estate and Finance
Finance, Real Estate, and Decision Sciences
W. Frank Barton School of Business
1845 Fairmount
Wichita, KS 67260-0077
316-978-7120; fax 316-978-3263
realestate@wichita.edu
http://realestate.wichita.edu

Degree	Year Program Began	Credit Hours	Years to Complete	Full-Time Students (2007–2008)	Degrees Conferred (2007)
BBA	1977	124	4	77	8
MBA	1954	36	2	205	58

Number of Faculty/FTE	Specialized Degree Accreditation	In-State Graduate Tuition	Out-of-State Graduate Tuition	In-State Undergraduate Tuition	Out-of-State Undergraduate Tuition
BBA: 5/2	AACSB			$115.40/credit	$400.30/credit
	AACSB	$207.90	$557.80		

Degree Specialization

Bachelor of business administration (BBA). Four options are available: a major in finance with an emphasis in real estate; a major in marketing with an emphasis in real estate; a major in entrepreneurship with an emphasis in real estate; and a major in economics with an emphasis in real estate.

Program Description

Wichita State University's real estate program is unique in that it allows students to tailor their curricula to meet their particular career goals. This is done by offering a real estate degree through four different departments. All courses heavily emphasize practical applications and provide frequent interaction with area professionals.

Core Curriculum

Principles of real estate, real estate law, real estate finance, real estate appraisal, real estate investment analysis, urban land development, urban economics.

Financial Aid

For information on general university undergraduate scholarships, call 316-978-3430. For information on undergraduate scholarships in real estate, contact Stanley Longhofer at 316-978-7120 or realestate@wichita.edu. For information on graduate assistantships, call 316-978-3095.

Lecture Series

Wichita State University real estate students are offered free admission to all events sponsored by the Kansas chapter of CCIM.

Program Advisory Group

The Center for Real Estate (CRE) Advisory Board meets approximately once a year. Members include developers, commercial and residential brokers, financiers, appraisers, title-company executives, and other real estate professionals.

Internship Placement Assistance

Students are encouraged to find part-time employment in the real estate industry during their program of study. The CRE maintains active ties with the professional real estate community to help facilitate placement. Cooperative education and internship credit are offered. Contact Trisha Gresnick at 316-978-6983 or trisha.gresnick@wichita.edu.

Job Placement Assistance

Call the University Career Services Office at 316-978-3435. The CRE provides Web and e-mail career assistance, and one-on-one help from faculty.

Clubs/Alumni Associations

Rho Epsilon Real Estate Fraternity. Active involvement with Kansas CCIM Chapter.

Other

Wichita State University offers the only undergraduate degree in real estate in the state of Kansas.

Faculty

Timothy Craft, assistant professor of finance. PhD, MS, University of Wisconsin–Madison; MS, University of Illinois; BS, Illinois State University. Real estate investments and portfolio theory; real estate investment trusts.

Stanley Longhofer, Stephen L. Clark Chair of Real Estate and Finance; director, Center for Real Estate. PhD, MS, University of Illinois; BBA, Wichita State University. Real estate finance, investment analysis, development.

Adjunct Faculty

Jeffrey Emerson, adjunct instructor. JD, University of Kansas; BS, Ohio State University. Real estate law, realty litigation, trusts.

David Lewis, adjunct instructor. BBA, Wichita State University. CPM.

Dan Unruh, adjunct instructor. BBA, Wichita State University. CCIM.

University of Wisconsin–Madison

Stephen Malpezzi, Department Chair
Department of Real Estate and Urban Land Economics
975 University Avenue
Madison, WI 53706
608-262-9816 or 608-262-6007; fax 608-265-2738
smalpezzi@bus.wisc.edu
www.bus.wisc.edu/realestate

Degree	Years in Operation	Credit Hours	Years to Complete	Full-Time Students (2007–2008)	Degrees Conferred (2007)
BBA	60	120	4	210	100
MBA	60	60	2	30	15
PhD	60	60+	4–6	5	2

Number of Faculty	In-State Graduate Tuition	Out-of-State Graduate Tuition	In-State Undergraduate Tuition	Out-of-State Undergraduate Tuition
Tenured faculty: 5 Senior lecturers: 3 Lecturers: 4 Visiting professors: 1	$5,549.20/semester	$13,268.24/semester	$3,505/semester	$10,505/semester

Degree Specializations

Students who wish to obtain a BBA with a specialization in real estate and urban land economics may apply for admission to the School of Business after completing their sophomore year at the University of Wisconsin (UW)–Madison and choose a major in real estate. Admission to UW is competitive, and admission to the School of Business is highly competitive. Admission is available to potential UW undergraduates both fall and spring; dates vary. Current details and application online at www.admissions.wisc.edu/admission/.

Candidates for an MBA with a specialization in real estate are admitted in the fall semester only. No minimum GMAT or GPA is specified, but admission is highly competitive. Application details are available at www.bus.wisc.edu/mba/.

Candidates for a PhD in real estate and urban land economics are admitted in the fall semester only. No minimum GRE or GPA is specified, but admission is very highly competitive. Application details available at http://bus.wisc.edu/graduateprograms/phd/phd/admissions/.

Program Description

The University of Wisconsin's real estate program is ranked as one of the top three real estate programs in the United States. One of the oldest academic real estate programs in the world, the program traces its history back to Richard T. Ely's 1925 program in Land and Policy Utility Economics. Other renowned faculty from previous years include Richard U. Ratcliff, Richard B. Andrews, and James Graaskamp.

The Department of Real Estate and Urban Land Economics, chaired by Stephen Malpezzi, is the academic home of the program and is the focal point for the undergraduate and PhD programs. François Ortalo-Magné is the PhD coordinator. The Center for Real Estate, under academic director Tim Riddiough, is the focal point for Wisconsin's MBA in real estate. The center also sponsors a program of applied research on a wide range of real estate and economic development issues. MBA students may focus on finance, development, or our unique Applied Real Estate Investment Trust (AREIT), in which students manage a $1,000,000 real estate securities portfolio.

For further information about undergraduate programs, contact Stephen Malpezzi (smalpezzi@bus.wisc.edu); for MBA programs, contact Timothy Riddiough (triddiough@bus.wisc.edu); for PhD programs, contact François Ortalo-Magné (fom@bus.wisc.edu). Or contact Dawn Hamre, Academic Department Associate (dhamre@bus.wisc.edu).

Core Curriculum

BBA: real estate process, real estate finance, real estate law, residential development, real estate economics, real estate valuation.

MBA: in addition to the MBA core, courses in real estate finance, equity investment, real estate economics, valuation and feasibility, and capstone seminars in real estate investment and international real estate. Course of study includes an international field trip.

PhD: coursework in microeconomics, econometrics, and finance, and advanced courses in urban economics and real estate finance. Students must pass comprehensive examinations after coursework and additional study, and successfully defend a dissertation. For further details, contact François Ortalo-Magné, PhD coordinator, at fom@bus.wisc.edu.

Financial Aid

All PhD students and some master's degree and undergraduate students are eligible for financial support. These range from partial funding to full fellowships and teaching and research assistantships.

Electives and Special Programs

Undergraduate electives include Computer Applications in Real Estate, International Real Estate, and Green Development, as well as a variety of related courses from finance, marketing, engineering, and urban planning.

MBA students choose electives to specialize in one of three suggested tracks in real estate finance, development and entrepreneurship, or the AREIT. Electives include managing the AREIT portfolio, Commercial Development, Commercial Mortgage-Backed Securities and Public Debt, Real Estate Law, Site Planning, and Entrepreneurial Finance.

Lecture Series

Both the graduate and undergraduate programs have an extensive program of guest lectures delivered by visiting real estate professionals and scholars. Joint lectures with foreign academic institutions are delivered through videoconferencing and Internet technology.

International Programs

The program offers a unique, three-week course in international real estate. Sample itineraries of past trips: Western Europe (Paris, London, Amsterdam, Berlin, Frankfurt); Central and Eastern Europe (Moscow, Prague, Budapest, Bratislava, Vienna); and Asia (Tokyo, Hong Kong, Seoul). Student groups attend international real estate conferences (e.g., MIPIM in Cannes, and ExpoReal in Munich). A capstone graduate seminar in international real estate is required of all MBAs. International examples also abound in other courses—for example, an urban economics course might include a comparative study of development regulation across countries.

Program Advisory Group

The Board of Trustees of the Center for Real Estate functions as an advisory group, with particular emphasis on the MBA program. The board is made up of distinguished leaders from the real estate profession nationwide. Its members are from the public, nonprofit, and private sectors, and represent a wide range of specialties within the field. The board advises and supports the center and participates broadly in center activities.

The Wisconsin Real Estate Alumni Association (WREAA) is an important source of advice for all aspects of the program, both through its board and through the many members who act individually.

Internship Placement Assistance

MBA students normally take an internship in the summer between their first and second years, and undergraduates are also encouraged to apply. Internship placement assistance is similar to job placement assistance.

Job Placement Assistance

The Career Center at the School of Business is a resource for graduate and undergraduate students, although its resources are directed mainly toward undergraduates. See www.bus.wisc.edu/career. The center's executive director takes special responsibility for career advice and mentoring for graduates of the MBA program. The WREAA works with the job coordinators of the Real Estate Club, the executive director of the Real Estate Center, and the Career Center to disseminate a regular e-mail newsletter of job opportunities at all levels.

Clubs/Alumni Associations

The University of Wisconsin Real Estate Club is an extremely active student organization with over 100 graduate and undergraduate members. Major activities include four-day field trips each semester to major markets, and an annual real estate job fair. Recent field trip destinations have included Chicago, Los Angeles, Minneapolis, New York City, and Washington, D.C. The club holds biweekly meetings with presentations by real estate professionals, as well as a full schedule of social and service events. See http://realestateclub.org.

Faculty

Morris Davis, assistant professor. PhD, University of Pennsylvania. Urban economics, macroeconomics.

François Ortalo-Magné, associate professor, PhD coordinator. PhD, University of Minnesota. International real estate, real estate finance, PhD-level urban economics.

Stephen Malpezzi, professor and chairman of the Department of Real Estate and Urban Land Economics; Lorin and Marjorie Tiefenthaler Chair. PhD, George Washington University. Urban economics, real estate process, computer applications, housing economics, real estate finance, international real estate.

Timothy Riddiough, professor; E.J. Plesko Chair; academic director, Center for Real Estate. PhD, University of Wisconsin. Real estate investment and finance.

Affiliated Faculty

Michael Dubis, lecturer. Public real estate.

Michael Johnson, lecturer. Computer applications, real estate process.

Thomas Landgraf, senior lecturer. Residential development, green development.

Sharon McCabe, senior lecturer. Valuation, real estate process, international real estate.

Barry Perkel, lecturer. Commercial development.

Arif Quershi, lecturer. Commercial development.

Peter Ritz, senior lecturer. Real estate law.

David Shulman, visiting professor. AREIT.

York University

James McKellar, Academic Director
Andre Kuzmicki, Executive Director
Schulich School of Business
Program in Real Property
4700 Keele Street
Toronto, Ontario M3J 1P3
Canada
416-736-5967; fax 416-650-8071
jmckella@schulich.yorku.ca
akuzmicki@schulich.yorku.ca

Degree	Year Program Began	Credit Hours	Years to Complete	Degrees Conferred (2007)
MBA	1991	60	2	13

Degree	Application Deadline	Minimum GRE or GMAT	Departmental Requirements
MBA	Fall: February 1 (early submission) Winter: October 1 Summer: February 1	550–790	Application; 2 letters of recommendation; resume; official GMAT score; supporting documentation, including official transcripts of previous academic work sent directly from the institution attended previously

Number of Faculty/FTE	Specialized Degree Accreditation	In-State Graduate Tuition	Out-of-State Graduate Tuition	In-State Undergraduate Tuition	Out-of-State Undergraduate Tuition
7/3	MBA: concentration in real property	$10,206/term	$15,000/term	$5,641/20/30 credits	$15,741.10/30 credits

Degree Specialization

The Program in Real Property is one of several industry sector specialization options available to MBA students at the Schulich School of Business. The program is intended to provide students with the real-world skills and knowledge to fulfill senior roles within the real estate industry, both domestically and internationally. The curriculum integrates theory with practice and relies extensively on actual case work. Electives are taught by leading practitioners in the field, and guest speakers from the industry are frequent visitors to the classroom. MBA students may take single electives or choose either a concentration or a diploma in real property. The concentration consists of a minimum of four real property electives. The diploma consists of seven half-course electives, completion of the Strategy Field Study at an approved real estate site; and either an internship or a major research paper. The diploma is awarded in addition to the MBA degree. Graduate students also qualify for RICS membership.

Program Description

The program is one of 17 areas of specialization that MBA students may pursue in year two. Since almost 50 percent of Schulich's international (IMBA) students are from other countries, the program has a distinct international focus. The program enjoys strong support from industry and offers a balanced approach to theory and practice.

Core Curriculum

Specialization options:
- Graduate Diploma in Real Property Development (MBA, IMBA, MPA)
- General Concentration (MBA, IMBA, MBA/LLB)
- Post-MBA Diploma in Advanced Management.

MBA Electives Course Descriptions: PROP 6 100.030, Real Estate Finance and Investment; PROP 6200.030, Development Prototypes; PROP 6400.030, Managing the Development Process; PROP 6500.030, Comparative International Property Markets; PROP 6600.030, Real Property Portfolio Management; PROP 6800.030, Structuring Real Property Transactions; PROP 4950 3.00, Real Estate Finance (undergraduate course only). For further information, call 416-736-5967; fax 416-650-8071; or e-mail prop@schulich.yorku.ca.

Financial Aid

Students entering, continuing in, or graduating from Schulich School of Business programs are eligible for a range of financial assistance options, including assistance programs administered by the Province of Ontario on the basis of financial need, and entrance scholarships and in-course awards given by the university in recognition of scholastic achievement. A number of additional awards, scholarships, prizes, and medals are also offered. Many of these are donated by corporations, associations and private individuals. The university may also provide academic fee deferments and short-term emergency loans. All awards are subject to change without notice. Contact acaulfield@schulich.yorku.ca or cshewell@schulich.yorku.ca.

International Programs

Students may enroll in the IMBA and pursue the concentration in real property. The school also has exchange programs with some 65 international universities, through which students can spend one term abroad. The IMBA also offers a joint degree with Peking University, through which students can spend a full year in China.

Program Advisory Group

The Real Property Advisory Board meets twice a year to discuss programs and curriculum issues. Membership represents leaders in the real estate industry in Canada.

Internship Placement Assistance

We do arrange for internship opportunities between the first and second year of the MBA program.

Job Placement Assistance

The program publishes a resume book each January containing information on students pursuing internships and full-time employment upon graduation. The school has a fully staffed career center, and the program itself offers assistance and counseling on an as-needed basis. Contact prop@schulich.yorku.ca.

Clubs/Alumni Associations

The Schulich School Real Property Association (SSRPA) is a student-run club that acts as a liaison between MBA students and the real estate industry. The SSRPA provides students with the opportunity to learn about the industry through a regular program of guest lectures and other events. Graduating students have the opportunity to continue their affiliation with the program through the Schulich School Real Property Alumni Association. Contact srpsa@schulich.yorku.ca.

Other

The Schulich School of Business is Canada's largest business school, graduating approximately 450 MBAs annually. It offers undergraduate, graduate, and post-graduate degrees, plus programs in executive education. It is consistently ranked the top business school in Canada in most international surveys, and is among the top 25 in the world. More than half of the MBA students are international, and alumni can be found throughout the world.

Faculty

Monica Contreras, sessional lecturer in real property development.

Tyler Hershberg, sessional lecturer in real property development.

Cynthia Holmes, full-time professor.

Patrick Iaboni, sessional lecturer in real property development.

Andre R. Kuzmicki, full-time professor; program co-director; professor of real property development. BA, MBA, McGill University.

James McKellar, full-time professor; academic director; professor of real property development. MArch, MCP, University of Pennsylvania; BArch, University of Toronto.

Neil A. Prashad, sessional lecturer in real property development.

Ron Rimer, CA. Sessional lecturer in real property development.

Other Universities Offering Real Estate Programs

University of Aberdeen
Aberdeen, Scotland, UK
www.abdn.ac.uk

University of Alabama
Tuscaloosa, Alabama, U.S.A.
www.cba.ua.edu

American University
Washington, D.C., U.S.A.
kogod.american.edu

University of British Columbia
Vancouver, British Columbia, Canada
sauder.ubc.ca

California State University, Fullerton
Fullerton, California, U.S.A.
business.fullerton.edu

California State University, Northridge
Northridge, California, U.S.A.
www.csun.edu/busecon

University of California at Berkeley
Berkeley, California, U.S.A.
haas.berkeley.edu/realestate

University of California at Los Angeles
Los Angeles, California, U.S.A.
www.zimancenter.com

University of Cincinnati
Cincinnati, Ohio, U.S.A.
www.business.uc.edu/realestate

Colorado State University
Fort Collins, Colorado, U.S.A.
www.biz.colostate.edu/ciref

Columbia University
New York, New York, U.S.A.
www.arch.columbia.edu/realestate

Concordia University
Montreal, Quebec, Canada
www.johnmolson.concordia.ca

University of Connecticut
Storrs, Connecticut, U.S.A.
www.business.uconn.edu/cms

DePaul University
Chicago, Illinois, U.S.A.
www.realestate.depaul.edu

Emory University
Atlanta, Georgia, U.S.A.
www.goizueta.emory.edu

ESSEC Business School
Cergy-Pontoise, France
www.essec.edu/home

European Business School
Oestrich-Winkel, Germany
www.ebs-immobilienoekonomie.de

Florida Atlantic University
Boca Raton, Florida, U.S.A.
www.fau.edu

Florida Gulf Coast University
Fort Myers, Florida, U.S.A.
cps.fgcu.edu

Florida International University
Miami, Florida, U.S.A.
business.fiu.edu

George Washington University
Washington, D.C., U.S.A.
business.gwu.edu

Georgia State University
Atlanta, Georgia, U.S.A.
www.robinson.gsu.edu/realestate

University of Guelph
Guelph, Ontario, Canada
www.uoguelph.ca

The Hong Kong Polytechnic University
Hong Kong, China
www.bre.polyu.edu.hk

Howard University
Washington, D.C., U.S.A.
www.bschool.howard.edu

University of Illinois at Chicago
Chicago, Illinois, U.S.A.
www.uic.edu/cba/lgradbiz

University of Illinois at Urbana-Champaign
Urbana-Champaign, Illinois, U.S.A.
www.business.uiuc.edu/finance

University of Kentucky
Lexington, Kentucky, U.S.A.
www.uky.edu

Louisiana State University in Shreveport
Shreveport, Louisiana, U.S.A.
www.lsus.edu/ba

Marylhurst University
Marylhurst, Oregon, U.S.A.
www.marylhurst.edu

Mississippi State University
Starkville, Mississippi, U.S.A.
www.cbi.msstate.edu

University of Missouri–Columbia
Columbia, Missouri, U.S.A.
business.missouri.edu

Morehead State University
Morehead, Kentucky, U.S.A.
www.moreheadstate.edu/business

University of New Orleans
New Orleans, Louisiana, U.S.A.
www.uno.edu

University of New South Wales
Sydney, New South Wales, Australia
www.unsw.edu.au

University of North Florida
Jacksonville, Florida, U.S.A.
www.unf.edu/ccb

University of North Texas
Denton, Texas, U.S.A.
www.coba.unt.edu/firel

Northwestern University
Evanston, Illinois, U.S.A.
www.kellogg.northwestern.edu/realestate

Ohio State University
Columbus, Ohio, U.S.A.
www.osu.edu

University of the Pacific
Stockton, California, U.S.A.
www.pacific.edu

Portland State University
Portland, Oregon, U.S.A.
www.pdx.edu

Université du Québec à Montréal
Montreal, Quebec, Canada
www.uqam.ca

Royal Melbourne Institute of Technology
Melbourne, Victoria, Australia
www.rmit.edu.au

San Diego State University
San Diego, California, U.S.A.
www.sdsu.edu

University of South Carolina
Columbia, South Carolina, U.S.A.
mooreschool.sc.edu/moore/sccre

Southern Methodist University
Dallas, Texas, U.S.A.
www.smu.edu

University of the South Pacific
Suva, Fiji
www.fio.usp.ac.fj

St. Cloud State University
St. Cloud, Minnesota, U.S.A.
www.stcloudstate.edu

University of St. Thomas
Minneapolis, Minnesota, U.S.A.
www.stthomas.edu/realestate

Texas Tech University
Lubbock, Texas, U.S.A.
www.ttu.edu

University of Texas at Arlington

Arlington, Texas, U.S.A.
www.uta.edu

University of Ulster–Jordanstown

Newtownabbey, Northern Ireland, UK
www.ulster.ac.uk

Washington State University

Pullman, Washington, U.S.A.
www.wsu.edu

University of West Georgia

Carrollton, Georgia, U.S.A.
www.westga.edu/~mktreal

University of Wisconsin at Milwaukee

Milwaukee, Wisconsin, U.S.A.
www4.uwm.edu

University of Wyoming

Laramie, Wyoming, U.S.A.
www.uwyo.edu

Faculty

Note: The names of adjunct and affiliated faculty members are shown in italics.

Aalberts, Robert (University of Nevada, Las Vegas)
Abaza, Hussain (Southern Polytechnic State University)
Abrams, Robert H. (Cornell University)
Addae-Dapaah, Kwame (National University of Singapore)
Adkinson, J. Daniel (Columbia University)
Adkisson, Amanda (Texas A&M University)
Agnew, David (University of Colorado)
Alcock, Jamie (University of Cambridge)
Allen, Peter (University of Michigan)
Allmendinger, Philip (University of Reading)
Almazan, Andres (University of Texas at Austin)
Altshuler, Alan A. (Harvard University)
Ambrose, Brent (Penn State University)
Amicucci, Ralph (New York University)
Anderson, Gary (The Johns Hopkins University)
Anderson, Sharon (The Johns Hopkins University)
Anderson, S. Kent (Texas A&M University)
Andersson, Roland (Royal Institute of Technology)
Andrus, Sherryl (Marquette University)
Anikeeff, Michael A. (The Johns Hopkins University)
Annese, Angelo (New York University)
Applegate, Ben (The John Marshall Law School)
Archer, Wayne (University of Florida)
Arena, Charles (University of Pennsylvania)
Arestis, Phillip (University of Cambridge)
Arku, Godwin (University of Western Ontario)
Armitage, L. (Bond University)
Asabere, Paul (Temple University)
Atkins, April (Georgia Institute of Technology)
Avello, Philip (New York University)
Azasu, Samuel (Royal Institute of Technology)

Bailey, Stephen (Florida State University)
Back, Shinn (New York University)
Baker, M. (Bond University)
Ballantine, John T., Jr. (University of Colorado)
Ball, Michael (University of Reading)
Baltin, Bruce (University of Southern California)
Banik, Gouranga C. (Southern Polytechnic State University)

Bao, Helen (University of Cambridge)
Barclay, Jeffrey (Columbia University)
Bardzik, Steven (New York University)
Barkacs, Craig (University of San Diego)
Barnes, Wilson C. (Southern Polytechnic State University)
Barnhart, Peter (Texas A&M University)
Barranca, Steven (New York University)
Barry, Alfred, III (The Johns Hopkins University)
Basu, Anirban (The Johns Hopkins University)
Battle, Thomas (Indiana University)
Baum, Andrew (University of Cambridge)
Baum, Andrew (University of Amsterdam)
Baum, Andrew (University of Reading)
Bausman, Dennis C. (Clemson University)
Bayfield, Natalie (University of Cambridge)
Bazzano, John (New York University)
Beal, Jeffrey (Baruch College, The City University of New York)
Becker, Franklin D. (Cornell University)
Bella, Michelle (The John Marshall Law School)
Beel, Charles (New York University)
Beller, Joseph (Temple University)
Bellman, David (Baruch College, The City University of New York)
Benedict, Robert (Clemson University)
Benton, Richard (Florida State University)
Bialkowski, Stephen (New York University)
Bierman, Leonard (Texas A&M University)
van de Bilt, Roel A.M. (University of Amsterdam)
Bin Ibrahim, Muhammad Faishal (National University of Singapore)
Blane, W.J. (Georgia Institute of Technology)
Bloch, Bruce (New York University)
Blumenthal, Robert (New York University)
Boggs, H. Glenn (Florida State University)
Bohman, Mats (Royal Institute of Technology)
Bond, Shaun A. (University of Cambridge)
Bond, Shaun A. (Penn State University)
Booth, Richard S. (Cornell University)
Boss, Mary (University of Cambridge)
Bostic, Raphael (University of Southern California)
Botein, Hilary (Baruch College, The City University of New York)
Boudry, Wally (University of North Carolina at Chapel Hill)
Bovill, Carl (University of Maryland)
Boykin, James H. (Virginia Commonwealth University)
Braconi, Frank (New York University)
Brady, Charles (New York University)
Breedveld, Hamith M.I.Th. (University of Amsterdam)

Brincefield, Steven B. (Virginia Commonwealth University)

Brinsden, Jonathan (Texas A&M University)

Brodie, M.J. (Jay) (The Johns Hopkins University)

Brody, Samuel (Texas A&M University)

Brown, David S. (University of Southern California)

Brown, David T. (University of Florida)

Bruner, Larry (University of Texas at San Antonio)

Brunes, Fredrik (Royal Institute of Technology)

Buck, René J.V.M. (University of Amsterdam)

Burke, Nancy (University of Southern California)

Burton, Donna (Baruch College, The City University of New York)

Busquets, Joan (Harvard University)

Butler, Jay Q. (Arizona State University)

Butler, Jim (Georgia Institute of Technology)

Buttimer, Richard (University of North Carolina at Charlotte)

Byrne, Emer (Dublin Institute of Technology)

Byrne, Peter J. (University of Reading)

Cahoy, Daniel R. (Penn State University)

Cancelliere, Thomas (New York University)

Cannon, Robert (The Johns Hopkins University)

Capozza, Dennis R. (University of Michigan)

Carman, Paul (The John Marshall Law School)

Carruthers, John (University of Maryland)

Caruso, F. Willis (The John Marshall Law School)

Cascioli, Kyle (University of Denver)

Castro, Daniel (Georgia Institute of Technology)

Castro, Elba (New York University)

Champion, Robert D. (University of Southern California)

Cheng Fook Jam (National University of Singapore)

Chernoff, David (The John Marshall Law School)

Chin Kein Hoong, Lawrence (National University of Singapore)

Chorman, Peter (New York University)

Chow Yuen Leng (National University of Singapore)

Christudason, Alice (National University of Singapore)

Cicero, John (New York University)

Cicero, Joseph (New York University)

Cinnamond, William (New York University)

Ciochetti, Brian (Tony) (Massachusetts Institute of Technology)

Clark, David E. (Marquette University)

Clarke, J. Joseph (The Johns Hopkins University)

Clauretie, Terrence "Mike" (University of Nevada, Las Vegas)

Cleary, Stephen (Roosevelt University)

Clements, W. (University of Denver)

Code, William R. (University of Western Ontario)

Cohen, James (University of Maryland)

Collins, Mark (Georgia Institute of Technology)

Colvin, John (University of Maryland)

Condlin, Andrew M. (Virginia Commonwealth University)

Congreve, Alina (University of Reading)

Conijn, Johan (University of Amsterdam)

Contreras, Monica (York University)

Conway, Delores (University of Southern California)

Cooper, S. (Bond University)

Corcoran, Frank (Dublin Institute of Technology)

Corgel, John (Jack) (Cornell University)

Corneal, David B. (Penn State University)

Cousins, Bruce (University of Denver)

Cox, Arthur (University of Northern Iowa)

Craft, Timothy (Wichita State University)

Crassee, Rob E.F.A. (University of Amsterdam)

Crawford, Margaret (Harvard University)

Crawford, Tim (Texas A&M University)

Crean, Michael J. (University of Denver)

Crosby, F. Neil (University of Reading)

Crunkleton, Jon R. (Old Dominion University)

Cumbie, Stephen (University of North Carolina at Chapel Hill)

Curry, Milton (Cornell University)

D'Arcy, Eamonn (University of Reading)

Datta, Jayanta (New York University)

Daugard, Michael (University of Maryland)

Davis, Morris (University of Wisconsin–Madison)

Davis, Paul (The John Marshall Law School)

Day-Marshall, Maria (University of Maryland)

Decker, Lisa (The Johns Hopkins University)

Dehring, Carolyn A. (University of Georgia)

Delaney, Charles J. (Baylor University)

DeLisle, James R. (University of Washington)

Demas, John (University of San Diego)

Deng, Yongheng (University of Southern California)

Dermisi, Sofia (Roosevelt University)

deRoos, Jan (Cornell University)

DeTraglia, Scott (New York University)

DeVries, Jon (Roosevelt University)

Di Sciullo, Alan (New York University)

Dickerhoff, Terri (University of Southern California)

Diskin, Barry A. (Florida State University)

Dixon, Martin (University of Cambridge)

Doak, Andrew J. (University of Reading)

Donnell, Cydney (Texas A&M University)
Dossani, Nazir (The Johns Hopkins University)
Douglas, Camille (Columbia University)
Downs, David H. (Virginia Commonwealth University)
Dubis, Michael (University of Wisconsin–Madison)
Dudney, Gretchen (The Johns Hopkins University)
Duff, Charles B., Jr. (The Johns Hopkins University)
van Duijvendijk, Jan (University of Amsterdam)
Dunkin, Terry R. (The Johns Hopkins University)
Dunne, Thomas (Dublin Institute of Technology)
DuPuy, Karl F.G. (University of Maryland)
Dyson, Ludwig M., Jr. (Baylor University)

Earl, G. (Bond University)
Early, Tim (Texas A&M University)
Eiseman, Neal (New York University)
El Itr, Zuhair (Southern Polytechnic State University)
Ellis, Cliff (Clemson University)
Ellis, Robert (Clemson University)
Elmore, O.E. (Texas A&M University)
Ely, Edward (The Johns Hopkins University)
Elzarka, Hazem (University of Denver)
Emerson, Jeffrey (Wichita State University)
Engebretson, Jeff (University of Denver)
Engelstad, Jeffrey L. (University of Denver)
Eppli, Mark J. (Marquette University)
Ercoli, Karen (The John Marshall Law School)
Eschemuller, John (New York University)
Eve, Holly Law (Virginia Commonwealth University)
Eyzenberg, David (New York University)

Fainstein, Susan (Harvard University)
Falk, David (University of Maryland)
Falletta, Elizabeth (University of Southern California)
Fallon, Emer (Dublin Institute of Technology)
Farrell, Michael (New York University)
Farris, J. Terrence (Clemson University)
Feigin, Philip (University of Denver)
Feng, Lei (University of Cambridge)
Fernandez-Solis, Jose (Texas A&M University)
Ferrandi, Stephen (The Johns Hopkins University)
Ferreira, Fernando (University of Pennsylvania)
Ferry, Michael (New York University)
Field, Charles (University of Maryland)
Fields, David (New York University)

Filippi, Anthony (Texas A&M University)
Fingleton, Bernard (University of Cambridge)
Finke, Robert (Roosevelt University)
Fisher, Jeffrey D. (Indiana University)
Fisher, Lynn (Massachusetts Institute of Technology)
Fitzmaurice, Michael (New York University)
Flesseman, Albert D. (University of Amsterdam)
Foerster, Mark (Cornell University)
Followill, Richard (University of Northern Iowa)
Ford, Mike (University of Cambridge)
Forsyth, David L. (Arizona State University)
Foster, Henry L. (University of Reading)
Foster, Iris (University of Denver)
Frame, David (Baruch College, The City University of New York)
Frankel, Merrie (New York University)
Franklin, Robert (Temple University)
Fraser, Donald R. (Texas A&M University)
Frenchman, Dennis (Massachusetts Institute of Technology)
Friedman, Sholem (New York University)
Fronapfel, Edward L. (University of Denver)
Fuerst, Franz (University of Reading)
Funk, David (Cornell University)
Furbish, Michael (The Johns Hopkins University)
Fu Yuming, National University of Singapore

Gabriel, Donald (The Johns Hopkins University)
Gabriele, Mauro (New York University)
Galles, Patrick (University of Northern Iowa)
Galuppo, Louis A. (University of San Diego)
Garfield, Spencer (New York University)
Garrison, Elena (The Johns Hopkins University)
Gatzlaff, Dean H. (Florida State University)
Gau, George W. (University of Texas at Austin)
Geltner, David (Massachusetts Institute of Technology)
Giaccardo, Marc (University of Texas at San Antonio)
Gibbard, Roger (University of Reading)
Gibson, Mark (New York University)
Gibson, Virginia A. (University of Reading)
van der Gijp, Boris (University of Amsterdam)
Giliberto, Michael (Columbia University)
Gilliland, Charles E. (Texas A&M University)
Gilliland, Jason (University of Western Ontario)
Gin, Alan (University of San Diego)
Ginsberg, Robert (New York University)
Giusti, Cecilia (Texas A&M University)

Glascock, John (University of Cambridge)

Glen, Alicia (University of Pennsylvania)

Glover, Joel (University of Denver)

Godat, Gordon (The Johns Hopkins University)

Godschalk, David (University of North Carolina at Chapel Hill)

Goering, John (Baruch College, The City University of New York)

Gómez-Ibáñez, José A. (Harvard University)

van Gool, Peter (University of Amsterdam)

Gordon, Marcia (University of Southern California)

Gordon, Peter (University of Southern California)

Gorman, Matthew (New York University)

Gottko, Edward (New York University)

Gouline, Jay (The Johns Hopkins University)

Graves, Bill (University of North Carolina at Charlotte)

Green, Milford B. (University of Western Ontario)

Griffith, Steve (Florida State University)

Grossman, Rachel (New York University)

Groth, John C. (Texas A&M University)

Guernier, William (New York University)

Guerts, Tom G. (New York University)

Gunnelin, Åke (Royal Institute of Technology)

Gyourko, Joseph E. (University of Pennsylvania)

de Haas, Peter (University of Amsterdam)

Hagy, James (The John Marshall Law School)

Hallman, Greg (University of Texas at Austin)

Hammond, Celeste (The John Marshall Law School)

Hamner, Clay (University of North Carolina at Chapel Hill)

Hanau, Paul (New York University)

Haney, Richard L., Jr. (Texas A&M University)

Hannigan, Pamela (New York University)

Hanratty, Martin (Dublin Institute of Technology)

Harris, Oliver O. (The Johns Hopkins University)

Hartley, Diane (The Johns Hopkins University)

Hartzell, David (University of North Carolina at Chapel Hill)

Hartzell, Jay (University of Texas at Austin)

Harvey, Tom (University of North Carolina at Chapel Hill)

Hassinger, Mark (The Johns Hopkins University)

Hass, Jerome (Cornell University)

Hauser, Thomas A. (The Johns Hopkins University)

ten Have, Tineke (University of Amsterdam)

Healey-Frosina, Cathleen (New York University)

Helman, Richard (New York University)

Hersh, Barry (New York University)

Hershberg, Tyler (York University)

Hicks, Harold (The John Marshall Law School)

Himschoot, Robert (University of Northern Iowa)

Hiney, Edward (New York University)

van Hoeken, Frans G. (University of Amsterdam)

Hoek-Smit, Marja (University of Pennsylvania)

Ho Kim Hin, David (National University of Singapore)

Holmes, Cynthia (York University)

Holtan-Brown, Kyle (University of Denver)

Hoogvliet, Adriaan (University of Amsterdam)

Hopkins, Jeffrey S.P. (University of Western Ontario)

Horowitz, Jacqueline (New York University)

Hover, Kenneth C. (Cornell University)

Howe, John (University of Cambridge)

Howland, Marie (University of Maryland)

Hoyt, Richard (University of Nevada, Las Vegas)

Huffman, Forrest (Temple University)

Hughes, Brian (Dublin Institute of Technology)

Hughes, Catherine (University of Reading)

Humphrey, Mewburn (New York University)

Iaboni, Patrick (York University)

Iezman, Stanley L. (University of Southern California)

Inman, Robert P. (University of Pennsylvania)

Jackson, Bryan C. (University of Southern California)

Jackson, Kevin (New York University)

Jackson, Thomas O. (Texas A&M University)

Jaconetty, Thomas (The John Marshall Law School)

Jaffe, Austin J. (Penn State University)

Jahn, Judson R. (Clemson University)

James, William M. (University of Denver)

Johnson, Eric (University of Northern Iowa)

Johnson, Johnnie (University of Cambridge)

Johnson, Michael (University of Wisconsin–Madison)

Johnson, T. (Bond University)

Jones, Keith (University of Northern Iowa)

Josephs, Julian A. (The Johns Hopkins University)

Justin, Thomas (New York University)

Kangari, Roozbeh (Georgia Institute of Technology)

Kasim, James (University of Southern California)

Kasindorf, Matthew (New York University)

Katzler, Sigrid (Royal Institute of Technology)

Kau, James B. (University of Georgia)

Kayden, Jerrold S. (Harvard University)

Keaveney, Myles (Dublin Institute of Technology)
Keel, Thom (Georgia Institute of Technology)
Kellenberg, Steve (University of Southern California)
Kelly, Hugh F. (New York University)
Kenison, Robert (University of Maryland)
Kent, P. (Bond University)
Kessler, Richard (New York University)
Keston, Michael I. (University of Southern California)
Kirkwood, Niall G. (Harvard University)
Klausner, Adam (Cornell University)
Klingborg, Kerstin (Royal Institute of Technology)
Kluft, Joop (University of Amsterdam)
Knegt, Mildred E.D.M. (University of Amsterdam)
Knoll, Michael S. (University of Pennsylvania)
Konsoulis, Mary (University of Maryland)
Kontokosta, Constantine (New York University)
Kontoleon, Andreas (University of Cambridge)
Korologos, Constantine (New York University)
Kostaras, James (Harvard University)
Koste, Byron R. (University of Colorado)
Kotin, Allan D. (University of Southern California)
Koutrouvelis, Demetri (The Johns Hopkins University)
Kovarik, John (New York University)
Kraft, Alon (University of Southern California)
Kraft, Elizabeth (University of Denver)
Kramer, Robin (New York University)
Krantz, M. Shawn (The Johns Hopkins University)
Krieger, Alex (Harvard University)
Krill, David (Marquette University)
Kuzmicki, Andre (York University)

Lachman, Gary S. (The Johns Hopkins University)
Lacilla, Jeff (New York University)
Lamb, Alastair (New York University)
Lambeck, Richard (New York University)
Lammendola, James (Temple University)
Landgraf, Thomas (University of Wisconsin–Madison)
Landis, John (University of Pennsylvania)
Langston, C. (Bond University)
Laposa, Steve (University of Denver)
Laria, Jon (The Johns Hopkins University)
Lawrence, Vanessa (Temple University)
LeBlanc, Steve (University of Texas at Austin)
Lee, Scott (Texas A&M University)
Lefenfeld, Robert (University of Maryland)

Leiber, Frank (New York University)
Lerner, Frederic (New York University)
Levine, Libbi (University of Denver)
Levine, Mark Lee (University of Denver)
Levy, Gerald M. (New York University)
Lewis, David (Wichita State University)
Lim Lan Yuan (National University of Singapore)
Lind, Hans (Royal Institute of Technology)
Ling, David C. (University of Florida)
Linneman, Peter D. (University of Pennsylvania)
Linnick, Shari (New York University)
Liow Kim Hiang (National University of Singapore)
Liow Wen-Chi (National University of Singapore)
Lippmann, John (New York University)
Liska, Roger W. (Clemson University)
Liu, Peng (Peter) (Cornell University)
Lizieri, Colin M. (University of Reading)
Lofredo, Andrew (New York University)
Lombard, John (Old Dominion University)
Lombardo, Edward (New York University)
London, Joseph (Temple University)
Lonegran, Andrew (University of Denver)
Longhofer, Stanley (Wichita State University)
Longua, Lawrence (New York University)
Lu, Chiuling (University of Cambridge)
Lum Sau Kim (National University of Singapore)
Lundgren, Berndt (Royal Institute of Technology)

Madden, Janice Fanning (University of Pennsylvania)
Maimis, Konstantinos (New York University)
Makarechi, Shariar (Southern Polytechnic State University)
Malczewski, Jacek (University of Western Ontario)
Malizia, Emil (University of North Carolina at Chapel Hill)
Malone-Lee Lai Choo (National University of Singapore)
Malpezzi, Stephen J. (University of Wisconsin–Madison)
Manaker, Stephen (New York University)
Mandell, Svante (Royal Institute of Technology)
Manekin, Robert (The Johns Hopkins University)
Maniscalco, Robert (Baruch College, The City University of New York)
Marcato, Gianluca (University of Reading)
Martin, Richard W. (University of Georgia)
Masciantonio, Andrew (New York University)
Massey, Adam (University of Colorado)
McAllister, Patrick (University of Reading)

McAuliffe, B. (Bond University)

McAuliffe, S. (Bond University)

McCabe, Sharon (University of Wisconsin–Madison)

McCoy, Douglas (Indiana University)

McDougall, Edgar J. (University of Florida)

McFarland, Margaret (University of Maryland)

McGram, W. Todd (Massachusetts Institute of Technology)

McGrath, Helen (Dublin Institute of Technology)

McKellar, James (York University)

McKenney, Eileen (New York University)

McKenzie, Evan (The John Marshall Law School)

McKeown, Declan (Dublin Institute of Technology)

McLellan, Harry (New York University)

McMillan, Jeffrey (Clemson University)

Meadati, Pavan (Southern Polytechnic State University)

Megbolugbe, Isaac F. (The Johns Hopkins University)

Mench, John (Southern Polytechnic State University)

Metzger, Dan (University of Denver)

Meuer, James (University of Denver)

Meyer, Carl F. (University of Southern California)

Miles, Mike (University of North Carolina at Chapel Hill)

Miletich, Dusan (University of Southern California)

Miller, Norm (University of San Diego)

Mobley, Linda Thomas (Georgia Institute of Technology)

Molloy, John (Dublin Institute of Technology)

Mok, Diana (University of Western Ontario)

Moore, Barry (University of Cambridge)

Morrison, Anne (New York University)

Mouchly, Ehud (University of Southern California)

Moynihan, Michael (New York University)

Mueller, Glenn (University of Denver)

Mulcahy, Vincent J. (Cornell University)

Muller, Tom (University of Southern California)

Munneke, Henry J. (University of Georgia)

Murdoch, Sandra E. (University of Reading)

Murray, Paula C. (University of Texas at Austin)

Nadenicek, Daniel J. (Clemson University)

Nakahara, Asuka (University of Pennsylvania)

Narwold, Andrew (University of San Diego)

Neuer, Philip (New York University)

Newburn, David (Texas A&M University)

Nickerson, David (Roosevelt University)

Nordlund, Bo (Royal Institute of Technology)

Norris, Ira C. (University of Southern California)

Novak, Paul (University of Southern California)

Nozeman, Ed F. (University of Amsterdam)

O'Hare, D. (Bond University)

Oler, John (New York University)

Oliver, Mark (University of Southern California)

Oliver, Ryan (University of Denver)

Oliveri, Carlos (New York University)

Olson, C. Bradley (Cornell University)

Ong Seow Eng (National University of Singapore)

Ooi Thian Leong, Joseph (National University of Singapore)

Op 't Veld, Hans (University of Amsterdam)

Ortalo-Magné, François (University of Wisconsin–Madison)

Ortwein, Richard (University of Southern California)

O'Shea, Cornelius (Dublin Institute of Technology)

Oswald, Lynda (University of Michigan)

Ott, Steve (University of North Carolina at Charlotte)

Pack, Janet R. (University of Pennsylvania)

Pape, Art (The John Marshall Law School)

Parker, Gavin (University of Reading)

Parker, Gene, Jr. (The Johns Hopkins University)

Parrish, William (New York University)

Patton, D. Kenneth (New York University)

Pearlman, Stephen (New York University)

Peca, Stephen (New York University)

Peiser, Richard B. (University of Cambridge)

Peiser, Richard B. (Harvard University)

Pendall, Rolf (Cornell University)

Peng, Helen (New York University)

Peng, Liang (University of Colorado)

Pennington-Cross, Anthony (Marquette University)

Perez, Andrew, III (University of Texas at San Antonio)

Perkel, Barry (University of Wisconsin–Madison)

Persson, Erik (Royal Institute of Technology)

Peters, Jordan (The John Marshall Law School)

Phillips, Debbie (Georgia Institute of Technology)

Phillips, Georgette (University of Pennsylvania)

Phillips, Patrick (The Johns Hopkins University)

Phillips, Richard A. (Virginia Commonwealth University)

Pickerill, Tracy (Dublin Institute of Technology)

Pierce, David R. (Southern Polytechnic State University)

Piskorski, Tomasz (Columbia University)

Pollalis, Spiro N. (Harvard University)

Pollock, Douglas (New York University)

Poon, Percy (University of Nevada at Las Vegas)

Porter, Douglas (The Johns Hopkins University)

Power, Thomas (Dublin Institute of Technology)

Prashad, Neil (York University)

Prendergast, Terry (Dublin Institute of Technology)

Procise, Donna (Virginia Commonwealth University)

Psilander, Kurt (Royal Institute of Technology)

Quan, Daniel W.C. (Cornell University)

Quercia, Roberto (University of North Carolina at Chapel Hill)

Quershi, Arif (University of Wisconsin–Madison)

Quinn, Jessica (University of Denver)

Rajewski, Robert J. (The Johns Hopkins University)

Ralston, Gary M. (University of Denver)

Randolph, Jeff (Clemson University)

Ray, James (New York University)

Read, Dustin (University of North Carolina at Charlotte)

Read, E. Stoney (Temple University)

Rector, Coleman G. (The Johns Hopkins University)

Redfearn, Christian (University of Southern California)

Retsinas, Nicolas P. (Harvard University)

Reynolds, Bob (University of Texas at San Antonio)

Richardson, Henry W. (Cornell University)

Riddiough, Tim (University of Wisconsin–Madison)

Riedy, Mark J. (University of San Diego)

Rimer, Ron (York University)

Ritz, Peter (University of Wisconsin–Madison)

Rivetti, Daniel (University of San Diego)

Robinson, Scott (New York University)

Rockoff, Jonah (Columbia University)

Rodriguez, Joe (Texas A&M University)

Rolfe, George (University of Washington)

Roloff, Kirk (University of Southern California)

Rome, Gerald (University of Denver)

Rompelberg, Lars (University of Amsterdam)

Roper, Kathy (Georgia Institute of Technology)

Rosenberg, Scott (The Johns Hopkins University)

Rosenfeld, Joel (New York University)

Rosenfeld, Robert (University of Maryland)

Roslyn, Burton (New York University)

Roth, Peter (Massachusetts Institute of Technology)

Rouhi, Soheil (Georgia Institute of Technology)

Rowe, Peter G. (Harvard University)

Rowley, Alan R. (University of Reading)

Rufrano, Matthew (New York University)

Rushman, Michael J. (New York University)

Russell, Anne (Dublin Institute of Technology)

Rutherford, Ronald C. (University of Texas at San Antonio)

Ruwiel, Patrick H.J. (University of Amsterdam)

Rybczynski, Witold (University of Pennsylvania)

Rypkema, Donovan (University of Pennsylvania)

Sadri, Saeid (Georgia Institute of Technology)

Saginor, Jesse (Texas A&M University)

Saiz, Albert (University of Pennsylvania)

Samuels, Tom (Cornell University)

Sarkis, Antoine Hashim (Harvard University)

Scanlon, Rosemary (New York University)

Scanlon, Tara A. (The Johns Hopkins University)

Scheffers, Wim J.M. (University of Amsterdam)

Schneller, Barbara (Temple University)

Schodek, Daniel (Harvard University)

Schuck, Gloria (Massachusetts Institute of Technology)

Schwartz, Michael (Baruch College, The City University of New York)

Scribner, David, Jr. (Baruch College, The City University of New York)

Scribner, David, Jr. (New York University)

Sears, Curtis (University of Colorado)

Segner, Robert (Texas A&M University)

Serruto, John (New York University)

Seslen, Tracey (University of Southern California)

Sessions, Stephen (University of Denver)

Shapiro, Marc (New York University)

Shapiro, Steven (University of Maryland)

Sharkawy, M. Atef (Texas A&M University)

Sharp, Jeffery M. (Penn State University)

Sherman, Scott A. (The Johns Hopkins University)

Shinn, M. (Bond University)

Shostal, H. Claude (New York University)

Shulman, David (University of Wisconsin–Madison)

Shultz, Steven (University of Nebraska at Omaha)

Shutkin, William (University of Colorado)

Siddiqi, Khalid M. (Southern Polytechnic State University)

Siedel, George (University of Michigan)

Silva, Elisabete (University of Cambridge)

Sim Loo Lee (National University of Singapore)

Simons, Robert A. (Cleveland State University)

Simril, Renata Smith (University of Southern California)

Sinai, Todd M. (University of Pennsylvania)

Sindt, Roger P. (University of Nebraska at Omaha)

Singer, Harvey (The Johns Hopkins University)

Singer, William (New York University)

Sing Tien Foo (National University of Singapore)

Sirmans, G. Stacy (Florida State University)

Sirr, Lorcan (Dublin Institute of Technology)

Sislen, David (The Johns Hopkins University)

Sklar, Stanley (The John Marshall Law School)

Slutsky, Lorence (The John Marshall Law School)

Smart, J. Eric (The Johns Hopkins University)

Smith, Brent C. (Virginia Commonwealth University)

Smith, J. (Bond University)

Smith, Julie (University of Maryland)

Smith, Peter (University of Reading)

Smith, Robert B. (New York University)

Smith, Walter (Arizona State University)

Smitheal, Jeremy (University of Texas at Austin)

Smyth, Karen (New York University)

Song, Han-Suck (Royal Institute of Technology)

Speetjens, Jan-Willem (University of Amsterdam)

Springer, Thomas (Clemson University)

Staiger, Roger, III (The Johns Hopkins University)

Stainback, John (University of Maryland)

Stark, Debra (The John Marshall Law School)

Stein, Sanford (The John Marshall Law School)

Stein, Stuart B. (University of Denver)

Steinberg, Norman (New York University)

Stockward, James (Harvard University)

Sullivan, Lenore M. (University of Texas at Austin)

Summers, Anita A. (University of Pennsylvania)

Sunderam, Arjuna (New York University)

Swenson, Bart (New York University)

Taltavull de La Paz, Paloma (Universidad de Alicante)

Tan Hock Chye, Harold (National University of Singapore)

Tangum, Richard R. (University of Texas at San Antonio)

Tatro, Kevin (New York University)

Tay, L. (Bond University)

Taylor, Philip (New York University)

Taylor, Robert W. (Virginia Commonwealth University)

Teske, Raymond H.C. (University of Texas at San Antonio)

Thibodeau, Thomas G. (University of Colorado)

Thomas, Catherine (Columbia University)

Thomson, Thomas A. (University of Texas at San Antonio)

Titman, Sheridan (University of Texas at Austin)

Tomlan, Michael (Cornell University)

Trancik, Roger T. (Cornell University)

Throupe, Ronald (University of Denver)

Tompaidis, Stathis (University of Texas at Austin)

Trotta, Ciro (New York University)

Trowbridge, Peter J. (Cornell University)

Truog, Nicole (Marquette University)

Tu, Charles C. (University of San Diego)

Tu Yong (National University of Singapore)

Turner, Jeffrey D. (The Johns Hopkins University)

Tyler, Peter (University of Cambridge)

Umphress, Elizabeth (Texas A&M University)

Unruh, Dan (Wichita State University)

Vaias, Emily (The Johns Hopkins University)

Valenza, Michael (Temple University)

Van Order, Robert (University of Michigan)

Van Tilburg, Johannes (University of Southern California)

Vetrano, Anthony (New York University)

Vick, Gerard (Arizona State University)

Vollmann, Alan P. (The Johns Hopkins University)

Voogt, James (University of Western Ontario)

Wachter, Susan M. (University of Pennsylvania)

Wallagh, Guido J. (University of Amsterdam)

Waller, Neil G. (Clemson University)

Walsh, Dennis (New York University)

Walsh, Stephen (Dublin Institute of Technology)

Wang, Bing (University of Cambridge)

Wang, Ko (Baruch College, The City University of New York)

Wang, Neng (Columbia University)

Ward, Charles W.R. (University of Reading)

Warsame, Abukar (Royal Institute of Technology)

Webb, James (Cleveland State University)

Weidner, Maureen (Georgia Institute of Technology)

Weiman, Brad (University of Denver)

Weiser, Jay (Baruch College, The City University of New York)

Weiss, Eli (New York University)

Weiss, Michael (New York University)

Welke, Gerd (Baruch College, The City University of New York)

Wertheimer, Robert (The Johns Hopkins University)

Wexler, Jack (Georgia Institute of Technology)

Wheaton, William (Massachusetts Institute of Technology)

Wilhelmsson, Mats (Royal Institute of Technology)

Wilson, Chris (University of Southern California)

Wong, Grace (University of Pennsylvania)

Wong, Kenny (New York University)

Wong Khei Mie, Grace (National University of Singapore)

Wood, Fred (University of Denver)

Woodruff, Richard L. (University of Colorado)

Woodyard, William (Florida State University)

Worzala, Elaine M. (Clemson University)

Yao, Rui (Baruch College, The City University of New York)

Yavas, Abdullah (Penn State University)

Yu Shi Ming (National University of Singapore)

Yuen, Belinda (National University of Singapore)

Zeigler, Christina (New York University)

Zhu Jieming (National University of Singapore)